$2.50

Lee Stafford

ONE WORD LEADS TO ANOTHER

MILTON PAISNER

ONE WORD LEADS TO ANOTHER

A LIGHT HISTORY OF WORDS

DEMBNER BOOKS   NEW YORK

Dembner Books
Published by Red Dembner Enterprises Corp., 1841 Broadway,
New York, N.Y. 10023
Distributed by W. W. Norton & Company, Inc., 500 Fifth Avenue,
New York, N.Y. 10110

Library of Congress Cataloging in Publication Data

Paisner, Milton.
    One word leads to another.

    Bibliography: p.
    Includes index.
    1. English language — Etymology.   2. Vocabulary.
I. Title.
PE1574.P22   422   82-2505
ISBN 0-934878-17-X   AACR2

To my wife, Martha,
without whose absence this book could not
have been written, but without whose presence
it could not have been completed

CONTENTS

PREFACE

There are people to whom words are a pastime, and there are people to whom they are a matter of life and death — it is obvious that to Milton Paisner they are both. No wonder, then, that his book is both light-hearted and enlightening.

ONE WORD LEADS TO ANOTHER must have been a pleasure to write. It certainly is a pleasure to read. It shows us again the charm of our everyday words; their deceiving simplicity; where they came from; how their meaning and form has changed; how our language, for nearly a millennium, has managed to stay *alive*.

To me, the message is reassuring. The decline-of-the-language mongers are wrong; language itself is right. There is no final way to spell a word and no absolute meaning in which we can use it. We have changed with every century, our language has changed with us. The end of this growth would be the end of our culture.

All we can do in our use of the language, here and now, is to do justice to its richness and beauty. But no stage can be ideal. A South Carolinian proverb says, "We ain't what we want to be, and we ain't what we're goin' to be, but we ain't what we wuz."

When we look at some of the baffling changes in spelling and the radical changes in meaning ("nice" — or *nyce* — meant ignorant, while "silly" — or *cillie* — was blessed), we see that English has survived changes considerably more severe than whatever may be happening to it in our age.

Some meanings come around a second time, and perhaps a third. I chuckle with approval when Mr. Paisner quotes from Captain Grose's *Dictionary of the Vulgar Tongue*. Here is a selection of mine from that book that may be a model example of growth and death and rebirth in language: The word "pig" is defined, in my 1811 edition, as "a police officer" — a meaning that disappeared by the midnineteenth century but which came very much alive in the nineteen-sixties (and already is heard less often today).

It is true that etymology, knowledge of a word's history, has little to do with its accurate use today. But it can help us respect the organic quality of each word, of language as a living whole. And if we have gained insight into a word's depth and often surprising dimensions of past and current meanings, we might, just might, also *use* it in a more sensitive, more creative, and more effective way.

Besides, it's fun just to browse, for the sheer adventure of it. Exactly two hundred years ago, William Cowper wrote of

> Philologists, who chase
> A panting syllable through time and space,
> Start it at home, and hunt it in the dark
> To Gaul, to Greece, and into Noah's ark.

In this book the changing forms and meanings of words — and phrases, we must add — are examined through a look at their etymology or through a passage in which they occur, or through both. Most of such passages are "citations," the rest are "quotations." Let's make this distinction:

A citation is a passage attesting the occurrence of a word or phrase in a context that demonstrates its spelling and meaning (often it is its first recorded occurrence); e.g., in Chapter IV, in the discussion of the word "scarf," William Painter is cited: "His wife Panthea brought him an armure of golde . . . and a crimsen skarfe" — hardly a candidate for a quotation anthology, but good as a citation. A quotation is a passage that is given because of its intriguing content or the poignant way it is phrased; e.g., in Chapter VI, on the subject of "abstinence," we are treated to an entry from Ambrose Bierce's *The Devil's Dictionary*: "Abstainer, n. A weak person who yields to the temptation of denying himself a pleasure."

Whether citation or quotation — Milton Paisner gives us a unique mix that is entertaining from end to end.

I am glad he chose to retain the spelling the way he found it in his sources. It is an intriguing feature of this book. If you have never read Middle English and early English forms of spelling, you will soon get the feel of it (reading *v* for *u* and the like). Here are some examples, from this book, approximately in order of difficulty: *loue* (love), *fornycacyon* (fornication), *deuorse* (divorce), *yvell* (evil), *lytylle* (little), *lyvande* (living), *lyynge* (lying, reclining), *werre and pes* (war and peace), *Soondaies* (Sundays), *olyues* (olives), or *iogelour* (juggler — in Chaucer). Sometimes the old form is briefer, like *dafter* for "daughter," sometimes it is longer, like *daunceynge* for "dancing." All are — *ynglysshe*.

In most centuries, different ways of spelling existed side by side; even the best authors used two or three versions of a word in the same paragraph. President Jackson was not alone in actually bragging he was a poor speller, saying he had no respect for anyone who knew only one way to spell a word.

And if we look at today's students — and many teachers, for that matter — we may wonder whether the social stigma that was attached until recently to "incorrect" spelling was just a brief interlude, of no more than a century and a half. A thought worth pursuing.

But, as you will see at the beginning of Chapter V, William Caxton had worried as early as the fifteenth century, "What sholde a man in thyse days now write, egges or eyren, certaynly it is harde to playse every man." And this reminded me of Chaucer's lament a century before Caxton (in *Troilus and Criseyde*):

> And for ther is so gret diversite
> In Englissh, nd in writyng of oure tonge
> So prey I God that non myswrite the [thee]

Spelling rules are fairly stable today, but dictionaries are far from agreeing on everything. For example, the preferred form is "kidnaper" (one *p*) in *The Random House Dictionary, The American Heritage Dictionry,* and *The Scribner-Bantam English Dictionary,* whereas "kidnapper" (two *p*'s) is preferred or at least given first in *Webster's New World Dictionary* and the Merriam-Webster books including *Webster's New Collegiate Dictionary.*

It may shock you to hear that there are at least 2,000 common words on whose spelling these dictionaries disagree. And along comes a Milton Paisner to add to our woes. In his Introduction he apologizes: ". . . your spelling may be affected after you finish your romp through old spellings of common English words!" So he *knows* it, but he publishes anyhow!

Let's be grateful he does. At least he has the decency and wisdom to stay away from giving us the older forms of *pronunciation.* When he asked me to write a Preface, I intended to say something about pronunciation in his book, and give some rules, but then I told myself it would not be in keeping with a work that is meant for reading pleasure. *Ye* (pronounced here "the") olde spellings are intricate enough.

Tracing the changes and meanings of a word or phrase is no easy task, and Mr. Paisner obviously had to rely on many sources — some better than others — and sometimes venture his own opinion. So, almost inevitably in a fun book on etymology, he treads on thin ice here and there, and occasionally he may even get a toe wet. But we don't necessarily have to go along on all details to find each page instructive and a pleasure to read.

Throughout, I can sense how Milton Paisner, fired with infinite enthusiasm for words and their possibilities, must have forced himself to write with restraint, to stay "sober" and not let puns and humorous asides interfere with what he has to say. Sometimes, fortunately, he relaxes and becomes "funny," as in Chapter V, when he quotes from a poem of 1839, "And lords made love — and ladies pies," and then asks us: "If the ladies were in the kitchen making pies, to whom were the lords making love?"

Looking at Milton Paisner's biography, I realize how multifaceted the man is: languages and translation, psychology, local politics, teaching, a business career . . . and I see he recently taught a course on "Fun With Words." As that was a college course, I don't think it was as refreshingly "unacademic" as this book; but Paisner being Paisner, he must have managed to blend all that talk of front and end clippings, backformation, cognates, doublets, and hypothetical forms with his special tone.

"Sit back and enjoy this book," as we say. But then, no, don't sit too long: I hope that reading for a while will whet your appetite, and you will be inspired to get up and search for yourself in other books on etymology (if you don't have any, look at the Bibliography and get at least one or two) and in your dictionaries (if you don't have any, you are not likely to be the person to read this book).

The quotation at the opening of Chapter I, by Justice Oliver Wendell Holmes, reminds me of what his father, the *poet* Oliver Wendell Holmes, had written: "When I feel inclined to read poetry, I take down my dictionry. The poetry of words is quite as beautiful as that of sentences."

WALTER D. GLANZE

INTRODUCTION

An introduction (Latin *intro*, into, and *ducere*, to lead) is usually designed to lead the reader into the subject of the book. In this case, however, it is my hope that the book itself will "lead" the reader "into" the beauties, the intricacies, and the joys of the English language. There are many dictionaries, thesauri, glossaries, compendia, etymological volumes, and collections and summaries of all kinds of groups of words and phrases. Most of them treat the language academically in one of two ways; they are either an *A* to *Z* listing of words for reference purposes or they are collections of special words such as place names, personal names, or specific derivations. Unless you are a logolept (word-nut!) of many years standing like me, you will generally go to one of these volumes, look up the word for its meaning, and close the book, satisfied.

Logolepts are a breed apart; they are afflicted with a malady not listed in the medical journals, "dictionaryitis." This disease has two symptoms. The first is a sense of incompletion; the word you are looking up is insufficiently defined or its derivation is cloudy, so you go on to another and another book until you are satisfied. The second symptom may be called getting lost. It manifests itself by the inability to leave the page where you found the word you were originally looking for. You continue to browse or, worse still, to read that page and continue on for pages more!

The aim of this book, then, is twofold: to make logolepts of those who hitherto have shown no particular interest in the derivation of words by stimulating their curiosity, and to make it easier for confirmed word lovers to succumb to their affliction within the groups of words offered in this volume.

The citations and quotations used for illustration are from a number of sources; they serve several purposes: to show some of the early uses, different spellings, and changes in the meaning of words from one time to another. Further, they explore different mores and customs as shown by word usage, and especially they are meant to entertain the reader.

It is my hope that there is something in this book for everyone and that readers will enjoy browsing through it at their leisure, savoring the ancient usages. I would like, however, to apologize to the reader in advance; your spelling may be affected after you finish your romp through old spellings of common English words!

In any case, may you derive from these pages the richness, humor, complexity, and above all enjoyment of our language that have led me to write them.

WORDS ON "WORD"

Pleynly at a word,
Thy drasty rymyng is nat worth a toord.
                                        Chaucer

Justice Oliver Wendell Holmes wrote in one of his decisions (*Towne* v. *Eisner*):

> A word is not a crystal, transparent and unchanging, it is the skin of a living thought and may vary greatly in color and content according to the circumstances and time in which it is used.

Throughout this volume we shall examine hundreds of words, their etymology and the way in which they may have changed their spelling and their "color and content" over the years. In this chapter we shall concentrate on the word 'word,' which is related to the Latin *verbum,* which meant word or verb.

Various writers have from time to time expressed their thoughts about words. Ernest Rhys (1859–1946) looked at words in a way very similar to that of Justice Holmes (*Words*).

> Words, like fine flowers, have their colours too.

Alice, in Lewis Carroll's *Through the Looking-Glass* (chapter 6), written in 1871, pondered over the power of men over words or vice versa.

> "The question is," said Alice, "whether you can make the words mean so many different things."
> "The question is," said Humpty Dumpty, "which is to be master — that's all."

17

Here are two opposing views on words: William Hazlitt wrote in 1822 (*Table Talk; or Original Essays on Men and Manners*):

> Words are the only things that last forever.

John Ray, however, quoted an English proverb in 1678 (*English Proverbs*) with an exactly opposite opinion:

> Words and feathers are tossed by the wind.

But Edmund Burke wrote in a letter in 1795 that it didn't matter whether words were ephemeral or eternal; they still caused problems:

> A very great part of the mischiefs that vex this world arise from words.

A book published in 1450 praised Chaucer's ability to make language convey a living reality ("The Boke of Curtasye" in *Babees Book*).

> His [Chaucer's] longage was so feyre and pertinent, That semed vnto mennys herying [hearing], Not only the worde, but verrely the thing.

The poet John Keats said in *Endymion* (IV) in 1818 that there are limits to language.

> Things for which no wording can be found.

Playing upon the generally accepted notion of his time that men were strong and women weak, John Florio wrote in 1578 in *First Fruites* (translating from the Italian):

> Deeds are males, words are females.

He may not have been aware of an old Hindu proverb with a similar thought as translated by Sir William Jones in 1794.

> Words are the daughters of earth, and deeds are the sons of heaven.

Florio also ascribed strong powers to words.

> Good words anoint a man, ill words kill a man.

John Davies in *The Scourge of Folly* in 1611 echoed the idea of the power of words as a cover for evil actions.

> Good words and ill deeds deceive wise and fools.

And a word about a much maligned kind of word — puns. Sir Sidney Smith (1771 – 1845) had high praise for them in *Elementary Sketches of Moral Philosophy* (lecture 10).

> I have mentioned puns. They are, I believe, what I have denominated them — the wit of words. They are exactly the same to words which wit is to ideas, and consist in the sudden discovery of relations in language.

We seldom use 'word' as a verb today, but it was once quite commonly employed that way. Cleopatra, in Shakespeare's *Antony and Cleopatra,* says of Octavius Caesar (act V, scene 2):

> He words me, girls, he words me, that I should not
> Be noble to myself; . . .

Christopher Nesse wrote of the Last Judgment Day in *A Compleat History and Mystery of the Old and New Testament* (1690 – 96, I).

> The judge . . . will not ask men . . . how they have worded, but how they have walked.

In a lighter vein James Howell wrote in his *Letters* (I, 1) in 1647 that he could suffer bores only if they spoke in Italian.

> If one were to be worded to Death, Italian is the fittest Language, in regard of the Fluency and Softness of it.

'Word' has accumulated many meanings over the years, meanings that derive from context, from combination with other words as well as in compound words. It is interesting to speculate why so many words have been written by so many writers, when so many other writers laud the man of few words. For example, here is the advice given in "How the Good Wijf Taught Hir Doughtir," *Babees Book,* published around 1430.

> Be noght of many wordes.

In the *Spectator* (#448, 1712) Sir Richard Steele described an all too familiar phenomenon.

> A wordy orator . . . making a magnificent speech to the people, full of vain promises.

Abraham Lincoln, speaking of a fellow lawyer, expressed a common view of the man of many words (Gross, *Lincoln's Own Stories*).

> He can compress the most words into the smallest ideas of any man I ever met.

News, report, rumor, fame or renown, authority are some of the meanings of 'word,' depending upon how it is used in a context. In *Measure for Measure* (act I, scene 4) Shakespeare used it to mean a simple report.

> Commend me to my brother; soon at night
> I'll send him certain word of my success.

Today we may speak of a rumor as "spreading like wildfire." In "The Queen's Marie" in *Child's Ballads* in 1400 (III) the spread of rumor was similarly described.

> Word is to the kitchen gane,
> And word is to the ha',
> And word is to the noble room,
> Amang the ladyes a'.

In *Layamon's Brut, or Chronicle of Britain* (1205) 'word' had the meaning of renown.

> Of hire wisdome sprong that word wide.

With the meaning of authority it appeared in these two instances over four hundred years apart. In 1450 it was the wife who was admonished (*The Book of the Knight of La Tour-Landry*).

> The wiff aught to . . . lete the husbonde haue the wordes, and to be maister.

Tennyson in *Dora* had similar advice for a child.

> In my time a father's word was law.

In the phrases 'the ten words' and 'word of God,' 'word' takes on a religious significance. In John Wyclif's translation of *Deuteronomy* of 1382, we find this verse.

> The ten wordis, that he wroot in the two stonen tablis.

A Proclamation of August 18, 1553, stated the following.

> Some euell disposed persons, which take vpon them . . . to interpret the worde of God, after theyr own brayne.

Shakespeare didn't need the full phrase 'word of God' to convey his meaning, as shown in these lines from *The Merry Wives of Windsor* (act III, scene 1).

> What, the sword and the word! do you study them both, master parson?

An example of 'word' used in a compound is 'wordless.' In 1633 Phineas Fletcher wrote a poem "Elisa" (II, 4) published in *The Purple Island, or the Isle of Man; Together with Piscatorie Eclogs and other Poeticall Miscellanies;* his subject was a sorrowing woman.

> So sat she joylesse down in wordlesse grief complaining.

Noctes Ambrosianae had a suggestion in April 1832 that is echoed by many therapists today: "Don't hold it in; give vent to your feeling."

> Silent people often get insane. It is not safe to have too many dealings with wordless thoughts.

Here is some encouragement from the *Spectator* (#560, 1714) for those called upon to speak in public for the first time.

> If I appear a little word-bound in my first . . . responses, I hope it will . . . be imputed . . . to the long disuse of speech.

Sir Francis Palgrave wrote in *The History of Normandy and of England* (1851– 64) of a quarrel between two men of authority.

> A silly, yet ferocious wordspite quarrel between Otho and Hugh-le-Grand.

'Word-catcher' in the early nineteenth century was one who "catches," "cavils," or "collects" words. R. Garnett used it in a derogatory sense in 1835 in his *Philological Essay*.

> Of this sort of knowledge — the very foundation of all rational etymology — our word-catchers do not seem to have had the smallest tincture.

In 1673 Andrew Marvell addressed words of scorn to a fellow-writer in *The Rehearsal Transprosed* (II).

> You are . . . a meer Word-pecker.

But by 1700 the word 'word-pecker' seems to have become respectable. Here is a definition from a dictionary published in that year (*A New Dictionary of the Terms Ancient and Modern of the Canting Crew*).

> "Word-pecker," one that play's with Words.

The word 'word' occurs frequently in our everyday language as part of a number of phrases such as "to keep one's word," "eat one's words," "hard words," and many more. There is a group of phrases that has to do with pledging one's honor or keeping one's promise. John Gower in *Confessio Amantis* (I) put it plainly, in 1390.

> It sit wel every wiht [person]
> To kepe his word in trowthe upryht.

When one carries out a promise made, he "keeps his word." When one makes a promise to another, he "gives his word." Sir Philip Sidney spoke of such a one in *Arcadia* (II) in 1586.

> I giue you my word, he for me shall maintaine this quarrell against you.

One who accepts a promise given "takes the word" of the speaker, according to William Meade Williams in 1587 (*Annals of the Worshipful Company of Founders of the City of London*).

> He givinge his fayth promyse to Mr. Alderman . . . Mr. Alderman tooke his worde.

Very often when we wish to assure another that we mean to do what we say, we use the phrase "word of honor," as it was used in 1814 by Donat H. O'Brien in *Narrative Containing an Account of His Shipwreck, Captivity, and Escape from France*.

> They suspected we were deserters. . . . We assured them upon our word of honour, they were very much mistaken.

Another way to say you will do as you promise is to guarantee that you will "be as good as your word."

The phrases "good words" and "fair words" have been used, not only to convey their literal meaning, but also to give a completely opposite meaning, evident from the context in which they are spoken or written. Jehan Palsgrave in 1540 and John Heywood in 1546 used them with their literal meaning. First Palsgrave in his translation of Fullonius' *Comedy of Acolastus* (act III, scene 1):

> [Thou] dyddest speke a good word for me, and dydst tourne away . . . the . . . strokes from me.

Then Heywood (*A dialogue conteynyng prouerbes and epigrammes*, I, 9):

> It hurteth not the tounge to geve fayre wurdis.

Looking at the other side of the coin we find Thomas Starkey writing in 1538 in *England in the Reign of Henry the Eighth, a Dialogue Between Cardinal Pole and Thomas Lupset* (II, 2):

> By hys dyssymulatyon and fare wordys.

And John Taylor (Water Poet) warned us in 1622 to look beneath the surface *(A Verry Merry Wherry-Ferry-Voyage)*.

> False hearts can put on good wordes and lookes.

Since words issue from the mouth, one would expect that there would be a number of phrases combining 'word' and 'mouth.' First is 'word of mouth,' used in its literal sense by Nicolas Udall in 1533 *(Ralph Roister Doister, a Comedy,* act III, scene 2).

> A little message vnto hir by worde of mouth.

To retract one's words is to take them back, or, put another way, to eat them. Ben Jonson, in *Epicoene, or the Silent Women,* written in 1609, described one who stood his ground.

> I'll eat no words for you, nor no men.

Eating or not eating one's words is something one does oneself; putting in or taking out words from one's mouth is done by others without one's consent. In John Wyclif's translation of the Bible (II Samuel 14:3), in 1382, he wrote:

> Forsothe Joab putte the wordis in hire mouth.

Palsgrave *(Acolastus)* was upset at another's bad manners and wrote:

> It is no good maner to take the worde out of my mouthe, or I have made an ende of my tale.

We have talked about "good words" and "fair words" used with opposite meanings, but with the phrases "sharp words" and "hard words" there can be only one meaning, made perfectly clear first by this citation from 1526 *(The Pilgrimage of Perfection).*

> Than [then] yf we be touched with a sharpe worde, we shall yelde a . . . gentyll answere.

Tennyson wrote in *Dora*:

> He and I
> Had once hard words, and parted.

In 1590 Richard Tarlton wrote of an inevitable sequence in *Newes out of Purgatorie.*

> Whereupon they grewe to woords, and from woords to blowes.

The word 'bandy' used to be used in tennis, to refer to hitting the ball back and forth. It is no longer used in that sense but has taken on the meaning of exchanging words back and forth, usually in argument. This is how William A. Black used it in 1872 in *The Strange Adventures of a Phaeton* (XXXI).

> Sharp words were being bandied about.

Today, however, 'bandy' is used in a much lighter vein as well — exchanging repartee or as a synonym for banter. Charles Dickens used it in *Nicholas Nickleby* (XXX), in 1834.

> The stories they invent . . . and bandy from mouth to mouth.

There are other phrases that use 'word' in the plural to convey their meaning. When we have a deeply felt experience or see a work of art that defies description, we are apt to say that we "have no words" to express our feelings or appreciation. The essence of a great orator or story-teller is that he makes us "hang on his words," unable to tear ourselves away, waiting for what comes next. Today we may say, "Tell it like it is"; in 1720 Daniel Defoe put the same thought into different words, using a phrase that is still current (*The Life, Adventures, and Pyracies of the Famous Captain Singleton*, XV).

> William told us in so many words, that it was impossible.

To express the idea that there are many things we take for granted, things we may be said to have imbibed with our mothers' milk, Shakespeare used a familiar phrase in *Henry V* (act IV, scene 3).

> . . . then shall our names,
> Familiar in their mouths as household words, . . .

Our next phrase using the plural 'words' is from Chaucer's Prologue to The Parson's Tale (I, 67). It has fallen into disuse but its meaning, 'to serve as spokesman,' is still clear, and it might very well have a resurgence someday.

> Our host hadde the wordes for us alle.

Stewart Chaplin wrote in the June 1900 issue of *Century Magazine* about a special phrase using the plural 'words.'

> Weasel words are words that suck all the life out of the words next to them just as a weasel sucks an egg and leaves the shell.

Certain phrases that use 'word' in the singular seem to refer to something even less than one word but actually mean several words of short duration. Dickens wrote in *Our Mutual Friend*

> Might I have half a word with you?

In the Prologue to the *Tales* Chaucer had one of his characters deliver a succinct piece of criticism.

> Pleynly at a word,
> Thy drasty rymyng is nat worth a toord.

In *Troilus* (III, 702) Chaucer used his own version of the phrase "beginning to end."

> Of al this werk he tolde hym worde and ende.

Spectator #75 gives us Sir Richard Steele's definition of a gentleman.

> In a word, to be a fine gentleman, is to be a generous and brave man.

Those of us who studied Latin in our youth might wish we had had the fluency expressed by Chaucer in *Dido,* c. 1385.

> I coulde folwe word for word Virgile.

To the hot-tempered, a word is sometimes not enough; it must be accompanied by action. Here is Mercutio's response to Tybalt's overture in *Romeo and Juliet.*

> TYBALT. Gentlemen, good den: a word with one of you.
> MERCUTIO. And but one word with one of us? couple it with
> something; make it a word and a blow.

There are times in the course of daily events when there might be engendered a response that is pure British. In 1857 C. Locker wrote the following in *London Lyrics*.

> Half London was there and, my word, there were few . . . but envied Lord Nigel's felicity.

And now, we come inevitably to 'the last word.' This phrase has had several meanings. In the sixteenth century, as today, it was used to refer to the final words of an exchange between two parties. John Foxe wrote in 1653 in *Actes and Monuments of these Latter and Perillous Dayes*.

> My Lorde of Lincolne . . . sayde thou were a frantike felow, and a man that wyll haue the last worde.

Gabriel Harvey used the phrase with a similar meaning in 1593 (*Pierce's Supererogation, or a New Prayse of the Old Asse*, II), but addressed it to a different audience.

> Come hee- and shee-scoldes, you that . . . will rather loose [lose] your liues, then the last word.

H. Harrison used the literal meaning of the phrase as part of a title of a book, *The Last Words of a Dying Penitent,* published in 1692.

Fashions in dress have their cycles; they come and go and come back again in slightly different form, and each time they return they are described by the fashion critics with a variant on the expression 'the last word,' as in the *Daily News* in London on September 21, 1888.

> The long mantles are the latest "word" of Paris fashions.

So, too, with words. We have seen how the word 'word' itself has changed its meaning and its form, too, over the years. The process never stops. The "latest" or "last" word in words is just for today. Tomorrow there will be other words to take its place. Those that are no longer in common use are called obsolete. Who knows whether or when they will emerge from obscurity to become once again "the last word."

CHAPTER II

A POTPOURRI OF WORDS

You've got me in between
the devil and the deep blue sea.

Why do we say 'pig in a poke' or 'apple pie order'? How did a friendship rift affect the name of the dish we call 'lobster New-burg'? What is an eponym? What is the irony behind the words 'tawdry' and 'dunce'? What does the ancient Celtic name for 'yew tree' have to do with the naming of New York? What is the origin of the word 'junket'?

Many volumes have been written (some are listed in the Bibliography) about common sayings, eponyms, geographical and personal names. In this chapter we shall sample some of the more interesting items found in these books in the hope that the reader will be encouraged to go further and more deeply into the amusing, enchanting, and fascinating world of words.

The word 'eponym' comes from two Greek words *epi* (upon) and *onoma* (name). It describes a class of words which come mostly from the names of people or places, and which have come into the language as common nouns, adjectives, or verbs.

First we will look at the word 'chauvinist,' a word very much in vogue today in the phrase "male chauvinist pig." The word comes from the name of Nicholas Chauvin, who was an officer in Napoleon's army. He believed, even after Napoleon's defeat at Waterloo and subsequent exile, that his emperor was the greatest man who had ever lived. Chauvin spent the rest of his life praising Napoleon and regaling his friends and neighbors with the glories and accomplishments of his hero; for Chauvin Napoleon could do no wrong. At first his patriotism and loyalty were celebrated far and wide, but finally the world tired of him, and he began to be ridiculed by his comrades for his unswerving devotion to the emperor. There were, however, many of the old soldiers who still revered the memory of their leader, and they began to be called 'chauvinists' for their idolatrous admiration for Napoleon's person and actions.

The word 'chauvinist,' when used alone, still refers to one who believes in the policy "My country right or wrong!" and who is ready to fight anyone who dares to criticize it. In the phrase "male chauvinist pig" the word 'chauvinist' identifies a man who believes that this is a man's world, that this is the way it should be, and that women are second-class citizens and should remain that way forever.

The British, not to be outdone by the French, have their own word for this kind of feeling about one's country. The word is 'jingoism.' It was originally used as a vigorous form of emphasis or agreement as "By jingo, that's right." The phrase "by jingo" was incorporated into the routines of the music halls in England as a refrain sung by the audience at appropriate times during the singing of a song by the stage performer. The phrase moved out of the theater in 1878 when Lord Beaconsfield sent the British fleet into Turkish waters to resist the advance of Russian troops. The supporters of this move, who advocated war, if necessary, to keep the Russians in their place, adopted the phrase "by jingo" as their rallying cry. Soon people were calling them 'jingoists.' 'Jingoism,' like 'chauvinism,' came into our language to describe the superpatriots for whom there is but one standard in foreign policy: "Whatever my country does is right." Their choice of the proper instrument to protect that policy is war.

The names of many well-known trees and flowers are eponyms, that is, their names come from the names of botanists and other scientists who were involved with their discovery and classification. The 'begonia' was named for Professor Bégon, a botanist, who encouraged the study of his specialty. The lovely 'magnolia' tree honors Pierre Magnol, a professor of medicine and prefect of the Botanical Gardens in Montpellier, France. That colorful herald of spring, the 'forsythia,' took its name from a Scottish gardener, W. Forsyth (1737– 1804).

Sometimes the naming of a plant is not as simple and straightforward as those discussed above. In 1787 the famous scientist Alexander von Humboldt found an interesting plant in Mexico, which he sent to his friend Professor Cavanilles in Spain. For some reason which is lost to us, Cavanilles named the plant for another friend and fellow botanist, Anders Dahl, and not for Humboldt. So the dahlia, of which there are over fourteen thousand named varieties, should properly have been called the humboldtia.

One of the most famous of the eponyms referring to food is 'sandwich.' Lord Sandwich, from whom the name came, was a compulsive gambler. He would not take time out from his gambling at cards to go to the dinner table, but directed his servant to bring him some slices of meat between two slices of bread. His aim was not only to save time for gambling, but also to avoid soiling his hands and thereby the cards.

One food item you cannot put into a sandwich is 'lobster Newburg.' The dish was invented by a regular patron of the famous restaurant Delmonico's in New York. The owner of the restaurant and the inventor of the dish had a falling out, and to spite his former friend, Delmonico named the dish for a nearby city, Newburgh, rather than for his erstwhile patron whose name was Wenberg. That is why we eat 'lobster Newburg' today instead of 'lobster Wenberg.'

In the first half of the nineteenth century in the United States there lived a minister named Sylvester Graham who forswore meat and became what we would call today "hooked" on vegetarianism, pure food, and unbolted (unsifted) flour. He traveled the countryside urging his fellow men to give up meat and fat and adopt his diet. The flour which he advocated is now called 'whole wheat' or sometimes 'graham' flour, and 'graham crackers,' made from sweetened whole wheat flour, still carry the name of a man who was born too soon. Think how popular he would be today with our emphasis on the elimination of adulterates in our food, our concern with organically grown food, and the increasing understanding of the influence of diet on our way of life.

Many of the eponyms in common use in our language come from the names of men and women of England. When we speak of

glittery, showy items of very little value, such as the souvenir trinkets on sale at most historical places and at summer resorts, we are
apt to describe them as 'tawdry.' There was once an Anglo-Saxon
princess whose name was Aethelthryth. She took a vow to remain a
virgin all her life, and even though she was married, she kept that
vow with such dignity that even her husband respected her. She
was eventually beatified and became St. Audrey. On her day, October 17, fairs were held in England and the inevitable trinkets of all
kinds were sold to the public. There were assorted souvenirs as well
as poor-quality laces. These were called, naturally enough, "Saint
Audrey's lace." This phrase was soon contracted to *sin t'Audrey lace,*
tawdrey lace, and finally 'tawdry.' Strange is the way of language by
which the name of an austerely religious woman came to be applied
to cheap, flashy adornments.

There is a parallel between the case of St. Audrey and that of
Duns Scotus, one of the most brilliant theologians of the thirteenth
century, who stressed proof above authority or doctrine, thinking
above mere knowledge. His followers were a predominant scholas-
tic sect and were called Scotists. When the new learning of the
Renaissance began to spread into England, the Scotists resisted its
growth and remained hidebound and conservative in their theol-
ogy, thus going completely counter to the teaching of their master.
Their opponents now began to refer to them as *Dunsmen, Dunce-*
men, or *Dunces.* Finally the word 'dunce' was born. From the name
of one of the most extraordinary of England's scholars came the
word to describe one who is stupid, ignorant, and slow.

The 'cardigan' sweater and the 'raglan' sleeve came from the
names of British lords who were generals in the Crimean War in
1855. The Earl of Cardigan was the commander of the ill-fated
Light Brigade. Lord Raglan lost an arm while fighting in the battle
of Waterloo and had a coat designed for his convenience without
tight sleeves, one that could simply be thrown on over the shoul-
ders. The style has since been modified but Raglan's name is still
attached to it.

Both Raglan and Cardigan always looked 'spruce,' a word
perhaps from the article of clothing called a 'spruce' (a leather
jerkin) made of leather brought from Prussia; an initial *s* was
added, and a new word was coined.

President Calvin Coolidge was spoken of as a 'laconic' man, that
is, a man of few words. For the origin of this word 'laconic' we must

go back to the ancient Greek province of Laconia, whose chief city was Sparta. When Philip of Macedonia, father of Alexander the Great, was besieging Sparta, he sent a message to the Laconians, "If we enter the city we will raze it to the ground." The 'laconic' answer that came back was — "If." (There are other famous examples of 'laconic' replies: When the Germans demanded that General McAuliffe surrender at the Battle of the Bulge in the Second World War, his answer was "Nuts." The English humor magazine *Punch* had this advice for those contemplating marriage: "Don't.")

'Sleazy' is another word used to describe cheap, poor quality goods. Many years ago cloth was imported into England from Silesia, then part of Germany. The cloth was of such poor quality that the English referred to it contemptuously as "that cloth from Silesia" or "Silesian cloth" and finally 'sleazy' cloth.

Some authorities say that the word 'bogus' came from a man named Borghese, a nineteenth-century counterfeiter. But in a letter to the editors of the *Oxford English Dictionary*, a Dr. S. Willard wrote that the word 'bogus' was the name of an apparatus for coining false money. He said it was shortened from "tantrabogus," a word his father had used in Vermont for any ill-looking object. Further, his father had told him that "tantrabogus" came from a word used in Devonshire in England, "tantarobobs," which meant "devil." The word 'bogy,' however, was also used extensively to mean the devil, as in "Old Bogey," and in that phrase used to frighten children years ago, "The bogeyman will get you if you don't watch out!" So it is probably a combination of this latter meaning with the Devonshire word which produced our current word 'bogus.'

The striped 'tabby cat' has a name that goes far back in history. There was a Prince Attab who lived in the section of Baghdad later named for him, Attabiya. This area was also the region where a special kind of striped cloth was woven, and thus the name of the Prince has been immortalized in the name of one of our most common domestic pets.

New eponyms are constantly being formed as the names and actions of individuals catch the public's fancy. Some will have a brief period of popularity, like 'Quisling' after a Norwegian who betrayed his country to the Nazis. Not too many people use that word today. Other words like 'McCarthyism' of our recent past, and 'Watergate' are examples of currently popular eponyms.

Others will emerge and become the eponyms of tomorrow, so firmly entrenched in the language that their very origin will not be known to those who use them.

The next few pages will provide an examination of some popular sayings, clichés, and maxims which, when taken literally, may not make much sense. That there are differences of opinion as to the origin of some of these phrases should not be surprising. Many of them go back several hundred years, and the historical record may be somewhat hazy.

A familiar old song contains the lyrics 'You've got me in between the devil and the deep blue sea.' One member of a class on the subject of words suggested that the origin of the phrase might have been, "You're caught between burning in hell or drowning in the ocean." While not correct, it is a fine example of folk etymology. The beginning of the explanation is in the phrase "the devil to pay and no pitch hot," which has nothing to do with paying anything to the devil. It goes back several hundred years to the days when the hulls of sailing ships were made of wood and were called in French *le diable* (which does mean "the devil" in modern French, but at that time had the other meaning as well). The French verb *payer,* from which the "pay" in our expression comes, meant then to "calk with pitch or tar." When the ship was fouled with barnacles so much that it was losing headway, or when the seams began to leak, the crew dragged it up on a beach and heated pitch for the calking operation. This had to be done very quickly between the flow of the tides. So the crew was caught with the necessity of calking (paying) the ship's hull (*diable*) before the water came and stopped the process; hence they were "between the devil," meaning the whole process of calking the ship's hull, "and the deep blue sea."

When you are tempted to buy something that is very cheap and do not examine it very carefully, you frequently get stuck with a bad bargain. You are said to have bought "a pig in a poke." At country fairs in England a cheat would put a mangy cat in a cloth bag called a 'poke' and hoodwink some not too bright countryman into thinking that there was a fine pig in the poke. The customer paid his money, the seller vanished in a hurry, and when the poke was opened there was no pig, just a cat. A smart buyer would insist on opening the bag first, the result being that the "cat was let out of the bag."

There are no fewer than five explanations for the origin of the expression 'apple pie order'!

1. The French expression *cap-a-pié* means head-to-foot order.

2. Another French phrase is *à plis* which means "in plaits," or neat and proper like the braids on a little girl's head.

3. *Order* is an Old English word for "row," and apple pies used to be made with a neatly cut border.

4. There is a phrase *alpha-beta order* which means the "order of the alphabet."

5. By far the most interesting explanation comes from the time when aristocratic French ladies who lived in England but spoke no English had English maids who spoke no French. When the lady of the house instructed the maid to arrange the linen in proper order, neatly folded, she said she wanted the *nappe pliée en ordre,* meaning "the linen folded in order." It was but a short step from *nappe pliée en ordre* to 'apple pie order,' giving us but another example of difficulty with pronunciation distorting the meaning of a phrase.

Place names derive from many sources: topography, people's names, incidents which may have taken place at a certain spot, and many others. Being a New Englander, I will concentrate on the names of the six New England states along with their next-door neighbor, New York. 'Vermont' has a principal mountain range which is called the Green Mountains, and it is from the two French words for these mountains, *vert* (green) and *mont* (mountain) that the state got its name.

The name for her eastern neighbor, 'New Hampshire,' came from the old country. In 1629 Captain John Mason of the British navy received a part of northern New England as a grant and decided to name it after the county in England where he had spent a good part of his life, Hampshire. However, in that same year, another charter for this area showed the name 'Laconia.' While this latter name was short-lived for the larger area, it remained as the name of a town, the first Greek place name in America. A friend of Mason, Sir Ferdinando Gorges, wrote (cited in George R. Stewart's *Names on the Land,* 1958):

Laconia, so called by reason of the great lakes therein.

and thereby pointed out that the name was also a pun.

When the famous Captain Smith wrote a book about the voyage

of Sir Francis Drake to the New World, he called his book *A Description of New England*. Drake had placed on his own map the name Nova Albion, meaning New Albion, Albion being a poetic name for England. Knowing that there were already a New Spain and a New France in the New World, Smith chose to call the area 'New England,' a prosaic rendering of the flowery Nova Albion of Drake. Smith is also responsible for the naming of 'Massachusetts' which he took from the Indian tribal name for the area, *Massadchu-seuk,* meaning "big hill people."

To the southwest we come across the first state to be named for the principal river flowing through it. The river was known to the English in Plymouth by the Indian name *Quinetucquet* or *Quenticutt*. At least this was how it sounded to English ears. After several changes the name came out to be 'Connecticut,' although no one knows where the extra 'c' came from, and to this day no one pronounces it.

In 1644 the Court of Providence Plantation decreed that Aquethneck (now called Aquidnick) Island be renamed the Isle of Rhodes or 'Rhode Island.' This name came either from the writings of a Dutch sailor named DeLaet, who made mention of a "little reddish island" (*Rood Eiland*) in the vicinity, or from the famous book of the Dutch traveler Hakluyt called *Voyages*. Hakluyt described the voyage of Verrazano along the coast of New England in 1524, in which he encountered an "island about the bigness of the island of Rhodes." The Massachusetts General Court, however, having very little regard for Roger Williams' Providence Plantations, the principal town in Rhode Island, usually spelled the name of the state 'Road Island,' as if it were simply an anchorage for ships (another meaning of the word "road"). Today we call the state 'Rhode Island.' Its official name, established by the state's legislature on July 18, 1876, is "The State of Rhode Island and Providence Plantations."

In a New England charter of 1620 the land north and east of Massachusetts was described as "the country of the Main Land." The use of the word "Main" was intended to mean the continent as opposed to the offshore islands. Before very long, Sir Ferdinando Gorges and Captain John Mason, the same two men who were involved in the settling and naming of New Hampshire, were granted a charter for this same land, which was to be called the 'Province of Maine.'

Some years later Sir Ferdinando named the land "New Somerset" after his own county in England, just as Mason had done with New Hampshire. However, he did not reckon with his king. King Charles didn't like the name "New Somerset" and decreed that it should be called "henceforth and forevermore by the name The Province or County of Mayne." A few years later, Massachusetts Bay Colony, using as its excuse a passage in its charter — "all the land north and south of the Merrimack and Charles Rivers or of any and every part thereof" — extended its claim to include Maine. All the northern area was made into one county called Yorkshire, and for a time the names of New Hampshire and Maine disappeared. In 1667 the Lord Chief Justice in England changed the name of Yorkshire County to the County of Maine, as King Charles had wished. Maine finally became a sovereign state in 1820.

The name 'New York' has very old roots. In ancient Britain the Celtic word for the yew tree was *eburos* and the place where it grew was known as *Eburacon*. The Romans latinized it into *Eburacum*, which gradually changed to *Eboracum* and then *Evorac*. When Anglo-Saxon pirates conquered the country, they called the area the "place of the wild boar," in their language *eoforwic*. In 865 the Danes seized the area, and because the last syllable *wic* sounded the *vik* in Danish, which meant bay or inlet, they changed the name to *Eoforvik*, which became *Yowik* and finally 'York.'

King Edward III of England married Princess Philippa of Belgium; they had seven sons and five daughters, and for his fifth son Edward created the title Duke of York. In the Wars of the Roses the Duke of York conquered and became king. When the Tudors overthrew the Yorkists, the title Duke of York was retained for the second son of the king, after the Prince of Wales. In the seventeenth century, James, second son of Charles the First, was both the Duke of York and Lord High Admiral of the navy. When a naval squadron under Colonel Nicolls took possession of New Amsterdam from the Dutch, Nicolls named it New York for his master.

After this brief sampling of place names, let us take a look at some personal last names. It has been common through the ages to name a son for his father. This was done by attaching a syllable of some sort either before or after the father's name, thus indicating whose son this was. The combination of the father's name with a prefix or suffix is called a patronymic.

The custom in Wales was to use the syllable *ap* before the father's name, as *ap Rhys,* meaning "son of Rhys." This combination gradually was shortened to 'Price'; likewise, *ap Howell* became 'Powell.' The Irish used *O* or *Mc;* the Scottish equivalent was *Mac,* but they did not use *O.* The Normans preceded the father's name with *fitz* from the Latin *filius* (son), giving us names like 'Fitzgerald' or 'Fitzmaurice.' In Sweden, Denmark, and Norway they added either *sen* or *son,* producing 'Anderson,' 'Peterson,' and 'Jensen.' The Spanish added *ez* to the end of the father's name, thus 'Alvarez' was the "son of Alva," while the Portuguese got the same result with *es,* as in 'Gomes,' "son of Gomo."

The Slavic peoples had a variety of equivalent endings; *ov* in 'Petrov,' "son of Peter," *wicz* in 'Danowicz,' "son of Dan," and 'Alexandrovich,' "son of Alexander." In Italy it was *de* or *di* preceding the name either separately or attached. The Greeks used the ending *poulos* to denote the son of the father, as in 'Theodoropoulos,' "son of Theodore."

Many of our common surnames derived from three personal or first names, John, Robert, and Richard. Let us look first at John, which in its original form meant gracios gift of Yahveh or Jehovah. From John we get names like 'Johnson' from England and 'Jones' from Wales. Other English forms are 'Jaynes,' 'Jennings,' and 'Jennison.' Another form of John is 'Hans,' and this led to 'Hancock' in England and 'Henschel' in Germany. Swedish names from Hans are 'Hansen' and 'Jensen.' The matching forms to John in Italian are *Gian* and *Giovan* leading to 'Gianuccio' and 'Giovanitti.' At times the first parts of the names were dropped and the names ended up as 'Nuccio' and 'Nitti.' Spain has 'Ibanez' and Greece 'Gianopolous.' The Russian 'Ivanov,' the Czech 'Janas,' the Hungarian 'Janosfi,' and the Polish 'Janik' all come from John.

From Robert the English derived 'Robertson,' 'Robinson' (from *Robin*, a diminutive of Robert), 'Robb,' and 'Robison.' From *Hob*, another diminutive of Robert, we get 'Hobbs,' 'Hopkins,' and 'Hobson.' *Dob*, a related form of Robert, led to 'Dobbs,' 'Dobson,' and 'Dobbins.' Related to Robert is *Roger,* which along with its diminutives led to 'Hodge,' 'Dodge,' 'Hotchkins,' and 'Dodson.' Its Dutch and Italian equivalents were 'Rutgers' and 'Ruggiero.'

Richard, with its diminutives *Rich* and *Richie* and its nicknames *Rick, Hick,* and *Dick,* have brought forth a variety of popular names such as 'Rickard,' 'Ricketts,' 'Hickox,' 'Hitchcock,' and 'Ickes.' A very common name from Spain and Portugal is 'Riccardo.' The Welsh *ap Richard* ended up as 'Pritchard.'

To conclude this chapter, we will look at some common English words with interesting histories. One word very much in the public eye in these days of continuing demand for reduction in government expenditures is 'junket.' Its original meaning was a basket made of reeds or rushes in which fish were caught and carried. Then it became the basket or mat in which cheese or other dairy products were served. Soon it was a basket for any sweet or confection. From being the carrier of sweets and confections, it came to be the banquet or feast at which such delicacies were served along with other foods. Such feasts or 'junkets' were accompanied by all kinds of entertainment. Finally we arrive at the current meaning of 'junket,' a trip whose ostensible purpose is business (especially government business), but whose real reason for existence is pleasure and whose expenses are borne by others, usually the taxpayers.

In Roman times the word *caminus* meant a room with a chimney; the modern version of the word *caminus* is 'chimney.' Religious services are often held in a 'tabernacle.' It is ironic that the Latin word *taberna,* the source of 'tabernacle,' is also the root of the word 'tavern.' Reading the 'Gospel' is part of the service in the tabernacle. 'Gospel' is derived from the Anglo-Saxon *godspel,* which meant "good tidings." At a funeral service a 'dirge' is often sung. It is called 'dirge' because it comes from the first word of the service for the dead, which starts, in Latin, *Dirige, Dominus* . . , "Direct, Lord" (our life in your path).

We have barely scratched the surface of the amusing, enchanting, and fascinating world of words, and we hope that these glimpses of that world have whetted the reader's appetite for more.

CHAPTER III

"THE BODY BEAUTIFUL" WORDS

Wype not thi nose nor thi nosthirlys,
Weare than mene wylle say thou come of cherlys.
Babees Book

Webster's New World Dictionary (see Bibliography) defines the 'body' as ". . . the whole physical structure and substance of a man, animal, or plant . . ." In this chapter we shall figuratively take apart the body and examine many of its parts, their functions, how they came by their names, and some of the ways they have been viewed throughout the years of English literature.

Let us start with the 'head' spelled *heed, hede, huede,* and *hide* by various Middle English writers. The head is very important in body language; it stands high in pride, it hangs down in sorrow, it nods in agreement, and it shakes from side to side in disagreement. Its importance was noted by John Heywood in 1562.

For when the head aketh, all the bodie is the wurs.

The head was treated very shabbily in this old English proverb as recorded by John Ray around 1670 (*English proverbs*).

Wash your hands often, your feet seldome, and your head never.

We currently use a description of a forgetful person which was put forth over one hundred years ago by George Eliot (*Adam Bede,* 1859, XXVII).

39

He'd leave his head behind him, if it was loose.

A high 'forehead' or 'brow' is commonly considered a sign of great intelligence, as evidenced by the word 'highbrow,' used to describe an intellectual; but in 1582 Thomas Watson had a different view of a high forehead. He spoke (*The ekatoupadia or passionate century of loue*) of

> malicious high foreheads.

Behind the brow and on top of the head is the 'scalp,' a word allied to the Middle Dutch *schelpe* and Old French *escalope* (shell).

From the American Indian custom of cutting the scalps off the heads of their victims (a practice learned from their white enemies) came a word used widely today when a Broadway hit is sold out; the man who has obtained tickets and is selling them at an exorbitant price is called a 'scalper.' The magazine *The Nation* used this word on October 15, 1882, to describe such a practice.

> With the eternal quarrel between railroads and scalpers passengers have nothing to do.

Unfortunately for many men the scalp loses its hair, producing 'baldness,' which gives the head a shiny appearance. It is from this shine that the word 'bald' gets its meaning. The Middle English *balled* or *ballid* seems to have had the original meaning of "shining" or "white" as in "bald-faced stag" and "bald eagle." The problem of baldness has plagued men since time began. John de Trevisa wrote about it in his translation of *Polychronicon Ranulphi Higden* (1387).

> The formests partye of the heede wyxeth soone balde.

Not many men take the advent of baldness as philosophically as did Caesar, according to William Caxton (*The game and playe of the chesse*, 1474).

> Julius Caesar was ballyd whereof he had displaisir.

Joseph Addison (1672–1719) noted that Caesar may have been displeased but he managed to overcome his feelings and make the best of a bad situation.

> Caesar . . . because his head was bald, covered that defect with laurels.

Like 'head,' 'eye' has been spelled many ways in English, *eize*, *eigh*, and *eyen*. The eye 'sees,' or put another way, has the power of 'sight.'

Both words are allied to the Teutonic *sean* (to see). We speak of a wise man as a 'seer,' one who we feel can see into the future. In addition to the function of sight, the eye 'cries' or 'weeps.' 'Weep' is from the Anglo-Saxon word *wepan* (clamor, outcry, loud lament), but we also weep 'tears' (Middle English *tere*) of joy. (The word 'tear' meaning to rip or rend is from another Anglo-Saxon word, *teran*.)

In 1450, as seen in *Morte d'Arthur,* men could weep and no one would think them unmanly.

> Thane the worthy kynge wrythes, and wepede with his enghne [eyes].

But by 1700, as noted by John Dryden, weeping was no longer acceptable behavior for men (*Sigismund*).

> Away, with Women weep, and leave me here,
> Fix'd, like a Man to die, without a Tear.

'Cry' comes from the Latin word *quiritare* (shriek, lament), which literally meant to implore the help of the Quirites (Roman citizens).

The eye not only receives messages, it sends them. It can cast a stern glance or send a tender thought. In *Merciles Beauté* Chaucer describes what we would call today a "femme fatale."

> Youre two eyn will sle [slay] me sodenly,
> I may the beaute of them not sustene.

The 'membrane' of the eye (Latin *membrana,* skin covering of a "member" of the body) is thick like a horn, and that is how it got the name 'cornea,' from the Latin *cornu* (horn). We all know blue-, brown-, hazel-, and green-eyed people. The Greeks remarked this profusion of color in that part of the eye and named it the 'iris' from the name of the goddess of the rainbow, Iris, who was also the messenger of the gods. In *Henry VI, Part II* (act III, scene 2) Shakespeare called upon Iris the messenger.

> . . . let me hear from thee;
> For whereso'er thou art in this world's globe,
> I'll have an Iris that shall find thee out.

'Pupil,' referring to a part of the eye, is an interesting word. It gets its name from *pupilla,* which may be a feminine diminutive of the Latin *pupa* (girl). The word 'pupil' meaning student is from *pupulus,* a masculine diminutive meaning little boy. But it is not the idea of boy or girl that gave rise to the meaning of the 'pupil' of the eye; it is the smallness of the images that register on the pupil that gave it its name. This was noted in 1398 by John Trevisa in his translation of Bartholomeus' *De proprietatibus rerum* (V, 7).

> The blacke of theye . . . is callyd Pupilla in latyn for smalle ymages ben seen therin.

Sir Roger L'Estrange, in 1642, used 'pupil' as "student" in his *Letter sent by an Oxford scholler to his quondam schoolemaster, [with] the schoolmaster's answer* (one can only imagine a modern teacher's response).

> Tutors should behave reverently before their pupils.

In Sanskrit the word *nasa* meant "dual," and it was from this idea of double that 'nose' (Anglo-Saxon *nosu, nos*) with its two 'nostrils' got its name. 'Nostril' is made up of two words: Anglo-Saxon *nos* and *thyrel* (perforation or orifice). Advice on good behavior in public is found in "Young Children's Book" in *Babees Book,* c. 1475.

> Wype not thi nose nor thi nosthirlys,
> Weare [lest] than mene wylle say thou come of cherlys [churls].

What we are told in this citation not to wipe away is 'mucus' (Latin *mucus, muccus,* slime from the nose). From the fact that it is a sticky, slimy substance we get the word 'mucilage.' Matthew Prior wrote a poetic description of the nostrils in *Alma,* around 1720.

> Wise nature likewise they suppose,
> Has drawn two Conduits down our Nose.

A well-known shape of the nose is the 'aquiline' sometimes called "Roman." This describes a curved or hooked nose shaped like an eagle's beak and is derived from the Latin word *aquila* (eagle). William Cowper described such a nose in *The Task* (III) in 1784.

> Terribly arched and aquiline his nose.

With the nose we 'smell,' 'sniff,' and 'sneeze.' 'Smell' (Middle English *smel*) is allied to the Dutch word *smeulen* (to smoulder), and it has the sense of the vapor given off by smoldering wood. 'Smell' has been used figuratively by many writers. John Fletcher wrote in *The Noble Gentleman* (act II, scene 1), c. 1625:

> Come, these are tricks; I smell 'em: I will go.

Shakespeare wrote in *King Lear* (act I, scene 5):

> . . . that what a man cannot smell out, he may spy into.

'Sniff' and 'sneeze' are from a variety of Scandinavian words with similar spellings and sounds. We often use 'sniff' in a figurative sense to express displeasure, as did Jonathan Swift in 1729 (*The Grand Question*, IV, 1).

So then you look'd scornful, and snift at the dean.

'Sneeze,' too, is used figuratively. Thomas S. Surr, in *A Winter in London; or sketches of fashion, a novel*, 1806, speaks of a young man who perhaps deserves to get whatever it is he thinks is beneath his dignity.

It's a sort of thing a young fellow of my expectations ought to sneeze at.

Many things are said or done out of habit and therefore lose any religious or other significance to the doers, sayers, or the hearers. One of these actions is uttering the phrase 'God bless you' when someone sneezes. Sir John Lubbock analysed this action in *The Origin of Civilization and the Primitive Condition of Man* in 1870.

Mr. Halliburton brings forward . . . the habit of saying "God bless you" or some equivalent expression when a person sneezes. He shows that this custom . . . is ancient and widely extended. It is mentioned by Homer, Aristotle, Apuleius, Pliny, and the Jewish rabbis, and has been observed in Koordistan, in Florida, in Otaheite, and in the Tonga Islands.

The 'ear' (Middle English *ere*, Anglo-Saxon *eare*) serves not only as the mechanism by which we 'hear' (Middle English *heren*, Anglo-Saxon *hyran*), but its 'lobe' (Greek *lobos)* is useful as place on which to display jewelry. The ear has also been useful to writers as a device to illustrate their ideas. In place of our modern phrase "head over heels," to describe someone fully committed either to love or to a project of some sort, the sixteenth century used 'ears' as the metaphor. Udall (*Ralph Roister Doister, a Comedy*, I,1) wrote in 1533

If any woman smyle, up is he to the harde eares in love.

Today we say 'his ears are burning'; John Heywood expressed the same thought in other words in *Prouerbes*, 1562.

Hir eares might well glow,
For all the towne talkt of hir.

Many are the ways in which lovers have expressed their desire to be near their beloved ones; Tennyson, in 1832, used the ear (*The Miller's Daughter*, XXII).

> I would be the jewel
> That trembles in her ear.

In 1833 Charles Lamb wrote an essay entitled "A Chapter on Ears" in which he had this figurative use of the ear.

> When therefore I say that I have no ear, you will understand me to mean —*for music.*

The word 'cheek' (Middle English *cheke, cheoke,* Anglo-Saxon *ceace*) has also served ethical and literary inspiration. Christ said, "Turn the other cheek." A reserved person is described by Sir John Harrington in *Epigrams both Pleasant and Serious* (#19), c. 1610.

> When others kisse with lip, you giue the cheeke.

Today we use the expression 'tongue in cheek' to indicate that what has been said is not to be taken too literally. In 1748 Tobias Smollett used the phrase with a somewhat different meaning in *The Adventures of Roderick Random* (LIV).

> I signified my contempt of him, by thrusting my tongue in my cheek.

For the meaning of 'tongue in cheek' as we use it today we go to Matthew Arnold (*Culture and Anarchy,* Preface), 1869.

> He unquestionably . . . knows that he is talking claptrap, and, so to say, puts his tongue in his cheek.

'Cheek by jowl' means both actual togetherness and figurative association. For an example of the former there is a translation by Meredith Hanmer of *The Aunciant Ecclesiasticall histories of the first six hundred years after Christ, written by Eusebius, Socrates, and Evagrius* (1577) in which appears

> Cheeke by iowle with the Emperour.

Josuah Sylvester, in his 1598 translation of *DuBartas his divine weekes and workes* (I), used the expression figuratively.

> Mercie and Justice, marching cheek by joule.

There are two other attitudes that have been described by the use of the 'cheek.' Insolence, generally from an inferior, is the attitude of a man observed by Frederick Marryat in *Poor Jack* (XXII) in 1840.

> The man, who was a sulky saucy sort of chap . . . gives cheek.

What is insolence in an inferior may be characterized as boldness or effrontery in an equal. This seems to be what Charles Reade was saying in 1861 in *The Cloister and the Hearth* (XLVIII).

> She told him . . . she wondered at his cheek.

'Dimple' (Middle English *dympull*) is probably allied to the Swedish word *dimpa* (to fall down, plunge) and therefore may have had the sense originally of a deep pool, from which came the idea of a hollow. Dimples occur on the cheek and on the 'chin' (allied to Sanskrit *hanu*, jaw). Theodore Winthrop (1828–61) penned a succinct description of the 'dimple' in *Cecil Dreeme* (XV).

> Dimple — that link between a feature and a smile.

There is something especially attractive about a dimple that has been known for ages. In what appears to be a description of the lovely Helen of Troy c. 1400 the anonymous translator waxes poetic (*Destruction of Troy*, 3060).

> Hir chyn full choise was . . .
> With a dympull full derne [deep], daynte to se.

For hundreds of years, men have tried to figure out a system to explain one's inner traits and characteristics from the shape of the various parts of the body. Here is an example from 1793 by Thomas Holcroft in his translation of Lavater's *Essays on Physiognomy* (XL).

> The pointed chin is held to be a sign of acuteness and craft.

The word 'mouth' (Old English *muth*) has its equivalents in Dutch *mond*, Icelandic *munur*, and Danish *mund*, all of which are related to the Latin *mandere* (to chew). There is an interesting metaphorical use of 'mouth' which reveals an early understanding of the law of supply and demand. In 1550 we find this plea for a reduction in the number of sheep in the country before the country is ruined (*Certayne causes gathered together, wherein is shewed the decaye of England . . . by the great multitude of shepe*, 97).

> So many mouthes goith to motton, whiche causeth motton to be dear.

Where today we would use the word "mouthpiece," Joseph Addison (1672 – 1719) simply used 'mouth' (*Coffee House Politicians*).

> Every coffee-house has some particular statesman belonging to it, who is the mouth of the street where he lives.

When our "mouths water" in anticipation of a good meal, we are, technically speaking, secreting 'saliva' (Latin *saliva*, spit, spittle). The word 'spit' is from the Middle English *spitten*. Whether one is waiting for animal or human food, the result is the same according to Richard Eden's translation of *The decades of the newe worlde or west India* in 1555.

> These craftie foxes [cannibals] . . . espying their enemies a farre of, beganne to swalowe theyr spettle as theyr mouthies watered for greedines of theyr pray.

Surrounding the mouth are 'lips.' We speak of upper and lower lips; in Middle English they were called *ufuveard lippa* and *nethere lippa*. When a good meal is brought to the table, it is not considered good manners to smack one's lips. So said F. Seager in *The schoole of vertue and booke of good nourture for chyldren and youth to learne theyr dutie by* in 1557.

> Not smackyng the lyppes, as commonly do hogges.

When we refrain from making a sarcastic or nasty remark, we are said to be 'biting our lips' in restraint. It is not a new expression. It was used in 1362 by William Langland in *The vision of William concerning Piers Plowman*.

> His body was to bolle [boil] for wratthe bat he bote [bit] his lippes.

If at some time we don't get something we feel we are entitled to, we involve the 'lip' in our reaction, as written by John Neal in 1833 (*Down Easters*, I).

> What's the use o' boohooin'? . . . Keep a stiff upper lip; no bones broke — don't I know?

Sometimes the 'lip' is used to show contempt. George P. James, in *The Life and Adventures of John Marston Hall*, 1834, said:

> A bitter smile curled the lip of the President.

And finally the 'lip' is used in certain phrases to convey a kind of insolence, as shown in Frank R. Stockton's *Rudder Grange* in 1879.

> I told him that I didn't want none of his lip.

On the upper lip some men wear a 'mustache,' spelled *mustachio* by Shakespeare. It is from the Greek *mustaki* (upper lip, mustache). Richard Sanders' advice to men in 1653 was to grow a *thick* 'mustache' if one were going to have one at all (*Physiognomie and Chiromancie, metoposcopie, the symmetrical and signal moles of the body, fully and accurately handled*).

> Those that have but a little mustache are of an ill nature.

Writing in 1596, Edmund Spenser indicated that the Spaniards concurred with Sanders (*A View of the present state of Ireland*).

> This was the auncient manner of Spaynyardes . . . to cutt of all theyr beardes close, save only theyr muschachoes, which they weare long.

In the movies the Native American indicates his distrust of the white man with the expression "White man speak with forked tongue." The use of the word 'tongue' (Anglo-Saxon *tunge*) to express this feeling was known in early English times. In William Caxton's translation of *The subtyl histories and fables of Esope, of Auyan, Alfonse, and Poge* (XXII) we find, in 1484:

> The felauship of the man whicke hath two tongues is nought.

There is a pseudo-Chinese saying, probably used by the fictional detective Charlie Chan, "Engage brain before putting tongue in gear." Heywood said in 1562 (*Prouerbes*):

> Thy tounge runth before thy wit.

"Enough talk," we say. "Actions speak louder than words." Almost six hundred years ago, in 1382, John Wyclif gave voice to the same thought in his translation of the Bible (I John, 3:18).

> Loue we not in word, nether in tunge, but in werk and treuthe.

There comes a time when we find it very difficult to hold back words that we might regret later on. We don't utter them; we do as York did in Shakespeare's *Henry VI, Part II* (act I, scene 1).

> So York must sit, and fret, and bite his tongue, . . .

A major function of the tongue is to 'taste.' The word 'taste,' however, was used in the fourteenth and fifteenth centuries to mean touch as well as taste. Here is an example of 'taste' used with the sense of "touch" (*Three prose versions of Secreta Secretorum*).

> The taste is a commyn witte Spraden thogh the body, but hit
> Shewyth hym most by the handys . . . by that witte we knowen hote,
> colde, dry, moyste and other Suche thyngs.

Further evidence of 'taste' meaning "touch" is found in *Merlin or the early history of King Arthur, a prose romance* (III, c. 1450).

> Merlin leide his heed in the damesels lappe, and she began to taste
> softly till he fell on slepe.

Even earlier than these two examples of taste referring to touch is this early-fourteenth-century excerpt showing the modern use of 'taste' with the tongue (*Richard Coer de Lion*).

> When he has a good tast, and eeten weel a good repast.

Figurative uses of 'taste' abound. In *Hamlet* (act II, scene 2) it means "to sample."

> Come, give us a taste of your quality; come, a passionate speech.

Richard Brinsley Sheridan used 'taste' as a synonym for "liking" or "preference" in *The Critic, or a Tragedy Rehearsed* (act I, scene 1).

> Now Mrs. Dangle, Sir Fretful Plegiary is an author to your own
> taste.

It is all very well to taste food, but to get nourishment out of it, we must bite or chew it, and to do that we need 'teeth.' The word comes from Latin *dens* (tooth); the verb is *dentire* (to teethe). From the same root comes 'dentist.' False 'teeth' have been made from wood and ivory among other substances. In Guillemeau's *French chirurgerye or the manualle operations of chirurgerye* of 1597 we find this reference.

> These artificialle teeth are sometimes made of Ivorye.

We commonly use the phrase 'tooth and nail' to describe a desperate kind of fighting, and it was so used by Sir Thomas More in 1534 (*A dialogue of comforte against tribulation*, III, 22).

> They would faine kepe them as long as euer they might, euen with
> tooth and naile.

Adam's original sin of disobedience was portrayed c. 1450 by using the idea of 'bite' (Middle English *bite, biten, bot, boot*, Anglo-Saxon *bitan*) in *Ludus coventriae; a collection of mysteries formerly represented at Coventry on the feast of Corpus Christi*.

Adam ffor thou that appyl boot [bit]
Agens my byddyng.

While women today are learning karate and other disciplines as a means of self-defense, their basic weapons were different in 1530, at least according to Jehan Palsgrave in *Lesclarcissement de la langue françoyse*.

A woman can defende her selfe no better than to scratche and byte.

The most important teeth in chewing are the 'molars.' They get their name from the Latin *mola* (a mill) — an example of the many cases where the name is derived from the function. The importance of these teeth and a recognition of the origin of the word was outlined by Thomas Fuller in *The history of the worthies of England* (I) in 1661.

How necessary these [mill stones] . . . are for man's sustenance is proved by the painful experience of such aged persons, who wanting their Molare Teeth must make use of their Gums for Grinders.

It is unfair to blame those Tartars of Central Asia for the word that describes the substance the dentist has to scrape off your teeth. The word has no connection with them; it is from the Arabic *durd* (dregs, sediment, the 'tartar' of wine), and was restricted to describing a by-product of one of nature's noblest achievements, wine. So said Trevisa (*Bartholomeus* XVI).

Tartar is wyn drastes [dregs], . . . and like to a softe ston cleuynge harde to the sides of the tonnes [tuns].

It was not until 1806 that the word 'tartar' was applied to teeth. An article in the *Medical Journal* (XV, 30) of that year stated:

We find that this coagulum has the greatest similarity with the tartar adhering to the teeth.

Babees Book was full of advice on deportment; here is its suggestion concerning teeth.

Nothur at thy mete thy toth thou pyke [pick].

There are many functions the mouth performs. Let us look first at two that normally do not involve the making of noise: 'smile' (Swedish *smila*, to smile, frown, smirk, simper), and 'swallow.' In Middle English the latter was *swolowen* or *swolwen*, related to the

German *schwelgen* (to eat or drink immoderately). Here is an excerpt from *Pilgrimage* by Samuel Purchase of 1613 showing two uses of 'swallow,' one figurative and one literal.

> The mother (not able to swallow her shame and griefe) cast herselfe into the lake to bee swallowed of the water . . .

All the other duties and functions of the mouth involve the making of some kind of noise. These include 'talk,' 'whistle,' 'sing,' 'chuckle,' 'giggle,' 'laugh,' 'sob,' 'scream,' and 'yell.'

An early version of "he who laughs last laughs best" was Heywood's in 1546 (*Prouerbes*).

> Better is the last smyle than the fyrst laughter.

We use 'laugh' (Middle English *laughen*) in several figurative ways today, all of which are found in early writings. Trevisa wrote in 1387 (*Polychronicon*):

> Men laughe hem selve to death.

And this warning about laughter appeared in England in 1560.

> You laugh — 'tis well — the tale applied
> May make you laugh on t'other side.

'Chuckle' and 'giggle' are imitative or onomatopoetic words; 'chuckle' is a variant and diminutive of *chuck* which was, according to Chaucer, the noise made by the cock when he found a grain of corn. Tennyson used it in speaking of a goose (*The Goose*).

> It clutter'd here, it chuckled there,
> It stirred the old wife's mettle.

Although Tennyson used 'chuckle' in describing a goose, he might have used 'giggle' which is from the Middle English *gagelen* (to make a noise like a goose). It is from this root that we get our word 'gaggle' to describe a flock of geese. In 1635 Francis Quarles wrote this ominous warning for those who giggled and frittered their lives away (*Emblems*, I).

> Fool, giggle on, and waste thy wanton breath;
> Thy morning laughter breeds an ev'ning death.

'Talk' (Middle English *talken*) is from the Anglo-Saxon *tal* (tale), something one might tell when one talks. Our word 'moan' was spelled *mone* in Middle English as we can see from this translation of

Froissart's *Chronicles* by John Bourchier Lord Berners in 1524.

> Than [then] they of the towne began to mone, and sayd, this dede ought not to be suffred.

'Sob' is also from a Middle English word, *sobben*, but it is related as well to an Anglo-Saxon word, *siofian* (to lament), and to an Old High German word, *sufan* (to sip, to sup).

Women have almost always taken verbal abuse from men. Back around 1509, when it really was a man's world, Alexander Barclay wrote this nasty bit about women in *The mirrour of good manners*.

> One woman chiding maketh greater yell
> Than should an hundred pyes [magpies] in one cage.

It is always interesting to look at Chaucer's spelling. Here is his version of 'yelled':

> They yelleden as feendes doon in helle.

'Yell' is from the Anglo-Saxon *gyllan, giellan* (to yell, cry out, re-sound), and both of these words are derived from the Old High German *galan* (to sing). It is from this latter word that we get 'nightingale,' a "singer in the night."

Being required by unfortunate circumstances to 'sing a different tune' is usually not a happy situation. This is how John Gower phrased it in 1390 (*Confessio*, I).

> O thou, which hast desesed The Court of France be [by] thi wrong,
> Now schalt thou singe an other song.

An odd contemporary meaning of 'sing' (Middle English *singen*, Anglo-Saxon *singan*) is to squeal or inform. Sir Walter Scott defined it in *Guy Mannering; or the Astrologer* (XVIII, note) in 1815.

> To sing out or whistle in the cage, is when a rogue, being apprehended, peaches against his comrades.

(The verb *peaches* in this citation is from Middle English *apechen*, which is a variant of *impechen*, 'to impeach.')

Allied to the normal meaning of 'sing' is 'whistle.' It is from a Teutonic base, 'hwist' (to imitate the hissing sound of whistling), and it is from this same root that we have the word 'whisper.' Whistling when in trouble is supposed to make us forget that there is a problem; so we have been advised by Robert Blair in *The Grave*, 1742.

> The Schoolboy . . . Whistling aloud to bear his Courage up.

While the winner of a contest may 'scream' with joy, the word was originally associated with terror, since it came from the Icelandic word *skreama* (to scare, terrify). The association of the word with terror is made clear in this citation from c. 1400 (*Laud troy book*).

> A dredful dreme that lady dremed,
> That in hir sclepe she cried & scremed.

We have spent much time on the head and particularly the mouth since so much of what we do, say, and perceive is carried on by the organs of the head. But it is now time to move on to the rest of the body, and next in line come the 'neck,' the 'nape,' and the 'collar bone.' Both 'neck' (Middle English *nekke*) and 'nape,' (Middle English *knappe*) are related to similar words in several Teutonic languages, for example, Dutch *nek* (nape of the neck) and Norwegian *nakke* (knoll).

Here is practical advice as to what to do to stay free from colds. In his translation of Vives' *Introduction to Wysedome* Sir Richard Morison, in 1540, suggested that you

> Kepe the nape of thy necke from cold.

In his *A compleat practice of physick* of 1656 John Smith had special words for those who find it hard to get going in the morning.

> Every morning rub hard the hinder part of the Head and Nape.

The 'collar-bone' or 'clavicle' (Latin *clavicula*, diminutive of *clavis*, key) got its name, according to Emile Littré's *Dictionnaire de la Langue Française*, 1863– 77, "because it was compared to the key of a vault, or, as others think, because its form is that of the ancient bolts." This tongue-in-cheek advice from Sir Richard Steele in *Spectator* #474 has particular relevance for skiers today.

> None should be admitted into this green conversation-piece, except he had broken his collar-bone thrice.

Like other parts of the body, the 'shoulder' (Middle English *shulder, shuldre*, Anglo-Saxon *sculdor, sculder*) is used figuratively in a number of expressions. Thomas Hood used 'shoulder' this way in *A Drop of Gin* (III) in 1845.

> [They] snub, neglect, cold-shoulder, and cut
> The ragged pauper, misfortune's butt.

A simple statement of fact takes on an interesting meaning when it appears in the proper context and with the right emphasis. Robert Louis Stevenson showed how in 1883 (*Treasure Island,* XXXII).

> "Well, that's so," he said, "you've a head upon your shoulders, John, and no mistake."

Stevenson might not have written that had he been able to accompany Sir John Maundeville on his travels. This is what Maundeville reported in his *The buke of John Maundeuill being the travels of Sir. J. Mandeville knight 1322 – 56,* c. 1400.

> On another Yle, toward the Southe, duellen folk of foule Stature and of cursed kynde, that han no Hedes, and here [their] Eyen ben in here Scholdres.

Descending from the shoulder is the 'arm,' a word from an Aryan root *ar* (to fit, join) referring to the motion of the arm from the joint between it and the shoulder. It figures in an expression we use to indicate a desire for solitude, 'to keep at arm's length.' It is fascinating to note that a similar expression was used back in 1669 by William Penn (*No Cross, No Crown*, XIII).

> Live loose to the World, have it at Arm's-End.

It is doubtful that a young woman of today would be flattered by this description of Charles Reade's in 1863 (*All Year Round,* October 3).

> A gentle timidity that contrasted prettily with her biceps muscle.

The word 'biceps' describes a muscle which has two heads or points of origin. It comes from two Latin words, *bis* (twice) and *caput* (head). Similarly it took two Anglo-Saxon words to give us 'elbow', *eln* (ell) and *bugan* (to bend). Here is a style note from 1676, written by Sir George Etheredge in *The Man of Mode* (I, 1).

> He was yesterday at the Play, with a pair of Gloves Up to his Elbows.

Today we say, 'Speak of the devil and he appears.' It was phrased differently by Sir John Vanbrugh in *Aesop* (II, 1 in 1698).

> Talk of the Devil, and he's at your elbow.

William Cowper warned, in 1784, all those who would deal with gamblers (*The Task,* III).

> The wings that waft our riches out of sight,
> Grow on the gamester's elbows.

Between the arm and the 'hand' (Middle English *hond, hand*) is the 'wrist.' Its original form was *handwrist* (that which turns the hand about). The 'wrist' part of the word is from the Anglo-Saxon *wrioan* (to writhe, twist). There was also a word *fot-wrist,* which referred to the instep or ankle, as seen in these lines from "Robin Hood rescuing the widow's three sons" (in *Child's Ballads*) where 'wrist' is substituted for the original *fot-wrist.*

> Then he put on the old man's hose,
> were patch'd from knee to wrist.

We call the inside of the hand the 'palm' from Middle English *paume* and Latin *palma*. A similar word in Anglo-Saxon is *folm,* and allied to it is the English word 'fumble.' This is not the place to argue the merits of palm-reading; suffice it to say that this practice has existed for many years. William Somerville wrote disparagingly in 1740 of gypsies and palm-reading (*Hobbinal, or the rural games, a burlesque poem,* III).

> She of the Gypsy Train, . . . artful to view The Spreading Palm, and with vile Cant deceive the Love-Sick Maid.

'Palm' was used by Eaton S. Barrett in 1807 (as quoted in *The Rising Sun* by Cervantes Hogg) as part of an expression involving bribes.

> You would imply that if we were greased in the palm, we should, like them, be ready to turn a courtier.

The 'fingers' (Middle English *fyngres*) of the hand serve to hold rings, utensils, and tools. As ring-bearers they were described by Langland (*Plowman*) in 1362.

> Hir fyue Fyngres weore frettet with Rynges.

Here is more advice from *Babees Book* on proper behavior while eating.

> Put not thy fyngerys on thy dysche,
> Nothyr in flesche, nothir in fysche.

There have always been busybodies. Here is Lusatia as depicted by Bartholomew Harris in his translation of Parival's *Historie of this iron age,* 1659.

> Lusatia . . . must needs, forsooth, have her Finger in the Pye.

This adage from John Ray (*A collection*) hasn't changed much since 1670.

> He hath more in's little finger, then thou in thy whole body.

Someone who is awkward and clumsy is described as being 'all thumbs' (from Middle English *thombe,* Anglo-Saxon *thuma*). John Heywood (*Prouerbes*) wrote of such a man.

> When he should get [something] ought [out], eche fynger is a thumbe.

Shakespeare ascribed a special sensitivity to the 'thumb' in *Macbeth* (act IV, scene 1).

> By the pricking of my thumbs,
> Something wicked this way comes . . .

Benjamin H. Malkin translated A. R. LeSage's *Adventures of Gil Blas of Santillane* (VII, 3), 1809, with this statement of support for all suffering authors.

> Authors . . . are under the thumb of booksellers and players.

The 'thumb' figures in a gesture of contempt which is still used in parts of Europe. The gesture and its meaning are clearly delineated in this comic interlude from *Romeo and Juliet* (act I, scene 1).

> SAMPSON. Nay, as they dare. I will bite my thumb at them; which is
>   a disgrace to them, if they bear it.
> ABRAHAM. Do you bite your thumb at us, sir?
> SAMPSON. I do bite my thumb, sir.
> ABRAHAM. Do you bite your thumb at us, sir?
> SAMPSON. [aside to GREGORY] Is the law on our side, if I say ay?
> GREGORY. [aside to SAMPSON] No.
> SAMPSON. No, sir, I do not bite my thumb at you, sir; but I bite my
>   thumb, sir.

The spelling of 'nail' on the finger and 'nail' meaning "spike," are identical today, but in fifteenth- and sixteenth-century England, there was much variation. *Babees Book*, which covered every part of the body in giving advice, used the spelling *nailes* in dealing with fingernails.

> Pare clene thy nailes.

Sir Richard Torkington used *nayle*, c. 1515, but he was referring to an iron nail as a religious relic (*Ye oldest diarie of Englysse travell: Being the hitherto unpublished narrative of the pilgrimage of Sir R. Torkington to Jersusalem*).

> And in the mydys of the Sterr [star] is on [one] of naylis that ower Savyr Crist was crucifyed with.

Hall and Donne also used the spelling *nayle* but they were speaking of human nails. Here is Edward Hall in 1548 writing in *Chronicle* (*The union of the two noble and illustre famelies of Lancestre and Yorke*, VI).

> A scoldyng woman, whose weapon is onely her toungue and her nayles.

John Donne was not much kinder to the fair sex. In 1639 he wrote in his *Poems*:

> She is all faire, but yet hath foule long nayles.

While we are on the subject of nails, it is appropriate to consider that very painful affliction that visits all of us at one time or another, the 'hangnail.' It was originally *angnail*, a word from two Anglo-Saxon words, *ang* (painful, compressed) and *naegl* (spike), which when put together meant something painfully fixed in the flesh like an iron nail. Confusion with two other words, Middle French *angonailles* (bumps, sores) and Latin *paronychia* (sore at the finger-nail), and perhaps a loss of the original sense of *naegl*, *angnail* developed into our word 'hangnail,' meaning the ripped skin at the fingernail. The agony of the 'hangnail' is demonstrated by Sir Roger L'Estrange in *Seneca's morals by way of abstract* (XXIII) in 1678.

> The ripping of a Hang-nail is sufficient to Dispatch us.

Some of the activitites we do with our hands are 'feel,' 'touch,' 'grasp,' 'squeeze,' and 'clutch.' 'Feel' (Middle English *felen*) is related to the Anglo-Saxon *folm* (palm of the hand) and the Latin *palma* (palm). It is difficult not to 'feel' envious of the perquisites enjoyed by kings in sixteenth-century England. Edward Hall reported in 1548 (*Chronicle*).

> By King Edward, which loved well both to loke and to fele fayre dammosels.

We also use 'feel' figuratively, and one of the earliest uses of 'feel like' is found in an article by James Grant in *Century Magazine*'s November 1865 issue.

> I now feel like ending this matter . . . before we go back.

We have discussed 'taste' used in the modern sense of 'touch.' Let us now look at the word 'touch' itself (French *toucher,* Italian *toccare*; German *zucken,* to twitch, draw with a quick motion). An early use of 'touch' with the idea of physical contact is found in a fourteenth-century reference to Midas, written by Gower (*Confessio*) in 1390.

> For he . . . preide,
> That wherupon his hond he leide,
> It scholde thurgh his touche anon,
> Become gold.

The word 'touch' has also been used with the connotation of sexual contact. A writer in the fourteenth century made this observation in *Cursor mundi (The cursor of the world, a Northumbrian poem of the fourteenth century in four versions).*

> Fra toche of hir [her touch] I saued be.

John Lydgate used 'touch' similarly in *Troy Book* (I), c. 1412 – 20.

> Sche [she] Ay kepte hir clene from touche of any man.

An expression involving 'touch' has crept into the language from the South. We speak of someone who is a bit strange as being 'tetched in the head.' It is not a new expression. It was used by Steele in *Tatler* #78.

> This touch in the Brain of the British Subject is . . . owing to the reading News-Papers.

A funny thing happened to 'grasp' on its way to modern English. It was originally the Anglo-Saxon word *graps,* but the *p* and the *s* were transposed, and in Middle English it had become *graspen.* Using the word 'grasp,' Sir John Denham gave a clue in 1642 (*Cooper's Hill*) as to how revolutions arise.

> Kings, by grasping more than they could hold,
> First make their subjects, by oppression, bold.

The same transposition happened to 'clasp'; it was originally *claps.*

Middle English *clucchen* gave us 'clutch' spelled *clouch* by Edmund Spenser in *The Faerie Queene* (III, 10).

> But all in vaine: his woman was too wise
> Ever to come into his clouch againe.

Another Middle English word, *queisen,* is the source for 'squeeze' with an *s* prefixed for emphasis. We have mentioned the lengths to which men and women will go for the sake of fashion. Here is an instance from 1779 in *The Mirror* #12 (by H. Mackenzie and others).

> Their bosoms . . . were squeezed up to their throats.

The word 'trunk' for the human body is not the same word as the 'trunk' of an elephant. The human 'trunk' is from Latin *truncum* (trunk of the body, stem, trunk), while the elephant's 'trunk' is a mistaken form of *trump,* which is an old word for a hollow stem or tube and from which we get the word for the musical instrument, 'trumpet.' Here is a definition of 'trumpet' from *Promptorium Parvalorum* in 1440.

> Trumpet, or a lytylle trumpe, that clepythe [calls] to mete, or men togedur.

Surrounding the trunk, as well as the rest of the body, is the 'skin' (Icelandic *skinn,* Danish *skind*). In the common expression "wolf in sheep's clothing," "clothing" is another word for 'skin.' It was stated more clearly and directly in 1526 in *The pilgrimage of perfection.*

> These by [be] welues [wolves] in lambes skynnes.

If the wolf turns out to be harmless, we will feel like the man described in 1584 in a translation of *The famous history of Herodotus* by B. Rich (I).

> Hymselfe as one ready to leape out of hys skynne for joy.

Under certain conditions one must weigh whether it is worth while to save one's skin; so said Daniel Rogers in 1642 in *Naaman the Syrian, his disease and cure.*

> Aequivocating with our conscience . . . for the saving of our owne skin, is abominable.

A traveler in New York in 1882 might have saved his 'skin,' but he could have lost something else if he weren't careful, according to James D. MacCabe in *New York by Sunlight and Gaslight* (XXXIX).

> The "skin game" is used, with the majority of the visitors, for the proprietor is determined from the outset to fleece them without mercy.

A miser probably would have stayed away from the places that used the 'skin game' on visitors since he would not be the spending kind. He might have been call a 'skinflint,' that is, one so tight with money that he would even skin a flint if that were possible.

One thing the skin does in profusion, particularly on a hot day, is 'sweat' (Middle English *swoot, swete*). We have all been brought up with the idea that we must earn our living with the 'sweat of our brows.' Here are two dissenters from that idea. Thomas Wilson, in 1553, had this question in *The arte of rhetorique* (Preface).

> Who would travaile and toile with the sweate of his browes?

Richard Brathwait was even more emphatic in 1621 as to the desirability of the easy life (*Natures embassie*).

> Liue on the sweat of others browes.

Whether for reasons of health, or because he didn't like after-exertion body odor, Richard Mulcaster laid down the following stricture in *Positions, wherein those primitive circumstances be examined, which are necessarie for the training up of children*, 1581.

> The rule is, change apparell after sweat.

It used to be said in polite society that a lady never sweats, she perspires. Perhaps this is what Nathaniel Fairfax meant when he wrote in 1667 in *Philosophical Transactions* (II).

> She affirm'd, she never swet in her life.

The situation is reversed with a female character of Dryden in his *Cock and Fox*, of 1700.

> With Exercise she sweat ill Humors out.

When all avenues but one are closed and that one risky, we are liable to sweat from nervousness. Alexander Pennecuik wrote of such a man in 1715 (*A geographical, historical description of the shire of Tweeddale, with a miscelany of Scotish poems*).

> This put our Conjuror in a deep sweet,
> Who now had only one Shift left him.

In another work Dryden and the Duke of Newcastle used sweat figuratively in 1667 (*Sir Martin Mar-all, or the feign'd innocence, a comedy*, act V, scene 2).

> If my shoulders had not paid for thi fault, my purse must have sweat blood for't.

Finally here is some drastic advice for dieters from John Arbuthnot written in 1713 (*Law is a bottomless pit, exemplified in the case of the Lord Strutt, John Bull, Nicholas Frog, and Lewis Baboon*, IV).

> He should be purged, sweated, vomited, and starved, till he come to a sizeable bulk.

The word 'sweatshop' for a place where people are forced to work inordinately long hours for little pay may have had its beginning in this citation from Henry Mayhew (*London Labour and the London Poor*, I), of 1851 – 61.

> I have many a time heard both husband and wife . . . who were sweating for a gorgeous clothes' emporium, say that they had not time to clean.

'Back' has its counterparts in Anglo-Saxon *baec* and Icelandic *bak*, while 'chest' has its roots in Middle English *cheste* and *chiste*. The latter word comes from the Greek word *kiste* (box). 'Breast' (Middle English *brest*, Anglo-Saxon *breost*) is related to the French word *bras* (arm), while 'bosom' is from Middle English *bosum* and *bosen*.

'Bosom' has been used with several meanings in the English language. Richard Hooker (1554– 1600) used it as a synonym for "family" (*Of the lawes of ecclesiastical politie*).

> They that live within the bosom of that church.

In the Book of Ecclesiastes (7:9) it is the abode of passion.

> Anger resteth in the bosom of fools.

John Fletcher and William Rowley employed 'bosom' in *The maide in the mill* (II), 1623, with the meaning of "intimate."

> I know you are his bosom counsellor.

The 'nipple' (perhaps from Middle English *nib*, *neb*) on the breast may be related to Old French *nifle* and Italian *niffa*, words which have the several meanings of beak, nose, and spout. The word 'nib' for the point of a pen may also be from these same roots.

'Waist' (Middle English *wast*, Anglo-Saxon *weaxan*, to grow) is tied in to the sense of growth, related to Scandinavian words with that meaning. Our word 'wax,' meaning to grow, increase, or become, is from the same Anglo-Saxon root. In the fluctuation of fashion over the years, the 'waist' has also fluctuated between thick and thin. A thin period was reported by John Bulwer in 1650 (*Anthropometamorphosis; Men transformed, or the artificial changeling, etc.*, XX).

> Young Virgins, who thinking a slender waste a great beauty, strive all that they possibly can by streight-lacing themselves, to attaine unto a wand-like smalnesse of waste.

An issue of *Sporting Magazine* (XLVIII) in 1816 carried a play on words which is highly appropriate for this volume.

> A lady observing her neighbour in a public room, dressed very tawdrily in a satin waist, drily remarked, it was a waste of satin.

'Navel' (Middle English *nauel*) is a diminutive of 'nave' (Middle English *naue*, Anglo-Saxon *nafu*) which means the central part of the wheel which holds the axle and at one time meant the center point of the body. (Note there is another English word 'nave', meaning the main, the middle part of a church; it comes from the Latin *navis*, ship.) Attached to the navel during gestation is the 'umbilical cord' (Latin, *umbilicum*, navel, middle, center). Ralph Waldo Emerson used it figuratively in 1847 in *Representative Men* (I).

> With a force of many men, he could never break the umbilical cord which held him to nature.

'Buttock' is a diminutive of the Middle English word *butt* (end), which is related to many Scandinavian words meaning stump, blunt, and clod. Among the first to use 'vagina' (Latin *vagina*, sheath, scabbard) in English was Thomas Gibson (*The anatomy of humane bodies epitomized*) in 1682.

> It has passages . . . for the neck of the Bladder, and in Women for the vagina of the Womb.

'Penis' (Latin *penis*, tail, 'penis') was defined in 1684 in an anatomical dictionary (S. Blancard's *Physical dictionary*) as

> "Penis," the Yard, made up of two nervous Bodies, the Channel, Nut, Skin and Fore-skin . . .

Connoisseurs of modern slang may recognize two terms from this definition which are in use today: 'yard' for penis and 'nut,' used in the plural, for testicles. Some etymologists connect 'testicle' (Latin *testis*) with the word "testimony" from the Biblical story concerning the placement of one's hand on one's testicles when testifying in order to certify as to the truth of what was being said. Others say there is not one grain of truth in this notion. Anyway, 'testify' is derived from the Latin *testis* (which also means witness, with or without the sexual connection) and *facere* (to make, do).

Inside the skin are the bony parts of the body which make up the 'skeleton' (Greek *skeleton,* mummy, skeleton, from Akkadian *shalamdu,* the whole [corpse]). It was defined in 1611 by Randle Cotgrave in his *Dictionarie of the French and English tongues.*

> "scelete" . . . a carkasse whereof nothing is left but the bones, which we call a Skelton, or Skeliton.

Thackeray seems to have been among the first to make use of the phrase 'skeleton in the closet.' In *The Newcomes; memoirs of a most respectable family* (IV) he wrote in 1855:

> Some particulars regarding the Newcome family, which will show us they have a skeleton or two in *their* closets, as well as their neighbours.

A principal part of the skeleton is the 'spine' (Middle English *espine* and Latin *spina,* thorn, spine, backbone), consisting of 'vertebrae.' This word is rooted in the Latin *vertere* (to turn). (From the past participle of this same Latin word, *versus,* we get our word 'verse,' so named from the turning at the end of each line in order to start a new one.)

The word 'bone' was spelled *boon* by Chaucer and *ban* in Anglo-Saxon. Everyone remembers from his youth the expression "Sticks and stones," etc. The idea is not new; in 1681 E. Sclater wrote in *A Sermon at Putney* (II):

> Weapons, that to be sure, draw no Blood, nor break any Bones.

It is probable that we get the phrase 'bone of contention' from the manner in which dogs fight over bones. Henry Lord Brougham used the phrase in 1839 in *Historical sketches of statesmen of the time of George III.*

Sardinia was one of the chief bones of contention between Genoa and Pisa.

Gamblers often refer to the dice they throw as 'bones.' Benjamin Disraeli used the word with that meaning in *The Young Duke* (II) in 1831.

He felt a little odd when he first rattled the bones.

The word 'bonfire,' incidentally, is not a "good" fire as it would appear from the French *bon* (good), but rather is made up of two words 'bone' and 'fire.' This is how it was used by Spenser in *Epithalamion* (I) in 1595.

Ring ye the bels, to make it weare away,
And bonefiers make all day.

The particular bone known as the 'femur' (Latin *femur*, thigh) gets its name from the location, while the collection of bones called the 'pelvis' (Latin *pelvis*, basin) gets its name from its shape. Bones connect or are joined at 'joints.' The source Latin word is *junctus*, past participle of *jungere* (to join).

Between the bones and the skin is the 'flesh' (Middle English *fleisch, flesch*, Anglo-Saxon *flaesc*) corresponding to words in many Scandinavian tongues meaning pork and bacon as well as flesh. A common figurative use of 'flesh' is found in Allan Ramsay's *The gentle shepherd a Scots pastoral comedy* (J, 1) in 1725.

A . . . dream . . .
That gars [makes] my flesh a' creep yet with the fright.

The next time you are tempted to call someone who irritates you a 'fathead' you ought to remember what Trevisa said (*Bartholomeus*).

The heed [head] hath lytell flessh and lytyll fatnesse.

Preachers and writers on religious subjects have often used the word 'flesh' to denote carnal as opposed to spiritual appetites. This is how Robert Burton put it in 1621 in *The Anatomy of Melancholy*.

Satan is their guide, the flesh is their instructor.

Running through the inside of the body are 'muscles.' This is a strange word, coming as it does from the Latin *musculus*, a diminutive of *mus* (mouse) and meaning literally "little mouse." It is from the creeping appearance as one moves one's muscles that they get their name. (*Mus* also gave us 'mouse,' and *musculus* also gave us 'mussel,' whose strong 'muscle' holds its two shells together.)

'Nerve,' spelled *nerfe* in Middle English, is from the Latin *nervus* (sinew) and may be related to the Greek *neira* (belly) and the Sanskrit *snara* (tendon). Shakespeare used 'nerve' with the Latin meaning of "sinew" in *The Tempest* (act II, scene 1) referring to the process of growing old.

> Thy nerves are in their infancy again,
> And have no vigour in them.

The 'blood' (Middle English *blod* and *bloude*) was once considered to rule our emotions, and we still speak of actions done "in cold blood" as well as those committed by "hotblooded" people. That we are ruled primarily by our emotions, that is, by our 'blood' and not our reason, was clear to Shakespeare. This is from *The Merchant of Venice* (act I, scene 2).

> The brain may devise laws for the blood; but a hot temper leaps
> o'er a cold decree: . . .

The semiprecious stone called the 'bloodstone' was once considered to have special powers, according to Thomas Wilson (*The rule of reason, conteinyng the arte of logique*), 1551.

> The bloodstone stoppeth blood.

One of the characteristics claimed by aristocratic families is that 'blue blood' flows in their veins. This claim originated with some of the old and proud families of Castille in Spain; they said their blood was blue, *sangre azul* in Spanish, and not contaminated with that of lesser and foreign peoples. The idea probably arose from the perception that veins in light-skinned people appear blue in contrast with the color of the veins in the darker-skinned. The phrase appeared in print in 1834 in *Helen* (XV-D) by Maria Edgeworth.

> One [officer] from Spain, of high rank and birth of the *sangre azul*,
> the *blue blood*.

The word 'blood' used to be used to describe a rake, a man of spirit and fire, or, in our terms, a playboy or jet setter. Oliver Goldsmith (1728–74) wrote about such men in *Reverie at Boar's Head Tavern*.

> The gallants of those times pretty much resembled the bloods of
> ours.

One of the first things a doctor requests from a patient is a sample of his 'urine.' The word is from the Latin *urina* (urine), whose Indo-European root, *wer,* is also related to Old Norse *ver* (sea) and *ur* (drizzling rain). The practice of examining 'urine' is an old one; Caxton wrote about it (*Histories*).

> Whan the medecyns had sene . . . his vrine also, they sayd that he had no bodyly sekeness.

Should you have trouble with your 'urine,' you might want to consult your physician to see if he agrees with the advice given by Arbuthnot in *Rules of diet* (I) in 1732.

> Cucumbers are useful in bloody Urine.

Another excretion which serves to rid the body of unwanted material is called 'feces.' It comes, appropriately enough, from the Latin word *faeces,* which means "dregs."

Twenty-two centuries ago, the Greek physician and philosopher Galen described 'four cardinal humours,' the latter word coming from the Latin *humor* (moisture), and said that they were responsible for one's health and disposition. The four are 'choler' (yellow bile), 'blood,' 'phlegm,' and 'melancholy' (black bile). It was considered important for good health to have the four 'humours' well-balanced in the body. We have seen how an excess of 'blood,' used in the sense of a 'humour,' led to passion's rule over reason. 'Bile,' from the Latin *bilis* (bile, anger), was the humour that regulated 'anger.' Its synonym 'choler' (Middle English *colere,* bile, anger) like the French word *colère* (anger) came from the Latin *cholera* (bile). In the sixteenth century in England, cholera was a nonfatal disease similar to our modern influenza. The Asiatic cholera, the deadly variety, was so named for the resemblance of the symptoms to its European cousin.

Chaucer worried about the balance of the 'humours' in the body and had one of his story-tellers give this sage advice to the listener (Nun Priest's Tale).

> I conseille yow . . . That bothe of Colere and of Malencolye Ye purge yow.

Shakespeare echoed this advice in *The Merry Wives of Windsor* (act II, scene 3).

> Throw cold water on thy choler.

It was not until the end of the seventeenth century that the word 'humour' (American spelling 'humor') acquired generally the modern meaning of something funny, diverting, or amusing. The following appeared in a translation of a work by Glanius (*Voyage to Bengala*), in 1682.

> The Cup was so closed, that 'twas a difficult matter for us to open it, and therefore the General gave it us on purpose, to divert himself with the humour of it.

In the fourteenth century, 'melancholy' was equated to insanity as shown in this use of the word from Gower (*Confessio*).

> Anone [anon] into melancolie,
> As though it were a fransie,
> He fell.

It was not until the seventeenth century that physicians recognized 'bile' or 'choler' for what it was, a bodily secretion with no special control over conduct as earlier physicians and philosophers had believed. T. Gibson made a simple medical statement in 1682 indicating this fact.

> Choler is separated by the Liver.

The supposed influence of 'melancholy' (Green *melas,* black, and *chole,* bile) is clear from its meaning: that is, a preponderance of "black bile" in the system leads to sadness and depression.

The fourth humour was 'phlegm' (Green *phlegma,* inflammation, heat), an excess of which led to what appears to be a contradictory state of health, a quiet or phlegmatic personality, becoming in extreme cases indolent or apathetic. Trevisa (*Bartholomeus,* IV) described the type of man in whom 'phlegm' was out of balance.

> A verry flewmatike man is in the body lustless [listless], heuy and slow.

By 1601 'phlegm,' like 'choler,' was recognized as another of the bodily secretions, as seen in Philemon Holland's translation of Pliny's *Historie of the world, commonly called the natural historie* (II).

> Wormwood . . . dischargeth the brest of tough fleagme.

According to a book on health published in 1788 (*Touchstone of complexions*) 'phlegm' was secreted not in the breast but in the stomach.

> For throughe cruditye and lack of perfect concoction in the stomacke is engendered great abundance of naughty baggage and hurtfull phlegme.

We will begin our journey through the internal organs with the 'stomach.' The word is from the Greek *stomachos* which was the mouth, opening, or gullet. From these several meanings the word came to have the sense of the opening or orifice of any organ but especially of the 'stomach.' Later it came to be the word for the 'stomach' itself. The 'stomach' has had two roles in medical and literary history. On the one hand it has been considered the receptacle for nourishment and therefore susceptible to disturbances from over- or underindulgence; consequently it became the object of all kinds of advice for the soothing of these disturbance. On the other hand it was the seat of feelings, emotions, and desires.

Let us look at its role as a receptacle first. Thomas Hoccleve wrote these comforting words in *La Male regle* in 1406:

> A draght of wyn . . . To warme a stomak with.

Woodall and Dryden had other suggestions for the well-being of the 'stomach.' In John Woodall's *The Surgions mate,* 1612, this line appears.

> Mace . . . strengtheneth the stomack.

In a work by John Dryden and Sir William Davenant (*Shakespeare's Tempest, or the enchanted island*), 1669, we find another remedy to comfort the stomach.

> This [Brandy] works comfortably on a cold stomach.

The *Daily Chronicle* of February 20, 1903, had some advice as to what not to put in one's stomach.

> Thus tea and coffe both retard stomach digestion powerfully.

Erasmus, the famous theologian, didn't like fish, and he expressed that dislike as follows.

> My heart is Catholic, but my stomach Lutheran.

Let us look now at the stomach in its other role. An unusual use of the word was as a verb with the meaning of "resent." Oliver Cromwell is quoted in Roger B. Merriman's *Life and Letters of Thomas Cromwell* (1902, I) as having said in 1523:

> I stomak as a sory Subiect may doo, the high injuries done by the said Francoys.

Most commonly, however, 'stomach' was used as a noun in these figurative descriptions of its role. Gower (*Confessio*, II) looked on the stomach as the seat of lust.

> Cupide . . . was the sire
> Of the stomak, which builleth evere,
> Wherof the lustes ben the levere.

Outside events made an impact on the stomach. Hall (*Chronicle*, IV) wrote:

> These reasons . . . sancke in the Dukes stomacke.

God himself was not exempt. Rogers (*Naaman*) wrote:

> Evill which causeth such a fulsomenesse and wearinesse in Gods stomacke.

The stomach was also considered to be the seat of desire or inclination. Bishop Gavin Douglas's translation of *The xiii bukes of Eneados of the famose poete Virgill* (XIII, 6), 1513, described one who acted against his own wishes.

> Agane [against] his stomak . . . the contrak is ybrokken.

'Belly,' virtually a synonym for stomach, is a perfectly good English word although considered somewhat vulgar and therefore not too commonly used in polite society. Shakespeare put it to good effect in describing a judge in *As You Like It* (act II, scene 7).

> And then the justice, in fair round belly with good capon lined, . . .

The word 'belly' is from the Anglo-Saxon *belig* (bag) and *belgan* (to swell out), which is of course what it does when we overeat.

We speak of someone willing to tackle a difficult job as having the 'guts' to do it. The word is related to an Indo-European root, *ghud* (to pour), and also had the sense of a channel. 'Guts' was once a synonym for bowel as reported by Trevisa (*Bartholomeus*, V, 42).

> The bowelles ben cominly called the guttes.

The source of the word 'bowel' is the Latin *botulus* (sausage). Today we speak of food poisoning as 'botulism,' literally a problem with the bowel. Like many of the words we have discussed, 'bowel' found its figurative uses. Shakespeare wrote in *Henry VI, Part I* (act I, scene 1)

> Rush'd into the bowels of the battle.

Sheridan, in *The School for Scandal* (act III, scene 3) viewed the bowel as the seat of pity, kindness, or compassion.

> What the plague, have you no bowels for your own kindred?

'Anus' is directly from the Latin *anus*. 'Rectum' is from the Latin *rectum* meaning "straight," from the form the 'rectum' takes in some animals. Robert Copland established its location in this anatomical note from his translation of Guydon's *The questyonary of cyrurgyens . . . or methode curatyfe of Claude Galyen* (H, 3), 1541.

> Fyrste it behoueth to begyn at the ars gut that is called longaum or rectum.

'Arse' (Middle English *aers, ears,* or *eeres*) was a respectable word in 1480 as used by William Caxton in *The cronicles of England* (CCXXVI).

> They lete hange fox tailles . . . to hele and hyde her arses.

By 1623 Philip Massinger and Thomas Dekker were using 'arse' in a slang sense *(The virgin martir, a tragedie,* act II, scene 1).

> The arse, as it were, or fag end of the world.

The 'kidney' (origin obscure; this organ may have taken its name from its shape which resembles an egg) secretes the liquid waste of the body and the bladder catches it. (An early English version of the word was *kideneiren,* and it has been proposed that *eiren* represents the plural of the old form of "egg," while the first part of the word may be from the Anglo-Saxon *codd,* bag.) We rarely see today a use of the word 'kidney' that was once quite common: to describe a class or sort of men. Hugh Latimer demonstrated this usage c. 1555 in *Sermons and remains*.

> To pronounce all to be thieves to a man, except myself, of course, and those men . . . that are of my own kidney.

Like other organs the kidney has had behavior traits ascribed to it. These lines appeared around 1400 in *Political, religious and love poems*.

> The Ire in the gawle [gall], Auaryce in the kydney.

Today we call those puffed-up, pretentious people who cannot stop talking, 'windbags.' They have always been around as illustrated in Calvin's *Sermons on the epistles to Timothie and Titus,* translated in 1579 by Laurence Tomson.

> Them that are harebraines and bladders full of winde.

The 'bladder' (Anglo-Saxon *bloedre,* blister, bladder) served as an inspiration for a marvelous curse written by Robert Burns in 1783 in *The death and dying words of poor Mailie.*

> May gravels round his blather wrench!

In addition to the kidney bladder we have a 'gall' bladder. 'Gall' (Anglo-Saxon *gealla*) gets its name from its color, being a yellowish material. The word 'yellow' is from a similar Anglo-Saxon word, *geolo,* and is allied to the Latin *heluus* (light red or yellow). Like virtually all the internal organs it has found its figurative uses. In the sense of bitterness it was used by Thomas Middleton and Thomas Dekker in 1611 in *The Roaring girle, or Moll Cutpurse* (act III).

> Loue sweets tast best, when we haue drunk downe Gall.

In the modern sense of impudence or assurance it appeared in the *Cambridge* (Massachusetts) *Frozen Truth* of November 28, 1890.

> And "gall," of which Joe always had plenty, especially as a politician.

The 'lungs' are porous, spongy, and very light organs. It is from this last characteristic that they get their name. The word is allied to the Sanskrit word *laghe* (light in weight). From this root we get not only 'lung' but also the words 'light' and 'levity.' Indeed lungs were at one time called "lights" as shown in this health note from Henry Lyte's translation in 1578 of R. Dodoens' *Niewe herball or historie of plantes.*

> Bitter Almondes doo open the stopping of the lunges or lightes.

The 'liver' (Middle English *liuer,* Anglo-Saxon *lifer*) has been associated with both lust and cowardice. In 1390 Gower (*Confessio,* III) saw the 'liver' as the seat of love.

> The livere makth him forto love.

Shakespeare echoed this sentiment in "The Rape of Lucrece."

> . . . To quench the coal which in his liver glows.

But Shakespeare also used the 'liver' in his descriptions of cowardice. In *The Merchant of Venice* (act III, scene 2) he used it with 'milk.'

> How many cowards . . .
> Who, inward searcht, have livers white as milk; . . .

In *Hamlet* (act II, scene 2) he varies the association by using 'pigeon.'

> But I am pigeon-liver'd, and lack gall
> To make oppression bitter, . . .

And finally in *Macbeth* (act V, scene 3) he used it with 'lily.'

> Go prick thy face, and over-red thy fear,
> Thou lily-livered boy.

The 'spleen' (Latin *splen*) has also had many traits and faculties attributed to it. An interesting "hair-of-the-dog" type recommendation for good health involving the 'spleen' was suggested by Robert Lovell in 1661 in his *A Compleat history of animals and minerals*.

> The Spleen [of a cow], eaten with honey . . . helpeth the paine of the spleen.

The 'spleen' has been considered the seat of melancholy, of laughter or mirth, of whim or caprice, of high spirits or courage, as a substitute for the heart, and as a holder of grudges! Taking them one at a time we find first this report from *Political . . . poems*.

> The mynde is in the Brayne . . . gladnes in the splene.

Francis Beaumont and John Fletcher in *The Maid's Tragedy* (act III, scene 2), 1611, ascribed full-fledged laughter to the spleen.

> I thought their spleens would break; they laugh'd us all Out of the room.

Bishop Francis Atterbury in his *Sermons* (I, 12), 1723 – 37, saw the spleen as the seat of a different emotion.

> Such [melancholic fancy] as now and then presents itself to musing, thoughtful men, when their spirits are low, and the spleen hath gotten possession of them.

In *Satirical poems of the time of the Reformation* (XXV), 1565 – 84, the spleen appears as a substitute for the heart.

When synneris repentis from the splene.

The capricious Hotspur is pictured by Shakespeare in *Henry IV, Part I* (act V, scene 2) as

A hare-brain'ed Hotspur, govern'd by a spleen.

Finally spleen was used as a synonym for "grudge" in the *Minutes of the Archdiocese of Colchester* (fol. 110), 1616.

There is a spleene betwixt one of the Churchwardens . . . and this partie.

The 'womb' (Anglo-Saxon *wamb, womb,* belly) has been referred to as the belly, the stomach, the bowels, and the uterus. As the belly or 'abdomen' (of unknown origin) it contained other organs as shown in *Nominale sive verbale,* c. 1340.

Inwyth the wombe of man . . . Is herte, liuer and longes.

The 'womb' was considered to be a different organ in *Secreta,* 1450 – 80.

A potage nesshe and laxatyue to the wombe.

Around this time it began to assume the meaning we give it today. A work of c. 1400 (*The tale of Beryn*) reports

A child gan stere in hir vombe.

In *The recuyell of the historyes of Troye* of 1471 Caxton employed 'womb' figuratively.

I had moche leuer that the erthe wold opene and swalwe me in to his wombe.

Shakespeare used 'womb' with its basic meaning but expanded its scope in *King Richard II* (act II, scene 1).

. . . this England,
This nurse, this teeming womb of royal kings . . .

'Ovary' is from the Latin *ovum* (egg); it is the female reproductive gland, in which the ova or eggs are formed. H. Sampson made an interesting comparison in 1677 (*Philosophical transactions of the Royal Society,* XII).

The right Testicle or Ovary was but small.

One of the earliest appearances in English of 'uterus' (Latin *uterus,* womb) was in 1615 when Helkiah Crooke wrote in *A description of the body of man* (IV, 13)

> It is called Vterus properly in women.

'Clitoris' is from the Greek word *klitoris* with the same meaning and may have come from the verb *klitein* (to shut).

Scattered throughout the body are the 'glands,' (Middle English *glande*, Old French *glandre*, from Latin *glans*, acorn). John Chamberlayne described one type of gland in *The religious philosopher* (I, 3), 1718.

> There are in the Mouth many Glands or Fountains of Spittle.

The word 'gland' was still being used for an acorn in 1836 (*Penny Cyclopaedia of the Society for the diffusion of useful knowledge*, V).

> *Gland*, . . . the fruit of the oak, hazel, etc.

A few of the better known glands are the 'pancreas,' 'lymph,' 'gonads,' 'thyroid,' 'pituitary,' and 'adrenal.' 'Pancreas' is from two Greek words, *pan* (all) and *kreas* (flesh). When the 'pancreas' glands of animals are used for food they are called 'sweetbreads.' This usage was current in 1681 in a translation of *Remaining medical works of Willis*.

> *Pancreas*, called in a hog the sweet bread.

'Lymph' should be spelled "limph" since it is from Latin *limpidus* (clear), but it was confused with a Greek word and the spelling became 'lymph' as in the Latin *lympha* (water, lymph, also waternymph). It was used poetically in 1630 in *The Roxburghe ballads* (I).

> Here rurall gods and tripping Nymphs
> Did bath their corps in the pure lymphs
> And christal streams.

Nicholas Robinson used it with its anatomical connotation (*A new theory of physick and diseases founded on the principles of the Newtonian philosophy*), 1725.

> The Pancreatic Juices, Lympha, and Bile are all fitted for their several Offices of Separation, Attenuation, and Dilution.

The 'gonads' are the glands that secrete sperm and get their name appropriately enough from the Greek *gonos* (generation, seed), through Latin *gonas* (plural, *gonades*). The 'thyroid' gland is named from its shape; it is from the Greek *thyreidos* (shield-shaped), from two words *thyreos* (shield, door) and *eidos* (form). Problems with the 'thyroid' bring about a certain condition according to Thomas Huxley (*Physiography: an introduction to the study of nature*, V), 1872.

> The thyroid gland . . . is that organ which when enlarged by disease gives rise to 'Derbyshire neck' or 'goitre.'

'Pituitary' from Latin *pituita* (slime, phlegm, rheum) was used in its adjectival form as a synonym for "phlegmatic" by Richard Baxter (*Saving Faith*) in 1658.

> My pituitous brain and languid spirits.

'Adrenal' is named from two Latin words, *ad* and *renes* (kidneys), but we now know that it affects many other organs in the body.

Fascinating as the interior organs of the body may be, it is time to leave them and go back outside to the lower extremities. 'Hip' comes from Middle English *hupe, hippe,* and *hipe*. 'Thigh,' related to similar words in Dutch, Icelandic, and Old High German, had originally a sense that is, unfortunately, all too familiar to many of us — fat, thick, or plump. 'Knee' is from the Anglo-Saxon *cneo* or *cneow* and is remotely related to the Sanskrit *janu* (knee), from which we also get 'genuflect,' the bending of the knee. The knee is part of the 'leg' (Icelandic *leggr*, leg, hollow, stem of a tree, shaft of a spear).

As we have seen many times previously, men have looked for all kinds of hints from the body to tell what kind of person inhabited it. There were, for example, legwatchers around 1450 (John Lydgate and Benedict Burgh, *Secrees of old philisoffres*).

> Smale leggys be tokne of symple konnyng.

'Legs' are to stand on, but the word 'leg' is also used as part of a phrase to mean a moral or factual foundation for a position taken. Jean Ingelow used this phrase in her *Poems* in 1863 in a rhyming style adumbrating Ogden Nash.

> Worthy but weak Mr. Brandon
> You haven't a leg to stand on.

Bishop Robert Sanderson was concerned with morals in 1621 when he warned men, particularly those who had the greatest opportunity, to beware (*Sermons*, XXXV).

It is never well when the Cobbler looketh above the Ankle.

'Ankle' is from the Middle English *ancle* which is related to Latin *angulus* (angle), with which it shares a Sanskrit root.

In its journey through time the *p* of the Latin *pes* (foot) became an *f*, and so *pes* ended up in English as 'foot.' Like 'leg,' 'foot' is used figuratively as part of a word which means base or foundation, the word 'footing.' That is the word we use now, but Horace Walpole in his *Letters* (II) in 1797 used simply 'foot' with the same meaning.

> I . . . shall take it ill if you don't keep up the correspondence on the same foot.

At the back of the foot is the 'heel' from Middle English *heele*. If your clothes are tattered and worn, you should follow the advice given by William Darrell in *A gentleman instructed in the conduct of a virtuous and happy life* in 1704.

> Sneak into a corner . . . down at heels and out at elbows.

Connecting the heel to the leg is a tendon called the 'Achilles tendon' (Latin *tendere*, to stretch). This 'tendon' got its name from the story in mythology concerning the warrior Achilles whose mother, holding him by the heel, dipped him in the River Styx to make him invulnerable to all weapons. However, a spear thrown at his heel hit the only part of him which had not been treated and thus brought him to his death.

The 'instep' (Middle English *instup, insteppe, instop*) seems to have been named with reference to the movement of the foot in walking. It was regarded as a love object by Philip Massinger in *The Parliament of love* (act IV, scene 5) in 1624.

> Is not this a pretty foot And a clean instep?

The 'toe' of the foot is from Middle English *too* and Anglo-Saxon *ta*. It should not be confused with the 'toe' (Old English *tan*, twig) of 'mistletoe'. According to one authority the 'mistle' part of the word 'mistletoe' is a diminutive of *mist* which in German has the sense of "dung," but other scholars hold that 'mistletoe' came from Old English *mistletan* (mistletoe plus twig). The reason for the former etymology is given in Pliny's *Natural historie* as translated by Holland.

> It (mistletoe) comes onely by the mewting of birds . . . which feed thereupon, and let it passe through their body.

When we wish to be flowery in our invitation to a dance partner we might say, "Come trip the light fantastic." We have left out an essential word, according to John Milton's *Allegro,* written in 1632.

> Com, and trip it as ye go
> On the light fantastick toe.

Thomas Nashe wrote in his preface to Sir Philip Sidney's *Astrophel and Stella,* in 1591 that it doesn't matter what you wear on your feet as long as your toes are properly decorated.

> 'Tis as good to goe in cut-finger'd Pumps as corke shooes, if one wore Cornish diamonds on his toes.

That painful excrescence on the toe called a 'corn' gets its name from the Latin *cornu* (horn). 'Corns' can be useful at times, at least according to Jonathan Swift in *Tatler* #238, 1710.

> A coming Show'r your shooting Corns presage.

The Duke of Wellington offered advice in *Nonconformist* (VI), 1846, which might be applicable today.

> The Duke begs to say that he has no corns and never means to have any. It is his opinion that if there were no boots there would be no corns.

In this recital of the words relating to the parts of the body we have left two of the most vital organs for the last, the 'brain' and the 'heart.' The word 'brain' is from the Middle English *brayne* and the Anglo-Saxon *braeden* or *bregen.* Gower (*Confessio,* II) summed up its importance succinctly around 1390.

> The wit and reson . . .
> Is in the celles of the brain.

While it is the 'brain' that directs man's physical and intellectual activities, it is the 'heart' that gives men life. 'Heart' is from the Middle English *herte.* It was pronounced at that time with two syllables, "her - te." The final letter was ultimately dropped and the word became the one-syllable word 'heart.' In addition to its role as life-giver, the heart has had many other functions and characteristics attributed to it through the years. It has been looked at as the stomach, as mind, as intent, will, or purpose, as the seat of emotions, as the home of love, as the seat of courage as well as of mental or intellectual faculty, and as a source of enthusiasm. For Thomas

Vicary (1548 – 77) the heart was the basic organ (*A profitable treatise on the anatomie of mans body,* VII).

> The Hart . . . is the principal of al other members, and the beginning of life.

One of the more unusual conceptions about the heart was as the stomach. Robert Godfrey wrote *Various injuries and abuses in chymical and galenical physick . . . detected,* in 1674, with this comment on the heart.

> So much is it the mode to call the Stomach the Heart, that people frequently say their Hearts were at their Mouths, when on a sudden fright or surprisal their Stomach's have been mov'd.

Gower (*Confessio,* II) equated the heart with the mind.

> His hert and tunge must accorde.

An early use of a currently common phrase may be found in a translation of the Bible by Miles Coverdale in 1535 (I Samuel 13:14).

> The Lorde hath soughte him out a man after his owne hert.

We have always looked on the heart as the seat of emotions, as pointed out in 1413 in *The pylegremage of the sowle* (from the French of G. de Guilleville, I, 3).

> The syght . . . gladyd moche my harte.

Shakespeare, on the other hand, wasn't quite sure. In *The Merchant of Venice* (act III, scene 2) we find this couplet.

> Tell me where is fancy bred,
> Or in the heart or in the head?

The use of the heart to depict one's inner thoughts has long been in vogue. This line appeared in *The Digby mysteries* (III), c. 1485.

> Now have I told yow my hart.

Shakespeare echoed that view in *Much Ado About Nothing* (act III, scene 2).

> . . . for what his heart thinks, his tongue speaks.

Around 1586, Sir Philip Sidney looked on the heart as the seat and symbol of love (*My true love hath my heart*).

> My true-love hath my heart, and I have his,
> By just exchange, one for the other given.

There seems to have been general agreement among all on th choice of the heart as the seat of courage. After all, the word 'courage' is from the Old French *cor* from the Latin *cor,* meaning 'heart' (modern French *coeur,* Spanish *corazón*). Well-known advice to lovers is given in "Jock O' the side" (*Child's Ballads*, VI).

> A faint heart ne'er wan a fair ladie.

Courageous men in war were depicted in *Godeffroy of Boloyne* as translated by William Caxton in 1481 (CXLIX).

> They ran on them with grete herte, and slewe them som of them.

A view of the heart as the seat of enthusiasm is found in the letters of Madame D'Arblay (Frances Burney) in *Diary and Letters,* January 22, 1780.

> I have so little heart in the affair, that I have now again quite dropped it.

Sir Thomas Browne noted in *Religio Medici* (I), 1642, that the heart could harbor evil thoughts as well as love and courage.

> The heart of a man is the place the Devil's in.

A fitting end for this chapter on the body might be the words of Juvenal, c. 100 B.C., "Mens sana in corpore sano" (a sound mind in a sound body). Francis Bacon (1561 – 1626) expressed the same idea somewhat more poetically (*Augmentis scientiarum: valetudo*).

> A healthy body is the guest-chamber of the soul; a sick, its prison.

WORDS TO CHANGE CLOTHES BY

History shows us people in full dress,
biography shows them in undress,
and diaries show them undressed.
George M. Dawson

Nature produces raw materials such as cotton, silk, wool, and leather. The spinner, weaver, tanner, and dyer treat these materials in various ways, and from them the tailor, seamstress, and shoemaker — either alone or with others in factories — produce the final product, wearing apparel, the principal subject of this chapter.

'Cloth' is from the Middle English *clath* and has had other meanings over the years in addition to that of a piece of goods. C. 1449 Reginald Peacock used 'cloth' to refer to clothing (*The repressor of over much blaming of the clergy,* III, 5).

Mete and drinke, hous and clooth.

To this day, the word 'cloth' is also used to refer to members of the clergy. Here is how it appeared in *English Gilds* around 1400.

That the worthy men of the seid cloth . . . witout the advise of the . . . comyners [commoners, i.e., laymen].

To get 'leather' (*lether* in Middle English), the hides of animals must be 'tanned,' a process that used to involve the bark of trees.

may be related to the German *tanne* and the French *tan,* both of which meant bark of a tree. Gradually it became a verb and assumed the meaning of the leather-treating process itself. An interesting use for leather, but only in a particular color, was described by William Langham in *The garden of health,* 1579.

> Binde the herbe to the body in Crimson lether, to stop bleeding.

Before they can be used in cloth and clothing, cotton, wool, and flax must be spun. 'Cotton' is from the Arabic *al qutun* (cotton), where *al* is the definite article ("the"). In Spanish the two were combined into the word *algodon.* By the time the word came into French, the *al* was dropped and the word became *coton* (printed cotton, cloth made of cotton).

The phrase 'to cotton to' has the meaning of fraternize, get close to, or associate with. In 1605 Richard Simpson wrote in *The school of Shakespeare* (2):

> John a Nokes and John a Style and I cannot cotton.

Richard Harris Barham used 'cotton' in relation to problem-solving (*The Ingoldsby Legends*, I), around 1845.

> For when once Madam Fortune deals out her hard raps,
>> It's amazing to think
>> How one cottons to Drink.

The flowers of the 'flax' plant (Anglo-Saxon *fleax*) were an inspiration to Longfellow in "The Wreck of the Hesperus," 1841.

> Blue were her eyes as the fairy flax.

'Wool' is from Middle English *wolle* and Anglo-Saxon *wull* or *wuln.* Let's look at some thoughts about 'wool' that have appeared over the years. Chaucer (*Lucrece*) concluded that it was a useful material, but not necessarily because it was warm.

> And softe wolle . . . she wroughte
> To kepe hire from slouthe & idilnesse

'Wools' from different countries were used, openly by women, secretly by men, for the same cosmetic purpose. In an issue of *Connoisseur,* #65, in 1755, there appeared the following confession.

> I am ashamed to tell you that we are indebted to Spanish Wool for many of our masculine ruddy complexions.

James Rennie revealed a similar cosmetic trick in *New Supplementary Pharmacy* in 1826.

"Oriental Wool." This colored wool comes from China in large, round, loose cakes . . . The finest of these gives a most lovely and agreeable blush to the cheek.

Our modern word 'spinster' (Middle English *spynnester,* from the verb *spinnen*), upon which the woman of today frowns, meant formerly a woman who spins, and by implication does nothing else such as have children and maintain a home for them and her husband. After the thread is spun, one 'weaves' (Middle English *weven,* Anglo-Saxon *wefan*) the cloth. To put color in the woven cloth it had to be 'dyed' (Anglo-Saxon *deah,* dye, color). Samuel Purchase (1577– c. 1628) wrote about makeup for the face (*Pilgrimage*).

Their [maidens'] cheekes were died with vermilion.

In the chapter on food there are several references to the problem of adulteration of food. Robert Southey echoed the concern with a warning to watch out for artificial colorings, in *Madoc (Madoc in Wales, Madoc in Aztlan* [XIV]).

Cheese of curd-like whiteness, with no foreign die Adulterate.

Once the cloth was woven and dyed it had to be fashioned into items for use, and the people who did this were the 'tailor' and the 'seamstress' who sewed it into garments. There has been considerable controversy over the years as to the influence of tailors and their clothes upon one's character and one's chance of success in the world. On one side of the argument we have Sir Thomas Overbury in *A wife now the widdow of Sir T. Overbury. A poem of the choice of a wife. Whereunto are added many witty characters,* of 1613.

Shee can easily turne a sempstresse into a waiting gentlewoman.

Allied with Overbury is Ben Jonson with this dictum in 1625 (*The staple of newes,* I).

Believe it, sir, That clothes do much upon the wit, . . . and thence comes your proverb, The Tailor makes the man.

Richard Brathwait disagreed completely with both Overbury and Jonson in *The English gentleman,* 1630.

A Gentleman is a man of himselfe, without the addition of either Taylor, Millener, seamster or haberdasher.

The weakness of women in respect to the dictates of fashion so upset Barnaby Rich that he wrote the following in 1614 (*The honestie of this age*).

> I doe see the wisedome of women to be still ouerreached by Taylers, that can euery day induce them to as many new fangled fashions as they please to inuent.

'Tailor' comes from the French word *tailler* (to cut) and the Late Latin *taliare* (to prune, split, cut). A 'seamstress' (Middle English *semster*, Anglo-Saxon *seamestre*, from Anglo-Saxon *seam*, seam) 'sews' (Middle German *sowen*, Anglo-Saxon *siwian*) a seam.

There are a number of words for clothing in general, and we shall look at them before we examine the individual items. 'Raiment,' usually reserved for a rather more elaborate set of clothes, is short for Middle English *araiment*, from which we get 'to array' (to set in order). Caxton warned against ostentation in 1483 in his translation of *Caton* (F, 2).

> Thou oughtest not to haue . . . ouer precyous Jewellys ne Raymentes.

But one of John Fletcher's characters in *Women Pleased* (act I, scene 2), 1625, thought otherwise.

> Do you think to . . . keep me like an alms-woman in such rayment,
> Such poor unhandsome weeds?

'Apparel' is a more common term for a set of clothing. What better use of the term can be found than in the famous advice of Polonius to his son in *Hamlet* (act I, scene 3).

> Costly thy habit as thy purse can buy . . . rich, not gaudy:
> For the apparel oft proclaims the man . . .

The Middle English form was *aparailen* (to dress), and it was taken from the Old French *apareil* (apparel) which was made up of *a* plus *pareillier* (to put like things together with like). The Latin root was *parilis* (like). 'Apparel' therefore means a matching set of clothes.

Included in one's apparel may be certain 'costumes' and perhaps a 'uniform' or two. 'Costume' comes from Latin *consuetudo*, custom, and is thus basically the same word as 'custom'; it meant to wear what was customary to the place and time. The word 'uniform' is made from two Latin words, *unus* (one) and *forma* (form), and means alike dress for persons who belong to the same group. Armies were not always clothed in uniforms, as pointed out in *Harper's Magazine* (LXXX) in the late nineteenth century.

> The practice of clothing soldiers by regiments in one uniform dress was not introduced by Louis XIV till 1665, and did not become general in our army for many years afterward.

A set of apparel has many 'garments,' a word from the Old French *garnir* (to adorn, protect). John Donne (*Letters,* XXXVII) used the term figuratively.

> I am not weary of writing; it is the coarse but durable garment of my love.

f064   The piece of furniture in which in earlier days one stored apparel was called a 'wardrobe.' 'Ward,' the first part of the word, is from the first half of the Old French *garderobe,* the word *garde,* which meant to keep or to preserve. In the transition from Old French to English the *g* became a *w.* Today the word 'wardrobe' refers more to a collection of clothing than to the place in which one keeps clothes. At one time, the word 'wardrobe' had an additional meaning, that of a room or large closet in which clothes were kept, as indicated in this citation from the *Paston Letters* (I) in the late fifteenth century.

> The last day of Octobre, the . . . yere of the reyne of King Henri the Sixt, Sir John Fastolf, Knyght, hath lefte in his warde-drope at Castre this stuffe of clothys, and othir harnays that followith.

By 1847, Charlotte Brontë used the word in *Jane Eyre* as a piece of furniture.

> Jane . . . open the top drawer of the wardrobe, and take out a clean shirt.

Richard H. Barham, writing at about the same time (*Ingoldsby,* I) used 'wardrobe' to refer to a set of clothing.

> The most important article of all in a gentleman's wardrobe was still wanting.

Now that we have assembled our clothing in a wardrobe, it is time to dress up in our 'finery.' The aim of such a maneuver would be to present a perfect picture to the world, and we get this idea from its Latin root, *finis* (end). In Late Latin it became *finus* (fine, pure), and it arrived into Old French as *fin* (perfect, exact), which is the way we are supposed to look in our 'finery.' Isaac Watts used 'finery' in warning students not to be deceived by the appearance of a particular school (*Divine and moral songs for children*), 1720.

Don't choose your place of study by the finery of the prospects.

Getting dressed involves for some of us a considerable amount of 'primping.' What we are doing is making ourselves 'prim' (Middle English *prym*, neat girl), which Cotgrave says was "slender" or "delicate."

One of the adjuncts of the perfect costume is the right 'purse' or, as more commonly said today, pocketbook. 'Purse' is from the Greek *byrsa* (hide or skin from which purses were made). There is a well-known expression, "Money may not be the most important thing in the world, but it's way ahead of whatever is in second place." Ben Jonson said it more succinctly in *The new inne, or the light heart* in 1630.

A heavy purse makes a light heart.

Shakespeare, bearing in mind the original root of 'purse' and having observed that skin and hide are often wrinkled, used the word as a verb in *Othello* (act III, scene 3).

. . . thou criedst, "Indeed!"
And didst contract and purse thy brow together . . .

The 'purser' or 'bursar' (having the *b* of the Greek *byrsa* instead of the *p*) is the officer in institutions and ships who is responsible for the handling of money. 'Purse,' that which holds money, became the French word *bourse,* meaning stock exchange.

Let us turn now to the specific materials and the various items of clothing in a woman's wardrobe. When they get dressed in the morning, they have a choice of materials like balbriggan, cambric, calico, gauze, crepe, crinoline, cotton, and others which we shall examine in detail, as well as current man-made materials such as nylon, orlon, and polyester. From these materials we get the chemise, slip, petticoat, brassiere, garter, girdle, corset, and bodice. Most of these may be grouped under the general term "lingerie." Three of the materials mentioned are eponyms, or suspected eponyms.

'Balbriggan' is a fine jerseylike cloth first made in Balbriggan, Ireland. 'Cambric' (also called 'chambray' or "lawn") is a delicate white linen named from Cambrai, the French version of the Flemish town Kambryk; 'calico' is named for the city of Calicut (now Kozhikode). Evidence for these last places of origin appeared in Philemon Holland's translation of W. Camden's *Britain, or a chorographicall description of England, Scotland, and Ireland* (I), 1610.

> Cameric, Calecut &c had . . . their denomination from the places where they were first invented.

'Gauze' has an uncertain origin, but it is possible that it is named for the town of Gaza in Palestine. Andrew Lang used the word figuratively in *Contemporary Review* (LIV) in 1920.

> Perhaps there are people who do see their own lives, even in moments of excitement, through this embroidered gauze of literature and art.

'Crepe,' also called 'crêpe de Chine,' is an outgrowth of the Old French word *crespe* (curled, crisp). The Latin word *crispus* had the same meaning, and our word 'crisp' is directly related to 'crepe.'

Those 'crinoline' skirts that keep coming back into fashion are so-called from two Latin words *crinum* (horsehair) and *linum* (flax). It was the stiff horsehair woven in with the linen that made the skirt stand up by itself. If long 'crinoline' skirts do come back, women would do well to be aware of the danger of wearing them. In *All Year Round* (#33), 1839, an incident was reported which should be noted.

> We hear . . . of a woman in crinoline being blown off a narrow ledge into the water.

The word 'jersey' for the cloth is an eponym from the Isle of Jersey where it was first knitted. In 1583, Philip Stubbes wrote of the fine quality of this material (*The anatomie of abuses*, I).

> Nether stocks . . . not of cloth . . . for that is thought to [too] base, but of Iarnsey worsted.

We have mentioned the slavish submission of men and women to the contemporary dictates of fashion. Mary E. Braddon (Mrs. Maxwell) described in 1880 a woman who refused to be coerced (*Just as I am*, VII).

> She was not the kind of woman to encase herself in a boating Jersey because the fashion book told her that Jerseys were universally worn.

The Latin word *linum* which we just mentioned as the flax from which linen is made, is the source of the French word *linger* (dealer in linen). What the dealer sells is 'lingerie,' things made of 'linen.' The word 'lingerie' made one of its earliest appearances in English in 1835, in the arbiter of London fashion, the *Court Magazine* (VI).

> It is expected that lingerie will be this season in very great request, both in morning and half-dress.

In the seventeenth century, linen stockings were fashionable, as worn, for example, by Samuel Pepys, the famous diarist. He wrote on May 24, 1660, in *Memoirs. Comprising his Diary from 1659 to 1669, and a Selection from his Private Correspondence:*

> Up, and made myself as fine as I could, with the linning stockings on . . .

Shakespeare used 'linen' in Macbeth to denote an ashen, pale appearance (act V, scene 3).

> . . . those linen cheeks of thine
> Are counsellors to fear.

What we call a 'chemise' used to be called a 'camisole'; both words are from the Arabic *gamis* (shirt). Thackeray used 'camisole' in 1848 in *Vanity Fair* (XXX) as an outer garment.

> Mrs. O'Dowd, the good housewife, arrayed in curl-papers and a camisole, felt that her duty was to act and not to sleep.

A 'slip', as its name indicates, is something slipped over the head, just as 'slippers' slip on over the foot. The first part of 'petticoat,' *petti* is related to the French word *petit,* which means small; the word 'petticoat' used to be written as two words, 'petty coat.' *Babees Book,* giving advice to servants, distinguishes between the short and long coats.

> Se [see] that your souerayne haue clene shurt and breche, A pety-cote, a dublett, a long coote [coat].

The French word *brassard* was used in the time of chivalry to mean the armor of the upper arm. It is believed that the modern word 'brassiere,' and its current short form, 'bra,' are derived from *brassard.* While women don't wear garters very much today, due to the advent of pantyhose, 'garters' used to be worn regularly. In this age of freedom in women's clothing, it is interesting to go back a few years for this passage from Sir Walter Scott's *Woodstock, or the Cavalier* (III).

> Lasses leaping till you might see where the scarlet garter fastened the light-blue hose.

The word 'garter' is from the Breton word *garr* (shank of the leg). Dante Gabriel Rossetti observed that garters for some girls served a different purpose from that of holding up stockings (*A Last Confession*) c. 1880.

> Our Lombard country-girls along the coast wear daggers in their garters.

Along with 'garters' women used to wear 'corsets,' a word which is a diminutive of the Old French word *cors* (body). The 'corset' gradually gave way to the 'girdle' (Middle English *girdel, gerdel;* Anglo-Saxon *gyrdel*). 'Bodice' is an old word which seems to be back in the fashion lexicon again, but this time as an outside garment rather than as underclothing. It may be a corruption of the word "bodies" as "pence" is of "pennies," and it originally appeared in the plural defined as 'a pair of bodies to a woman's petticoat.' It is referred to in this note from Nehemiah Grew in 1674 (*The Anatomy of Plants,* V).

> A Flower without its Empalement, would hang as uncouth and taudry, as a Lady without her Bodies.

With the underclothing in place, it is time to select those items of clothing that go on over them. Materials like muslin, silk, lace, gingham, poplin, organdy, and others are turned into a great variety of items like the dress, smock, frock, skirt, blouse, and many more. Eponyms furnish the names of some of the materials mentioned, such as 'muslin.' According to Marco Polo, the famous traveler to China and other places, the word is from Mosul, the Syriac name for a city in Iraq; the Arabic name for the city is Mawsil. William Biddulph was in general agreement with Marco Polo; in his *The Travels of Certaine Englishmen into Africa, Asia, etc.* he merely changed the name of the originating town.

> A little towne called Muscia, from whence the inhabitants . . . bring a kinde of linnen cloath called Muslina to Aleppo.

'Organdy' is of uncertain origin, but it has been suggested that it might have come from the altered name of some Chinese town or locality. 'Poplin' is from the French word *popeline,* a later form of the word *papeline* (the French word for the pope is *pape*). These words describe cloth made at Avignon, France, which was once the seat of the popes. From France to Malaysia in a long distance, but words have a way of ignoring time and space; and so it is from the

Malay word *ginggang* (striped or checkered cotton) that we get our modern word 'gingham.'

Those women who put on 'lace' with the hope of snaring a partner (men do it, too), are probably not aware that the origin of the word 'lace' lies in the Latin word *laqueus* (noose, snare, knot). It is, of course, from the meaning of "knot" that 'lace' gets its name. Chaucer used 'lace' or, as he spelled it, *las,* with the meaning of snare or noose (The Knight's Tale, I).

> Lo, alle thise folk icaught were in hire [her, i. e., Venus'] las,
> Til they for wo [woe] ful often sayde allas [alas].

Let's look at some one-piece garments, then two-piece outfits, and finally some accessories. (Men's clothing will have its turn later.)

'Pinafore' used to be a child's garment, but it has its place in the wardrobe of the grown woman. However, before it was a garment, it was a bib. So said Miss Frances Burney (Madame D'Arblay) in *Cecilia, or Memoirs of an Heiress* (VI, 8) in 1782.

> A pin-a-fore for Master Mortimer Delvile, lest he should daub his pappy when he is feeding him.

It was called 'pinafore' because it used to be *pinned* to the front of —*afore* — a child; it was afterward enlarged and made to be tied behind. 'Shift' used to be a change of clothes, as in "six shifts of apparel." Shakespeare used it simply as a change of clothes from one outfit to another. It then became a change of linen, particularly the chemise, and then a simple garment in one piece. James Bruce so used it writing of people of the Nile in *Travels to Discover the Source of the Nile* (I) in 1790.

> At home they [the women at Loheia] wear nothing but a long shift of fine cotton-cloth, suitable to their quality.

Today 'shift' has had a resurgence in fashion as a simple, straight, short dress.

It is always interesting to note how words respond to cultural changes through the years; in the seventeenth century, the word 'smock' was replaced by 'shift,' viewed as a more delicate-sounding word. In the nineteenth century, however, even 'shift' was not delicate enough, and it was replaced by 'chemise.' In 1850 L. Hunt Barhan wrote in his *Autobiography* (III, 24):

> That harmless expression [shift] . . . has been set aside in favour of the French word "chemise."

'Dress' comes from the Old French word *dresser* (to set up, arrange, direct, dress). Chaucer used 'dress' as a verb to mean arrange or direct with the sense of to improve or to correct (Tale of Melibeus).

> Thou schalt blesse God and pray hym to dresse thy ways.

There is a wonderful epigram involving 'dress' which ought to be better known. In 1876 George M. Dawson wrote in *From Memory*:

> History shows us people in full dress, biography shows them in undress, and diaries show them undressed.

'Frock' is a word which conjures up a gay, dress-up garment, worn on festive occasions. It hasn't always had that meaning; a 'frock' was seen as something quite different in *The Girl's Own Paper,* June 28, 1884.

> I think "frock" seems to be applied to the morning costume, and "dress" to that of evening only.

'Frock' was originally another word for a monk's or friar's habit — hence, 'to unfrock,' for to deprive (someone) of priestly function. The men whose clothes used to be called in French *froc de moine* (monk's cowl or hood) would be quite surprised to see how their somber outfits have developed into our modern 'frocks.' Thomas Gray (1716– 71) pointed out very clearly the original meaning of 'frock' (*Letters,* I).

> All the confraternities resort thither . . . habited in linen frocks, girt with a cord, and their heads covered with a cowl all over, that has only two holes before to see through.

The 'smock,' in the world of fashion, is some distance removed from the 'frock.' It is a very simple, everyday garment, and it lives thereby up to its origin. It is from the Teutonic root *smeug* (to creep). The original 'smock' was a garment which had only a round hole for one's head and which fell as a cover over the body. In other words, it was what we now call a 'poncho,' a word from the Spanish and the Araucan Indians of Chile. Painters and others used the 'smock,' a loose cotton garment which hung shapelessly over their clothes and kept them clean. The 'smock-frock,' of which 'smock' is a shortened form, was a long, loose-fitting garment of coarse linen or similar material, which farm laborers wore over a coat, or instead of a coat. The 'smock-frock' was the source of the word for the ornamental work called 'smocking.'

> To gather by means of sewing done in lines crossing each other diagonally, after a pattern common on smock-frocks.

The grandest of the one-piece garments is the 'gown,' and the origin of the word is equally grand. The Latin word *gunna* was a skin or fur or garment of fur. We tend to forget that men wore gowns in days gone by, as pointed out in "Death of Queen Jane" (*Child's Ballads,* VII).

> He came with all speed,
> In a gownd of green velvet from heel to the head.

The 'tunic' (Latin *tunica*), a term now chiefly used to denote a British soldier's undress uniform coat, was originally an under-garment for Romans of both sexes. Along about 1670, it became an outer garment as defined by Thomas Blount in *Glossographia, or a Dictionary Interpreting Such Hard Words . . . as are Now Used.*

> "Tunick" or Tunicat, a Jerkin, Jacket, or sleeveless coat, formerly worn by Princes.

By 1800 'tunic' had advanced to dress-up wear for women as seen in the *Hull Advertiser* of October 4.

> Paris fashions . . . tuniques of black crape are coming into wear.

The revolving wheel of fashion brought 'tunics' back into the limelight recently as an outer garment reaching to the knees, worn over pants or a long skirt, as part of the "layered" look.

From the tunic developed the 'blouse,' which is a word of uncertain etymology; it may have come from a French word *bliaut* or *bliaus,* another name for a surcoat or supertunic. There is a special kind of blouse, the 'middy,' It is named from the kind of top garment worn by *midshipmen* aboard ship. (Midshipmen were so-called because they were quartered "amidships" on sailing vessels.) Blouses may be worn with 'skirts' (Icelandic *skyrta*, Danish *skjorta* — both of which mean 'shirt' with the sense of the lower part of the shirt or garment).

Dresses, skirts, and blouses have 'collars,' 'sleeves,' and 'cuffs.' 'Collar,' like many words we have seen, is something worn with or used with the thing it originally was. In this case it was the Latin word *collum* (neck) that became the word for that which was worn around it.

Our enslavement to fashion has been noted in previous citations. Here is further evidence provided by Samuel Rowlands in 1612 (*The Knave of Harts*).

> Let us have standing collars in the fashion;
> All are become a stiff-necked generation.

'Sleeve' (Anglo-Saxon *slyf*) is allied to "slip"; it is something one creeps or slides into while dressing and undressing. At one point in our history this was literally true. John Skelont described a gentleman's outfit in *Magnyfycence, a Goodly Interlude and a Mery*, c. 1520.

> His gown: so wyde That he may hyde his dame and syre Within his slyue [sleeve].

'Cuff' has two meanings; as a blow it is from the Swedish word *kuffa* (to thrust, push). As part of a sleeve it is from Middle English *cuffe, coffe;* but before it became part of the sleeve it was originally a glove or mitten as defined in *Promptorium,* 1440.

> "Cuffe," glove or metyne.

Final touches to one's outfit may take the form of a 'kerchief,' 'veil,' 'shawl,' 'stole,' or 'scarf.' The two components of 'kerchief' (we get the meaning of the word when we see its Middle English antecedent *coverchef* or *couerchef*) are *ker* from the Old French *covrir* (to cover) and Old French *chef,* from its Latin root *caput* (head). Many men today would welcome the same kind of governmental assistance in limiting what their wives spend for clothes that was given them by the government of Edward IV in 1482 (acts 22, Edward IV, c,1).

> They shall not suffer their wives to wear any reile called a kercheffe, whose price exceedeth twentie pence.

(Reile was a piece of linen or other cloth that women used to wear about the neck — a neckerchief.) A woman described by Chaucer in the General Prologue to the Canterbury Tales (I, 453) did not appear to have been constrained by cost.

> Hir couerchiefs ful fyne weren of ground I durste swere they weyeden ten pound That on a Sonday were upon hir heed.

(Ground was a piece of cloth used for embroidery or other decoration.)

The original sense of 'veil' was a covering, cloth or sail, from the

Latin *velum* with those meanings. The Persian *shal,* the root of our modern word 'shawl,' was a mantle made from the very fine wool from Shaliat in India. The 'stole,' like the frock, was originally clothing for members of the clergy. The Greek word *stole* (robe, stole) came to be both an ecclesiastical vestment for a priest and a long robe. This is how Chaucer used it in The Merchant's Tale.

> Forth cometh the priest with stole aboute his neck.

That 'stole' had another meaning can be seen from its use by John Wyclif in 1382.

> Forsoth the fadir seyde to his servantis, Soone bryng ye forth the first stoole, and clothe ye him.

'Scarf' is from the Dutch and Low German *scherf,* meaning a military scarf or girdle. This was worn over one shoulder and around the waist as a sling in which to carry assorted items. One of the earliest recorded appearances of 'scarf' is this from William Painter in 1566 – 67 (*The Palace of Pleasure,* I).

> His wife Panthea brought him an armure of golde . . . and a crimsen skarfe.

There are two special sets of clothing which have a very close relationship to each other, the 'trousseau' and the 'layette.' While one would hardly expect the bride walking down the aisle carrying a little bundle, that is what the French word *trousse,* of which *trousseau* is a diminutive, means. There is also an English verb 'to truss' (to pack up in bundles) from the same root. 'Trousseau' is a relatively modern word; it was used by Lady Moyan in *France I* (I) in 1817.

> An "armoire" . . . held the bridal wardrobe, or rustic "trousseau."

At some point during or after the assembling of the 'trousseau,' the 'bride' (Middle English *bride, bryde,* Anglo-Saxon *bryd*) will walk down the aisle in a 'bridal' gown. The word 'bridal' literally means "bride-feast," since the word *ale* was a common word in Middle English for a feast. Thomas Warton, in 1774, referred to *ale* with that meaning in *The History of English Poetry* (III).

> Lamb-ale is still used at the village of Kirtlington in Oxfordshire, for an annual feast or celebrity at lamb-shearing.

In Middle English 'bridal' was spelled *bridale* and *bruydale;* Shakespeare used *bridall* in *Othello* while Ben Jonson in 1609 wrote *bride-ale* in *Silent Woman*. Further evidence of the old use of 'bridal' as a wedding feast was given by John Heywood (*Prouerbes*).

> It is, as telth vs this old tale,
> Meete, [proper] that a man be at his own brydale.

However, in 1596, Edmund Spenser used the word with our modern meaning in *Prothalamion:*

> Against their bridal day, which is not long:
> Sweet Thames, run softly, till I end my song.

After marriage, when a baby is expected, the mother-to-be begins to assemble a 'layette.' It meant originally a drawer, box, or tray, and it is only since 1874 that 'layette' took on its present meaning of a collection of all the items that a baby might need. In her *Memoirs* (April 26), Princess Alice wrote to a donor of a baby gift.

> Let me thank you . . . for the present toward the layette. . . . a most kind assistance.

Men, it is your turn now! As we did for women, we will look first at some of the materials used in the manufacture of men's clothing, and then at the garments themselves. Some of the more common materials found in men's wear are lisle, denim, flannel, wool, seersucker, khaki, corduroy, and polyester and other synthetics. As with some of the materials we discussed previously, two of these are eponyms. 'Denim' is a compound word made up of the French *de* (of, from) and the city of Nîmes in France (pronounced "neem"). 'Denim,' therefore, means "(cloth) from Nîmes," where it was first manufactured. So said the *London Gazette* #3885 in 1703.

> A pair of Flower'd Serge de Nim Breeches.

'Lisle' is also named for a French city, Lille. Staying with the French, we find what appears to be the source of still another cloth, 'corduroy.' On the surface the word seems to be an Anglicization of the French *corde du roi* (king's cloth). Some authorities point out, however, that this word has never been used in French. On the contrary, a list of materials manufactured in France in 1807 contains the word "kingscordes," obviously an English, not a French word.

For the word 'flannel' we have to cross the Channel to Wales where the probable root is the Welsh word *gwlan* (wool) and a word derived from it, *gwlanen* (article made from wool). Do we still think of flannel as Francis Fuller did in 1704? He said in *Medicina gymnastica: or, a Treatise Concerning the Power of Exercise with Respect to the Animal Oeconomy*:

> Flannel is scarce necessary or convenient On this side o old Age.

We must take a much longer trip to find sources for our next two words — to India. 'Khaki' comes from the Hindi word *khaki* (dusty), and 'seersucker' is from the Hindi word *shirshaker*. This word is based on the Persian compound word *shir o shakar* (milk and sugar), a very apt description of the striped cloth known as 'seersucker.' (And our 'sugar' comes, in fact, from *shaker*.)

Following the same format we used for women, we observe men as they wake up in the morning and prepare to put on their clothes. Men used to wear a garment of underclothing called the 'union suit.' One authority says that it was called that because it was made from textile fabric woven of two or more materials *united*, especially cotton and linen or cotton and flax. George Dodd wrote in 1844 of this material in *The Textile Manufacturers of Great Britain* (V).

> A mixture of flax and cotton called "union."

Another view is that it was called a 'union suit' because it was a top and bottom *united* in one piece. For convenience the one-piece garment was later separated into two units, the long drawers and the shirt. 'Drawers' probably got the name from the way in which they were put on; they were drawn on over the feet and legs. In 1567 they were equated to hose by Thomas Harman in *A Caueat or Warening for Commen Cursetors, Vulgarely Called Vagabones*.

> Here followyth their pelting speche ... Whyche language they terme Peddelars Frenche ... a commission, a shierte; drawers, hosen; stampers, shooes.

In recent years, the legs were cut off the drawers and the result was 'shorts.' Soon these were made smaller and tighter, and 'briefs' were born. Part of the sleeve was cut off the undershirts and the 'T shirt' was born. If there are no sleeves at all it is called a 'jersey.'

After underwear the next item one might put on is 'stockings' or 'hose.' In medieval times, men wore long leg coverings called 'hose' (Anglo-Saxon *hosa*). These were afterward cut in two at the knees, leaving two items of clothing, knee breeches or upper stocks and netherstocks or 'stockings,' where the 'stock' (Middle English *stok*, trunk of a tree) refers to the trunk of the body. Samuel Purchas (1577 – c. 1628) used 'hose' with the meaning of 'breeches' (*Pilgrimage*).

> And he had on yet all this while a paire of hosen of Deere-skinnes with the haire on.

In his *Masque of Middle Temple and Lincoln's Inn* George Chapman (who died 1634) used 'stockings' as we do today.

> Their legges were adorn'd with close long white silke stockings, curiously embroider'd with golde to the midde-legge.

John Gay had advice for men in 1732 in his *Shepherd's Week, in Six Pastorals* (J). Before you pop the question ask

> Will she thy linen wash, or hosen darn?

The next step after stockings is something to put on over them. Men used to wear 'breeches.' This word is an interesting example of a double plural. The origin of the word is the Anglo-Saxon *broc*, a singular form meaning a one-pant leg. The plural of *broc* was *breec*, just as the plural of "foot" is "feet." But *breec*, which, along with the Middle English *breche*, didn't sound like a plural, was made into one by adding an *s* and changing the sound a bit. The result was 'breeches.' We don't wear 'breeches' today, except at royal courts, but we do wear 'jeans,' from the fabric called *jean*, which is an eponym from the city of Genoa via its Old French form Gênes (prounced "zhane"). The word 'jeans' is quite old, having appeared as early as 1567. The spelling is strange, but this item did appear in a book in that year (*Churchwardens' Accounts of S. Edmund and S. Thomas, Sarum*,II, edited by Henry J. F. Swayne).

> . . . yerdes of Jene fustyan.

In 1807, in *The Parish Register,* George Crabbe still spoke of 'jean' as a material.

> Clean was his linen, and his jacket blue:
> Of finest jean his trousers, tight and trim.

For somewhat more formal occasions we wear 'trousers,' spelled *trowsers* in 1676, and taken from the Gaelic word *triubhas* (trunk-hose, breeches). In his *Cyclopaedia of Costume,* published in 1879, James Robinson Planche defined 'trousers'

> ... these large breeches, or sloppes became an important and splendid part of apparell; and while the long hose were either supplanted by or new christened the trauses (read trouses), the upper stock or the breeches worn over them received the name of trunk hose.

For less dressy occasions men put on 'slacks' instead of trousers from a suit. The word 'slack' means loose or lax, and such pants have been called 'slacks' because they fitted loosely or because they were worn during periods of re*lax*ation. The word 'slack' gets its meaning and form from an Anglo-Saxon word, *sleac* (slow, slack). Our words 'lag,' as in "to lag behind," and 'lax,' said of someone who is careless in his work, are from the same root. To hold up jeans, slacks, or trousers we use either a 'belt' (Latin *balteus,* sword belt) or 'suspenders,' a compound word from the two Latin words *sub* (under) and *pendere* (to hang).

On the 'shirt' we have already discussed we are likely to tie a 'tie,' or, as it was called in an earlier day, a 'cravat.' The word 'tie' is related to the Icelandic words *tang* (string) and *tigan* (to tie, fasten). The first 'ties' were strings; they are still worn out West as well as by square-dancers. Barham (*Ingoldsby Legends,* I) used 'tie' in the sense of a bow.

> A very smart tie in his smart cravat.

'Cravat' is another eponym, this one from the Croatians, the French word for whom is *Croates* or, more commonly, *Cravates*. It was they who introduced the style into France in 1636. In 1676 Sir George Etherege waxed sarcastic on the subject of cravats (*The Man of Mode,* I,1).

> That a man's excellency should lie in Neatly tying of a Ribbond, or a Crevat!

The required 'garb' (Middle French *garbe*, good fashion, comeliness, Italian *garbo,* grace, handsomeness, Old High German *garwi, garawi,* preparation, dress, gear) for business wear in most sections of the country is the 'suit.' The word is derived from the Latin *sequor* (to follow). In Old French it became *suite,* and then our modern word 'suit.' It was used in the sense of uniform wear for members of the same retinue or fraternity, that is, "followers" of a creed or a man. At one point 'suit' was used for a set of church clothes (chasuble, dalmatics, and cope), all of the same color. In the modern meaning the word goes back at least to 1738 when it was used in *Gentleman's Magazine* (VIII).

> One that . . . doth not put off his Religion with his Sunday's Suit.

It was even used for women's apparel as early as 1761 when *British Magazine* (II) reported:

> A suit of cloaths is weaving for a lady of quality . . .

The word to denote a group of followers normally takes the form of 'suite,' but it was *suit* in 1586 as noted by Sir Philip Sidney (*The Countess of Pembrokes Arcadia,* II).

> Had there not come in Tydeus and Telenor, with fortie or fiftie in their suit, to the defence.

Still another 'suit' is the one used to describe the four groups of cards in an ordinary deck of playing cards. *In Martins Months Minde, that is, a Certaine Report . . . of the Death and Funeralls of Olde Martin Marre-Prelate,* 1589, described a new card game in England.

> Leaving the ancient game of England (Trumpe), where every coate and sute are sorted in their degree, [they] are running to Ruffe.

'Blazer' is a less formal coat for use with slacks. It is from the Middle English word *blase,* meaning fire, and it must have been used to refer to color or decoration in men's clothing. For example, the *London Times* of June 19, 1880, had this sentence.

> Men in spotless flannel and "club" blazers.

Notes and Queries in the mid-nineteenth century gave its version of the origin of the word 'blazer' as applied to men's clothing.

> The origin of the word is as follows; The uniform of the Lady Margaret Boat Club of St. John's College, Cambridge, is bright red, and the Johnian jackets have for many years been called blazers. Up to a few years ago the inaccurate modern use of blazer for a jacket of any other colour than red was unknown.

Going from the informal to the truly formal takes us to 'tails' and the 'tuxedo.' The traditional 'tailcoat' has a slit in the back which was put in originally to facilitate the wearing of a sword. The dinner jacket or 'tuxedo' is apparently an eponym, perhaps from an exclusive part of New York State, called Tuxedo Park, where it was probably first worn. (The location probably got its name from *tuksit*, an American Indian name for a wolf, literally meaning "he has a round foot.")

To protect their feet both men and women wear 'shoes' (Middle English *shoo, schon,* Anglo-Saxon *sceon*) or 'boots' (Late Latin *botta*). 'To die with his boots on' is deemed a proper and brave way for a man to end his life; it means he is in the midst of the action and does not yield, but fights on to his death, if that is necessary. Compare that noble thought with this version from Barham (*Ingoldsby Legends,* I) who uses 'shoes' instead of 'boots.'

> And there is M'Fuze,
> And Lieutenant Tregooze,
> And there is Sir Carnaby Jenks of the Blues,
> All come to see a man die in his shoes! [that is, to be hanged]

One of the leathers used for shoes and gloves is 'suede,' another eponym, this time taken from the French word for the country Sweden, *Suède,* where gloves of this ultrasoft leather were first made.

'Brogues,' the heavy shoes one usually associates with Great Britain, are named from the Gaelic and Irish word *brog* (shoe), a derivative of the Anglo-Saxon *broc,* which is also the root for 'breeches' as we have already noted. For more informal wear, men and women both wear 'sandals,' which derives from *sandalou,* from Asia Minor, meaning originally a shoe of the Lydian god *Sandal.* 'Moccasin' is a word that appears in several Algonkian Indian languages — Powhatan *mockasin,* Micmac *mkasun,* and so on.

For formal occasions, men used to wear 'pumps'; women wear them at all times today. The shoe was called a 'pump' because it was worn with ribbons for fancy dress occasions, that is occasions of "pomp" from the French *pompe* (magnificence, ostentation). In 1848, Thackeray described what the gentleman should wear (*The Book of Snobs,* (l).

> The usual attire of a gentleman, viz. pumps, a gold waistcoat, a crush hat, a sham frill, and a white choker.

Outerwear worn by men and women, although differing greatly in cut and material, is called by the same names, as coat, hat, boots, etc. Therefore in discussing these garments we will treat men's and women's items as one. To go outside in snowy winter weather one used to wear 'galoshes,' called overshoes or boots today. In early French *galoche* was a wooden shoe made in one piece, with no ties or laces, designed to be worn in winter. Perhaps the Latin precursor of *galoche* was *kalopedila* from the Greek words *kalon* (wood) and *pedila* (sandals).

The practice of wearing 'hats' (same word in Middle English and Anglo-Saxon) comes and goes with the trends in fashion. Over the years, many different materials have been used to make coverings for the head, such as felt, voile, chiffon, satin, velvet, wool, and silk. 'Felt' is made by pounding or beating wool into a matted cloth, and the word is probably allied to the German *falzen* (to fit together). Richard Hakluyt in his *Diuers Voyages Touching the Discouerie of America*, 1582, reported that camel's hair was used instead of wool, but the 'felt' served the same purpose as it does today — to keep one warm.

> Howbeit, they are of discretion to make feltes of Camels haire, where with they clothe themselves, and of which they protect against the wind.

The word 'silk' (Anglo-Saxon *seole*) is from the Latin *serica* (silken), a form of the proper adjective *Sericus* (Chinese) and is therefore an eponym once removed. Whether for protection of native industry (cotton and wool manufacturing), or because wearing luxurious materials was considered sinful, sixteenth-century England did take action against 'silk.' William Wilkinson pointed out in 1579 (*A Confutation of Certaine Articles Deliuered vnto the Familye of Loue*) that

> They . . . affirmed, it was vnlawfull to weare silke.

'Velvet' is from the Latin *velluetum* (Chaucer's plural of 'velvet,' *veluettes*, like its Latin root, was pronounced in four syllables) which meant woolly or shaggy stuff, from its nap. It is allied to the Latin *vellus* (fleece). 'Velvet' was considered anything but shaggy by Thomas Starkey in 1538 (*England*, I,4).

> Yf the nobyllys [nobles] . . . be not appayraylyd in sylkys and veluettes, they thynke they lake [lack] much of theyr honowre.

The Latin *seta* (bristle), known to crossword puzzle fans, gave rise to the word *satinus,* which became our 'satin.' *Promptorium,* c. 1440, equated 'satin' with 'silk.'

> "Satyne," clothe of sylke, satinum.

'Chiffon' is from a French word *chiffe* (rag, piece of flimsy stuff). That 'chiffon' was anything but a rag, but was rather a material of elegance in 1711, was clearly pointed out in the *Spectator* #3018.

> The love of Chiffons ingrained in the female mind is amply satisfied on every opportunity by elaborate descriptions of the toilettes of Court beauties, singers, and dancers.

'Voile' is French for "sail" and comes from a Latin word, *velum* (sail, curtain). Our word 'reveal' means literally to pull back the curtain.

A dealer in small notions used to be called a *Milaner,* named for the city of Milan in Italy. It is from this usage that we get our word 'millinery.' The Latin word *capa* (cape) gave rise to our modern word 'cap,' while 'bonnet,' which in Old French, *bonet,* meant the stuff of which caps were made, came from the Latin *bonneta* (stuff). Its origin is unknown, but it may be allied to a word from India, *banat* (woolen cloth). According to Charlotte Brontë in *Shirley* (VII), the words 'hat' and 'bonnet' were virtually interchangeable.

> I want to finish trimming my hat (bonnet, she meant).

In the United States words from England occasionally took on different meanings. Here is George Sala writing to the *London Daily Telegram* on June 10, 1864, from the United States.

> By the way, they call a lady's dress here [New York], a "robe," and a bonnet a "hat."

Among other head coverings is the 'coif' (compare the word 'coiffure', meaning styled or dressed hair) which comes from Middle High German *kopf* (cup, head). From *kopf* came the word *kuffe* or *kupfe* meaning the cap worn under the helmet.

To convey to the opposite sex the fact that she is unmarried and unattached, the single woman has from time to time worn various items of 'jewelry' (Middle English *iowel,* Old French *joiel, joel, jouel*). The origin of the word is disputed. It is either from Late Latin *jocalia* (jewels, trinkets), Latin *jocare* (to play) and *jocus* (play), or it is a diminutive of French and Old French *joie* (joy, pleasure) so that the sense is a "little joy," that is, a toy or a trinket.

Perhaps single women might start as a new fad the custom of single girls in Scotland as reported by Thomas Pennant in 1771 (*A tour in Scotland*).

> The single women wear only a ribband round their head, which they call a snood.

'Ribbon' (Middle English *riban*), when used in the form *riband* or *ribband,* had a *d* added from a connection with "band," with which, according to the etymologist Skeat, it may be allied. In a famous couplet in *Lost Leader* Robert Browning used the word 'riband' to signify overweening ambition.

> Just for a handful of silver he left us;
> Just for a riband to stick in his coat.

The Frenchman's favorite head covering is the 'beret.' This is an eponym from the fact of its being worn by those from the Béarnais section of France. Our final head covering is native to the great Southwestern part of the United States. It is the 'ten-gallon hat,' which would fill up long before you could put even half that amount of liquid in it. It gets its name from an Americanized pronunciation of a Spanish word. It seems that that the Spaniards were fond of decorating their sombreros with silver braids; the more braids, the fancier the hat. The Spanish word for this type of braid is *galon,* and if a sombrero had ten braids on it, it was very fancy indeed. From *galon* to 'gallon' was but a very short step, and so the 'ten-gallon' hat was born.

Outerwear for cooler weather for both men and women is made from heavier materials like serge, worsted, mohair, tweed, and fur as well as man-made materials. The material we call 'serge' is a cloth made of twilled worsted or silk, but it was originally made only from silk, and the word 'serge' is from the same root as 'silk,' whose origin has been discussed previously in this chapter. For the narrator in Chaucer's The Knight's Tale (I) 'serge' was an inferior material.

> By ordinaunce thurghout the citee large,
> Hanged with cloth of gold, and nat with sarge.

'Worsted' (Middle English *wurstede*) is a well-twisted, smooth yarn made from long-staple wool. According to no less an authority than Chaucer, 'worsted' is an eponym from the town of Worsted, now spelled Worstead.

We use the term 'gabardine' for a material, but it was formerly a garment. The Spanish *gabardina* was a coarse frock. 'Gabardine' is related to two Middle High German words, *wallen* (to wander) and *faran* (to go). These two were combined to produce the word *Wallfahrt* (pilgrimage), and the early meaning of what we now call 'gabardine' was probably a pilgrim's frock. In *The Tempest* Shakespeare used 'gabardine' with its original meaning of garment (act II, scene 2).

> Alas, the storm is come again! my best way is to creep under his gaberdine . . .

'Mohair' has had an interesting development from the Arabic word *mukhayyar* (coarse cloth, goat's hair). In what one authority calls a ridiculous attempt to connect the Arabic word with the English word "hair," the spelling of the final *yar* was changed and the middle part of the word was dropped, leaving 'muhair' or 'mohair.' Government control, or interference, whatever your preference, continued into the seventeenth century. Anthony Wood reported in 1674 (*Life, from 1632 to 1672, Written by Himself; Continued till 1695*) that

> License was given to gent. commoners and commoners to weare silk and mohaire round caps.

Another error seems to have been made with the word 'tweed.' Its first form was as the Scottish *tweel* (twill). This is how the *Border Advertiser* explained its origin in 1850 (*The Imperial Dictionary*).

> It was the word "tweels" having been blotted or imperfectly written on an invoice which gave rise to the now familiar name of these goods. The word was read as tweeds by the late James Locke of London, and it was so appropriate, from the goods being made on the banks of the Tweed, that it was at once adopted, and has been continued ever since.

'Fur' (Middle English *forre*, with the original sense of casing) is from the Old Low German *fodr* (sheath, scabbard). There is even today something about 'fur' that brings out feelings similar to those reported c. 1460 (*The Towneley Mysteries*).

> Thay are so gay in furrys fyne.

While a 'vest' is not necessarily an outer garment, it can help to keep one warm. In addition to keeping one snug, the 'vest' has returned as a fashion item for both men and women. It might have also served as an economy measure, according to Pepys writing in his *Diary* on October 8, 1666.

> The king hath yesterday, in Council, declared his resolution of setting a fashion for clothes . . . It will be a vest, I know not well how; but it is to teach the nobility thrift.

The word 'vest' is from the Latin *vestis* (garment), which goes back to the Sanskrit root *wes* (to clothe). Corollary words are 'vestry,' which was a place to keep clothes, just as pantry is a place to keep bread, and 'vestments,' which refers particularly to liturgical garments. The original meaning of 'travesty' was to shift clothes from man to woman or vice versa, a practice we now describe with the word 'transvestism.' 'Travesty' was also used to describe a disguise by change of clothing. In 1678 Edward Phillips defined the adjective made from 'travesty' (*The New World Of English Words; or, A General Dictionary*).

> "Travested," shifted in apparel (dressed in the habit of a different sex, ed. 1706), disguised.

Dr. Charles Burney in *A General History of Music* (I), a century later, used another variant of the word to mean disguised.

> Aristophanes, in the beginning of his comedy called the Knights . . . introduces the two generals Demosthenes and Nicias, travestied into Valets, and complaining of their master.

'Caftan' is a loose outer garment worn in milder climes (it is once again in fashion for modern women) and comes from the Turkish word *qaftan* (dress). 'Coat' is from the Latin *cota;* but 'cloak' has a much more interesting history. The late Latin word *clocca,* meaning a bell was extended to mean a horseman's cape, because the shape of the cape resembled a bell. From this same word came the French word *cloche,* which still means bell. In English, however, it finally lost its meaning of bell, but kept that of cape or 'cloak.' Our word 'clock' is from the same root, and gets its name from the striking of the time on a bell. In *The Faerie Queene* Spenser used 'cloak' figuratively.

> Thenceforth she sought for helps to cloak her crimes withal.

'Jacket' is from the French word *jaque* (coat of leather reinforced with metal, a sleeveless coat). The 'pea-jacket' certainly doesn't look at all like a pea; it gets its name from the Dutch word *pij* (rough coat). So a 'pea-jacket' is really a "coat-coat" or "jacket-jacket." 'Ulster' was the most northerly of the four provinces of Ireland, and from there came the heavy outercoat that was first called, in 1867, the 'Ulster Overcoat'; by 1879 the name had been shortened to 'ulster.'

The 'Chesterfield' overcoat, generally worn on formal occasions, was named for one of the Earls of Chesterfield in the nineteenth century.

Auxiliary winter wear includes the 'glove' (Anglo-Saxon *glof*). It may have been taken from a combination of a common Gothic prefix *ge* along with *lofa* (palm of the hand), and may have meant something put on the flat or palm of the hand. Manner of dress was much more rigidly prescribed in the eighteenth century than it is now. Daniel Defoe, in 1715, outlined the proper attire for attendance at church on Sunday (*The Family Instructor,* I,1).

Another Sunday, for want of a pair of gloves, you stayed at home.

'Mitten' is an old English word and was used by Chaucer with two different spellings, *mitaine* and *miteyn*. The word 'muffler' is from the Medieval Latin *muffula* (furred glove) via the Old French *mouffle* (a winter mitten). In our time it has moved from the hand to the neck, whereas 'scarf' (discussed above) has moved an even longer distance from the waist to the neck.

After a long and tiring day, worn out from all the changes of clothing, we slip into 'pajamas' (spelled 'pyjamas' in England), from two Hindi words, *pa* (foot) and *jama* (garment), or into a nightgown worn under a 'negligee,' a French word meaning originally neglected, unnoticed, unheeded, careless, and even slovenly (how it has changed its meaning), we take off our 'slippers,' (Anglo-Saxon *slype-scoh,* a slip-shoe) and go to bed.

CHAPTER V

EAT YOUR WORDS

What sholde a man in thyse days now write,
egges or eyren, certaynly it is harde to
playse every man.

William Caxton

When an unusual fact or event presents itself to us, we are likely to describe it as 'food for thought.' In this chapter we shall devote our thoughts to food and specifically to the words we use to describe the food we eat. In examining the origins of these words, we will note their changing meanings and spellings as seen in the writings of English literature over the years.

First will be the words that have to do with the occasions of eating and drinking; today we call them 'meals,' in earlier, more leisurely times, people sat down to a 'repast.' In *The Comedy of Errors* Shakespeare had advice to those about to sit down to eat (act V, scene 1).

. . . unquiet meals make ill digestions. . .

The word 'meal' (from Anglo-Saxon *mael*, a stated time or a portion of time) implied a time for food rather than the current meaning of the food itself. We have retained this sense of time in the modern phrase "regular meals."

While the word 'repast' signifies a more elaborate meal and is usually reserved for festive days, the word itself has a very simple origin. It comes from the Latin words *re* (again) and *pastus* (food), and its literal meaning is to eat again. The general word for that which we eat is 'food' (Middle English *fode*, Anglo-Saxon *foda*). It does not normally refer to the kind of 'food,' at least for humans, that Shakespeare mentioned in *King Lear* (act III, scene 4).

> . . . But mice, and rats, and such small deer
> Have been Tom's food for seven long year.

On awakening in the morning we have 'breakfast,' and its origin is clear, 'break' (Middle English *breke,* end, snap) and 'fast,' an abstention from food, from the Middle English *fasten,* which is a very early derivative from the Teutonic stem *fast* (to be firm, observe, be strict). Thomas Langeley translated *An abridgement of the notable woorke of Polidore Vergile conteignyng the deuisers and firste fynders out . . . used in the churche* (VI, 3), 1546, and in it were these words about one who strayed.

> He kepeth not the true fast whyche forbeareth flesh, or forgoeth his supper.

The next meal of the day is 'luncheon.' The original word was *nunchion,* which was made up of two Middle English words, *none* (noon) and *schenche* (pouring out or distribution of drink). 'Noon' is from the Latin word *nonus* (ninth) and was the ninth hour of a day that began at six A.M. Thus the distribution of drink came at three o'clock in the afternoon as noted in Bishop White Kennett's edition of John Cowell's *The interpreter: or booke containing the signification of words,* 1701.

> "Nooning" beavre, drinking, or repast *ad nonam,* three in the afternoon, called . . . in the North parts a *noonchion,* an afternoon's *nunchion.*

The *nunch* of *nunchion* became confused with the word 'lunch,' a word of Scandinavian origin which meant a large piece or lump. John Gay used the word with this latter meaning in *Shepherd's Week Tuesday* (I), 1714.

> I sliced the lunchion from the barley loaf.

If we don't have time for luncheon we may stop for a 'snack,' a modern equivalent of "snatch." This is how Sir Walter Scott put it in *The Heart of Midlothian* (XXXVIII), 1818.

> And so . . . I have been waiting this hour for you, and I have had a snack myself.

We come now to the most elaborate meal of the day, the 'dinner.' Around 1450, it was not the toss of a coin that determined who paid for dinner; it was, as observed by an anonymous author in *La Tour-Landry,*

Whos wiff [wife] that obeieth worst,
Let her husbonde paie for the dener.

The word 'dinner' is from two Latin words, *dis* (away) and *jejunare* (to fast), which, when put together, mean to break one's fast. As the word traveled through time and space, it became the French word 'dîner' (to dine). Thus we see that breakfast and dinner mean essentially the same thing, to eat after a period of noneating.

There are several food groups that make up the items we eat at our various meals. We may have 'fish,' 'meat,' or 'fowl.' These dishes are cooked with 'spices' to give them flavor, and served to us with 'vegetables' and 'grains.' During the meal we may have 'drinks,' and afterward we might enjoy some 'fruit.' We will examine each of these words in turn.

The meaning of 'fruit' (Latin *fructus,* fruit or enjoyment) has changed over the years. It used to refer to what we now call vegetables. In 1722 Daniel Defoe described an ordinance of the Lord Mayor of London in *A journal of the plague year.*

> That no . . . musty corn, or other corrupt fruits . . . be suffered to be sold.

In 1791, in *A tour in England and Scotland in 1785,* Thomas Newte discussed the produce of Scotland.

> At Aberdeen, turnips, carrots, and potatoes, pass, among the common people, by the name of fruit.

However, as long ago as 1475, in DuGuez's *Introductorie,* quoted in *Babees Book* (index), 'fruit' was used much as we do today.

> But of all manner of meate, the moost daungerous is that whiche is of fruites, as cheres, small cheryse, great cherise.

(Note the three spellings of "cherries" in a single sentence.)

'Fish' (Middle English *fisch,* Anglo-Saxon *fisc,* both from Latin *piscis,* fish), was not always considered a desirable part of one's diet according to Sir Thomas Browne in *Pseudodoxia epidemica or enquiries into very many received tenents* [vulgar errors] (III, 25), in 1646.

> We mortifie ourselves with the diet of fish.

(The word 'mortify' in this citation should be understood as having the literal meaning of "kill," from the Latin *mors,* death.)

'Meat' (Middle English *mete*) is the general term used to describe the edible flesh of animals. It is probably allied to the Sanskrit root *mad* (to be glad) and a Gothic root, *mats* (food). Chaucer used the word 'meat' with the idea of food from plants but also brought out the sense of gladness when he wrote the following (*Boethius*, II, meter 5).

> Blysful was the fyrst age of men; they helden hem apayed [appeased] with the metes that the trewe feeldes browhten forth.

In Shakespeare's *King Lear* (act I, scene 4) the word 'meat' was used differently.

> Why, after I have cut the egg i' th' middle and eat up the meat, the two crowns of the egg.

The kind of 'meat' that comes from a cow or steer we call 'beef' (Middle English *beof*, Anglo-Saxon *bef*, ox), both of which words had their origins in the Latin *bos* (ox). A popular kind of 'meat' is 'fowl' (Middle English *foul, fowel*, Anglo-Saxon *fugol*), which had the general meaning of bird in Middle English. It comes from the Teutonic *fleugan* (to fly) and is but one of many instances where the word gets its meaning from an action. We might just as well have ended up with an English word "fliers" for chicken instead of 'fowl.' In *The romance and prophesies* of Thomas of Erceldoune, c. 1425, the word was used in a way that shows its original meaning (I).

> In Huntlee bannkes es mery to bee,
> Whare fowles synges both nyght and daye.

The 'spices' that are used in cooking some of these foods are quite varied, and we shall look at them individually later on. Now we are concerned with the origin of the word 'spice' itself. It is from the French *espice* (spice) and the Latin *species* (kind, sort, 'species'), meaning types within a general class or genus. Chaucer used 'spice' with this latter meaning in The Parson's Tale.

> The spices of penance ben three.

In the Middle Ages, however, the word 'species' was used for the four kinds of ingredients traded by the druggists of the period (we would call them grocers). These four were saffron, cloves, cinnamon, and nutmeg, items which we now call 'spices' rather than 'species.'

The well-balanced meal has an assortment of 'vegetables.' The word 'vegetable' is from the Latin *vegetabilis,* meaning animating, full of life, or growing. Randle Cotgrave gave the following definition of 'vegetable' *(Dictionarie),* 1611.

> Vegetable (F.), vegetable, fit or able to liue; hauing, or likelie to haue, such life, or increase in groweth, as plants, &.

In earlier days, the term 'vegetables,' like 'fruits,' referred to a variety of items. Even as late as 1822, John Mason wrote in *The study of medicine* (I)

> The expressed oils of mild vegetables, as the pistachio, olive, and almond.

In addition to vegetables, 'grains' are a very important part of our diet. The word 'grain' is used in other areas than food; for example, we speak of the 'grain' of wood or stone. Both meanings come from the Latin *granum* (grain, seed, small kernel). The lines in wood and stone resemble the waving fields of grain, and therefore the word was used to describe these lines. We also use the word 'ingrained' to mean something which is deep inside us, such as duty or respect. The meaning in that usage comes from a time when objects were dyed different colors; if the dye was deep enough to color the 'grain' it was considered to be a good dye job and likely to hold its color permanently.

The word 'drink' is to be found in pretty much the same form in several of the Indo-European languages, except that it might change its initial letter; in German it is *trinken* and in Dutch and early English it was *drinken.* Alexander Pope used 'drink' in a figurative sense when he wrote, in 1709, his *Essay on Criticism* (I), which has these well-known four lines.

> A little learning is a dangerous thing;
> Drink deep, or taste not the Pierian spring.
> There shallow draughts intoxicate the brain,
> And drinking largely sobers us again.

Now that we have whetted our appetites, our mouths must be watering and we are ready to eat some meals. When we take the time to eat breakfast we may start with any of the following: 'orange' juice, 'grapefruit,' or some form of 'melon' like 'canteloupe.' 'Grapefruit' are called that because they grow in clusters like grapes, not because they are members of the grape family. The word 'grape' is an outgrowth of two words, Old French *graper* (to gather clusters with a hook) and Middle High German *krappe* (a hook).

The generic term 'melon' is from the Greek *melon* (apple) and the Latin *melo* (apple-shaped melon). 'Canteloupe' is an eponym from Cantalupo, the name of a castle in Italy. 'Melons' were not always accepted as nourishing food according to Andrew Boorde (*A compendious regyment or a dyetary of helth*), 1542.

> Mylons doth ingender evil humoures.

But by 1661, as Pepys wrote in his *Diary* (September 27), 'melons' had become a delicacy.

> Some grapes and millons from my Lord at Lisbone.

The word 'orange' is particularly interesting because it illustrates a phenomenon in English which we could call "noncing," the dropping or adding the initial letter *n*, in particular when a word is taken over from another language. 'Orange' comes from the Spanish and Persian words *naranja* and *naranj* respectively. In English we have taken the letter *n* away from the beginning of the word and have added it to the end of the article which precedes it, and so we say "an orange" instead of "a norange." This change may have come about because of the connection with the Latin *aurum* (gold) and the notion that the word for the fruit denoted its golden color. On this basis it was assumed that the word should correspond to its supposed Latin root *aurum* and therefore have no initial *n*. An odd metaphorical use of the word occurs in a work by Hawley Smart (*From post to finish, a novel,* I, 7), of 1884.

> It is rather rough on the boy . . . to suddenly discover that his father had sucked the orange, and that he has merely inherited the skin.

(While the following words do not necessarily have anything to do with breakfast foods, we might note here another example of the noncing phenomenon. The words are 'napkin' and 'apron,' both of which come from the French word *nappe,* which means drapery or linen. In the former case the word has retained the initial *n*, while in the latter the *n* has been dropped.)

Many of us eat 'cereal' for breakfast. The word 'cereal' is also an eponym, taken from *Ceres,* the Roman goddess of corn and produce. On our cereal we put 'milk' (Anglo-Saxon *meolc, meoluc,* allied to the Old High German *miluh*). It has an Indo-European root meaning to stroke, the action required to get the 'milk' from the cow. If waistline bulge is not a problem, we may use 'cream' instead of milk on the cereal. 'Cream' is derived from the Greek word *chrisma* (unguent) from which we also get the second name or epithet of Jesus, 'Christ' (Greek *christos*), meaning the anointed. *Chrisma* became *cresme* or *chresme* in Old French and *creme* or *crayme* in Middle English, thus dropping the *s,* which is not pronounced in the French form, and finally 'cream.' It was not always considered a desirable food, at least that is what John Russell wrote in *The boke of nurture, folowyng Englondis gise* c. 1460.

> Bewar at eve of crayme of cowe.

We use the phrase 'the cream of the crop' to mean the best out of any group, which is how it was used in Cervantes' *History of Don Quixote* (II), as translated by Thomas Shelton, 1612.

> Welcome, O flower and cream of knights-errant.

From the Portuguese we have the name of a fruit we are likely to slice and put on our cereal, the 'banana.' From Alphonse de Candolle, quoted in the 1962 edition of the *Encyclopaedia Britannica,* we learn that the banana has been known since antiquity.

> The Greeks, Latins and Arabs have mentioned it as a remarkable fruit tree. Pliny speaks of it distinctly. He says the Greeks of the expedition of Alexander saw it in India and he quotes the name "pala" which still persists in Malabar. Sages reposed beneath its shade and ate of its fruit. Hence the botanical name "Musa sapientum." "Musa" is from the Arabic "mouz" or "mawoz," which we find as early as the thirteenth Century in Eba Baithar.

In 1597 Abraham Hartwell in *A report of the kingdome of Congo* (II) pointed out the relationship between the words 'banana' and *mouz.*

> Other fruits there are, termed banana, which we verily think to be the Muses of Egypt and Soria.

Another item we might put on our cereal is the 'berry' (Middle English *berye,* Anglo-Saxon *berige, berge,* which seemed to imply "edible fruit" and may be connected to the Sanskrit word *bhas,* to eat). The 'raisin' we find in some breakfast cereals is taken from Old French *raizin* and Latin *racemus,* both of which meant a bunch of grapes.

In addition to, or instead of cereals and fruits, we may decide to have 'eggs' for breakfast. The custom of throwing rotten 'eggs' at people is very old. Around 1300 in *King Alisaunder* there appeared

> Men to heom [him] threowe drit and donge,
> With foule ayren [eggs].

The spelling of the word 'egg,' as one can see from the above citation, was varied to say the least. It bothered no less an authority than Caxton, the famous printer, who in 1490 translated *The boke yf [of] Eneydos* (prologue).

> What sholde a man in thyse days now write, egges or eyren, certaynly it is harde to playse every man.

The word 'egg' is of Scandinavian origin and may be related to the Latin word *ovum* (egg), from which we also get the word 'oval' (egg-shaped). 'Poached' eggs are so-called because after they are cooked the yolk of the 'egg' is contained in a pocket, pouch, or *poke* of white. The modern version of *poke* is 'pouched' or 'poached.' A more appropriate word might be "pouched" eggs. Ben Jonson used a slightly different spelling in *The staple of newes* (III), 1626.

> THOMAS. . . . has drest his excellence such a dish of eggs.
> PENNYBOY [JUNIOR]. What, potched?

In the word 'omelette' we have another example of a word deriving its existence from a shape. The Latin word *lamella* means a thin plate; from it came the Old French word *alemelle* (thin plate, blade of a knife), which led to 'omelette.' The 'omelette' thus was named from its thin, flat shape. One of the earliest uses of a common saying with this word occurred in the *London Times* of January 23, 1898.

> Omelettes cannot be made without breaking eggs, and war cannot be waged without losses of this kind occurring.

'Bacon' and 'sausage' are often eaten with eggs at breakfast. When we eat 'bacon,' I don't suppose that most of us worry as much as did Tobias Venner in 1620 (*Via recta ad vitam longam; also the true use of our famous bathes of Bathe*, III) when he warned that

> Bacon is not good for them that haue weake stomacks.

The Middle High German *backe* (hinder part or piece, ham, bacon) became in Middle English *bacoun* and finally 'bacon.' The part of the body we call the 'back' is from the same root.

We send someone to participate in a game, struggle, or contest with the exhortation, 'bring home the bacon,' meaning "come home a winner." There are two sources given for this phrase; the first is simple and very undramatic. A feature of country fairs is the greased-pig contest. The one who catches the pig takes it home. The second explanation is much more appealing. In A.D. 1111, in the little town of Dunmow, England, a noblewoman announced that a side of 'bacon' would be given to any man who would come to Dunmow, humbly kneel on the two stones at the entrance to the church, and swear that for twelve months and a day he had never had a fight with his wife or wished himself unmarried. While some authorities say that it had to be a man and his wife who took the oath together, Chaucer's Wyf's Prologue took note of this custom but seems to indicate that it was the husband alone who did not meet the standards set by the noblewoman of Dunmow.

> The bacoun was not set for hem . . .
> That some men fecche in Essex at Donmowe.

We sometimes refer to a slice of bacon as a 'rasher.' This word could have come from a meaning of the word *rash* as "quick," referring therefore to the quick cooking of 'bacon,' or if 'rasher' referred to a slice, it could have come from *rash* meaning to cut or scrape. It is from this latter word that we get our word 'razor.' The word 'rasher' was used to describe a strip of meat in *A worlde of wordes, or most copius and exact dictionarie in Italian and English* by John Florio in 1598.

> "Carbonata," a carbonada, meat broiled vpon the coles, a rasher.

'Sausage' is a casing stuffed with salted and seasoned meat. The word is from the French *saucisse* and the Late Latin *salsicia*, from Latin *salsicius* (seasoned with salt). It is the Latin root *sal* (salt) that gives us the meaning of the word.

With breakfast it is customary to have 'toast.' This word is from the Latin *tostus* (parched). We also use the word 'toast' in another sense: to offer words to a person being honored. This custom derives from an interesting incident in English history. It was the custom in England in the sixteenth century to place a piece of 'toast' in a glass of whisky before drinking it. One day during the Restoration of Charles II, a noted beauty of the time decided to take a bath in a vat of wine in a public square, much to the amusement and delectation of the onlookers. One of those, slightly inebriated, tried to climb into the vat with the bathing beauty. He was restrained by the crowd, whereupon he is supposed to have exclaimed, "If I can't have the liquor, I'll take the toast." Therefore whenever we give a 'toast' at a party we should remember that it was the object of the words who is the 'toast,' not the words themselves. Sir Richard Steele used a phrase with 'toast' which is virtually synonymous with making a debut in society. In an issue of the *Tatler, #95*, in the early eighteenth century, he wrote:

> Her eldest daughter was within a half-a-year of being a toast.

On the toast we might put 'butter,' 'cheese,' or 'margarine.' 'Butter' is a word from the Latin *butyrum* (butter), from two Greek words, *bous* (ox, cow) and *tyros* (cheese). The latter word became also the Latin *caseus* — our 'cheese.' 'Butter' is used in several phrases today in a figurative sense. One of them appeared in a play by John Ford (*The Ladies Triall,* act II, scene 1), in 1638.

> I know what's what, I know on which side my bread is butter'd.

'Margarine,' in its original form, was a white pearllike substance extracted from hog's lard, and got its name from the Latin *margarita* and the French *marguerite,* all with the meaning of 'pearl.'

For some people the day doesn't begin until they have had their 'coffee,' a word from the Turkish *qahve* and Arabic *qahwa* (wine, coffee). Perhaps what William Parry wrote in 1601 in *A new and large discourse of the travels of Sir Anthonie Sherley* is still pertinent today.

> A certain Liquor which they call Coffe — which will soon intoxicate the brain.

To serve this purpose, the coffee had to be imbibed in the fashion described by George Havers in his translation of *The travels of Pietro della Valle into East India and Arabia Deserta, Whereunto is added a relation of sir Thos. Roe's voyage into the East Indies,* 1665.

> For drink, water and cahu (coffee), black liquor, drank as hot as could be endured.

Also in 1665, we find that special qualities are ascribed to the drink by Gideon Harvey (*A discourse of the plague,* XII, 12).

Coffee is recommended against the Contagion.

What may have been one of the first blue laws involved the 'coffee men,' the keepers of coffee houses, as quoted by Narcissus Luttrel in *A brief historical relation of state affairs 1678 – 1714.*

> The lord mayor has declared no coffee men in London shall receive guests on Sunday.

In addition to its protection against the plague as outlined by Harvey above, Alexander Pope saw additional benefits that might be derived from drinking coffee (*The Rape of the Lock,* III, 1712).

> Coffee (which makes the politician wise,
> And see through all things with his half-shut eyes).

Another morning drink is 'tea,' which is from a Chinese word pronounced *tay* (to rhyme with "obey"). On September 30, 1658, 'tea' was mentioned in the column Mercurius Politicus in the *Gazette.*

> That excellent and by all physicians approved China drink called by the Chineans Tcha, and by other nations tay, alias tee, is sold at the Sultana Head Coffee House, London.

Pepys wrote about 'tea' in his *Diary* on September 28, 1660.

> I did send for a cup of tee, a China drink, of
> which I never had drank before.

And finally, Colley Cibber (1671 – 1757) became quite eloquent about tea (*Lady's Last Stake,* I).

> Tea! thou soft, thou sober, sage, and venerable liquid! . . . thou female-tongue-running, smile-smoothing, heart-opening, wink-tipping cordial, to whose glorious insipidity I owe the happiest moment of my life, let me fall prostrate.

'Cocoa' is a drink made from 'chocolate,' which is composed of ground nuts from the *cacao* tree; none of these is in any way related to the coconut tree. The word 'chocolate' is from the Mexican Indian *chocolatl;* it is not derived from the word 'cacao,' which has its origin in another Mexican Indian word, *cacauatl.* 'Cocoa' is a corrupt form of the word *cacao* and came into the language through a spelling confusion with a similar sounding word, *coco* (the cocoa-nut, now spelled 'coconut,' palm tree). According to tit,' which is merely toasted cheese and has nothing to do with either "rare" or "rabbit." *MacMillan's Magazine* explained the origin of the terhe etymologist Skeat (see Bibliography), the tree was "called 'coco' by the Portuguese in India on account of the monkey-like face at the base of the nut, from 'coco,' a bugbear, an ugly mask to frighten children." We are all familiar with the cartoon showing complete absorption in the morning paper to the exclusion of everything else. Jane Austen added a new dimension to the picture in *Northanger Abbey* (II, 10), 1798.

> The General, between his cocoa, and his newspaper, had no leisure for noticing her.

A Mr. Edmund Hickeringill showed the sentiments of Protestant England in the late seventeenth century concerning the morning drinks we have been discussing (*Priest-craft, its character and consequences* (II, 6).

> Bless the Mahometan Coffee and the Popish Spanish Chocolate.

Breakfast is over, time has passed, we must consider what we shall have for lunch. We could start with some 'soup' (French *soupe*), from a Teutonic word meaning to drink in. Perhaps we have a 'mushroom' soup, from the Old French word *mousse* (moss), where mushrooms grow, or a 'tomato' soup, from the Spanish *tomate*, borrowed from the Mexican Indian word *tomatl*. The rapidly growing characteristic of the 'mushroom' makes it appropriate for this figurative use by Samuel Richardson in *Clarissa (Harlow); or the history of a young lady*, (I), 1748.

> The prosperous upstart mushroomed into rank.

Before you eat a mushroom, however, you ought perhaps to consider the advice of Sir Thomas Elyot in 1533 (*The castel of helth,*).

> Beware of musherons . . . and al other thinges, whiche wyll sone putrifie.

Emerson, the American philosopher, didn't worry about any evil effects from 'tomatoes,' but he did have to get used to them in 1856 (*English traits*).

> I find the sea-life an acquired taste, like that for tomatoes and olives.

A special kind of soup is 'chowder,' a word probably from the French *chaudière* (pot). The 'chowder' might be with 'clams,' a word closely allied with the word 'clamp' as derived from the Anglo-Saxon *clamm* (bond, fetter). In the late nineteenth century, 'chowder' was used in a much broader sense than merely a soup, as reported in *The Century* (XXVIII).

> A chowder was given a few weeks ago at the head of our little bay.

Another simple luncheon dish could be 'Welsh rabbit' or 'Welsh rarebm.

> Welsh rabbit is a genuine slang term, belonging to a large group which describe in the same humorous way the special dish or product or peculiarity of a particular district. For examples: . . . an Essex lion is a calf; . . . "Glasgow magistrates" or "Norfolk Capons" are red herrings.

If we are going to have a sandwich for lunch it would be on 'bread' (Middle English *breed, bred*). ('Sandwich' as an eponym is discussed in Chapter II.). 'Bread' has been called "the staff of life," and in 1655 Thomas Boufet and C. Bennet agreed, but put it differently (*Healths improvement*).

> Bread and Cheese be the two targets against death.

Most everyone will recognize this proverb even though it was slightly changed by John Heywood in 1562 (*Prouerbes*).

> Better is halfe a lofe than no bread.

'Pumpernickel' is a coarse black bread, and the word is from the German, meaning a "farting devil" or a "devil's fart" — a coarse name for a coarse bread.

Popular luncheon 'salads' (Dutch *sla,* salad) are made with 'tuna' (Middle English *tunny*), a word from the Greek *thynnos* (tuna, with the literal sense of to dart, rush along). Another salad ingredient is the 'sardine.' There is some doubt about the origin of this word, but most authorities believe that it is an eponym from the island of Sardinia. The 'tuna' or 'sardines' could be combined with 'lettuce,' from the Latin *lactuca* (lettuce), *lac* (milk). Today we look to 'lettuce' as a healthful source of vitamins with very few calories, but it was not always so regarded. William Turner had no use for it in 1562 (*A new herball 1551; the seconde parte 1562; the first and seconde partes lately ouersene, with the thirde parte, also a booke of the bath of Baeth*, II).

> Muche vse of lettes hurteth the eysight.

Both Alexander Pope and John Cooke saw soporific qualities in 'lettuce.' In 1614 Cooke asked (*Greenes tu quoque; or the cittie gallant,* L, 3).

> Did I eate any Lettice to supper last night, that I am so sleepie?

while Pope wrote in 1733 (*Satires and epistles of Horace imitated,* II, 1).

> If your point be rest, [take] Lettuce and cowslip-wine.

Whatever its qualities, lettuce has been known for a long time. In *The early South-English legendary or lives of saints,* I, 18) this appeared, c. 1290.

> A fair herb that men cleopez [call] letuse.

The salad could also include 'cucumber,' from the Latin *cucumis* (cucumber). There is a possible connection between this word and the Latin *cucuma* (cooking kettle), which gives rise to the explanation for the word 'cucumber' that "it ripens in the heat." Whatever it might have done in the heat, John Arbuthnot was concerned in 1732 with what it might do in the stomach *(Rules of diet,* I).

> The Juice of Cucumbers is too cold for some Stomachs.

This "coldness" quality of cucumbers is used in a popular saying today and was so used by George Colman (the Younger) in 1797 (*The Heir at Law*).

> When the wife of the great Socrates threw a . . . teapot at his erudite head, he was as cool as a cucumber.

A raw 'spinach' salad is frequently served. In Arabic the vegetable is called *aspanakh* or *isfanaj,* in Spanish *espinaca,* in Old French *espinache* or *espinage,* in Middle English *speneche,* and in modern English 'spinach.' Popeye and many mothers would take issue with John Arbuthnot's opinion of 'spinach' as expressed in *Rules of diet.*

> Spinage emollient, but not very nourishing.

Whatever the composition of the salad, it was not the specialty of the English according to Richard Ford in 1846 (*Gatherings from Spain*).

> The salad is the glory of every French dinner, and the disgrace of most in England.

Instead of salad we might be served 'coleslaw' — 'cole' from the Latin *caulis* (cabbage) and 'slaw' from the Dutch *sla* (salad). 'Coleslaw' was probably a favorite dish of Victor Hugo's because he had one of his characters say (a translation of *Les Misérables*, 1862, III).

> To leave my whole plateful without touching it! My coleslaugh which was so good.

A little heavier dish for luncheon would be either 'spaghetti' or 'macaroni.' 'Spaghetti' is the plural of the Italian word *spaghetto*, which is a diminutive of *spago* (small cord). 'Macaroni' may be from the Middle Italian *maccare* (to bruise, batter, pound), but the etymology is obscure. Ben Jonson wrote in 1627 in *Cynthia's Revels* (II)

> He doth learne . . . to eat aenchouies, maccarone, bouoli, fagioli, and cauiare.

Lord Chesterfield wrote to his son in 1750 (*Letters*, III) suggesting an inexpensive way to feed certain people.

> You would do very well to take one or two such sort of people home with you to dinner every day; it would be only a little "minestra" and "macaroni" the more.

The anonymous "Yankee Doodle" has a couple of lines in it that seem to make very little sense.

> He stuck a feather in his cap,
> And called it macaroni.

To find out why 'macaroni' was used this way, we have to go back to the eighteenth century. Horace Walpole, writing to Hertford in February and May of 1764, made quite clear how the word 'macaroni' was used in his time and what it meant. In a letter of February 6, 1764, he said:

> On Saturday, at the Maccaroni Club (which is composed of all the travelled young men who wear long curls and spying-glasses) they played again.

The May 27 letter described a friend.

> Lady Falkener's daughter is to be married to a young rich Mr. Crewe, a maccarone, and of our loo.

('Loo' was a card game, and the reference is to a group of card players who regularly played together.) Evidence that the word 'macaroni' traveled to the colonies with the same meaning is noted from its application to a body of Maryland troops in the American Revolutionary Army, which was noted for its showy uniforms. Now we can see that the word 'macaroni' in "Yankee Doodle" was meant to convey the idea of a dandy or a fop; by putting a feather in his cap and calling it 'macaroni,' the gentleman proclaimed himself a part of a very special group. Associated with 'macaroni' is the word 'macaroon,' since it was made with the same pounding process though not with the same ingredients. According to Skeat, Cotgrave defined the word as follows.

> little fritter-like buns, or thick losenges, compounded of sugar, almonds, rose-water, and musk, pounded together and baked with a gentle fire, also [the same as] the Ital. *macaroni*.

Lunch was early and light, and dinner won't be until much later, so it is time for a snack. We could have 'biscuits' and 'jelly' or an assortment of fruits, such as 'apricots,' 'cherries,' 'apples,' 'peaches,' 'pears,' 'pineapples,' or 'grapes.' Let us start with 'biscuits.' The word is made up of two French words, *bis* (twice) and *cuit* (cooked). A 'biscuit' is hard because it is baked twice. This explanation of the derivation of the word was known back in 1569 when Crawley wrote:

> The bread was such as was prouided to serue at neede, or in warres, for it was Bisket, that is twice baked, and without leauen or salt.

Note the spelling *bisket*. This is the way it was pronounced from the sixteenth to the eighteenth centuries. We still pronounce the word in the same way, but we have reverted to the French spelling. We should not confuse the "twice-baked" bread with the modern 'biscuit.' This is a small, round, soft cake made with yeast or soda batter, and sometimes shortened with lard, butter, or margarine.

'Hardtack' used to be a principal food of the crew on sailing ships during long ocean voyages. The 'hard' of 'hardtack' refers to the technique of baking 'biscuits'; it meant bread that was baked very hard to preserve it. 'Tack' seems to have been a corruption of *tact*, which itself derived from the word *taste*. By extension from *taste*, 'tack' came to be used generally for food. 'Hardtack,' therefore, was hard-baked food. In 1612 Michael Drayton used the word 'tack' with meaning of taste (*Poly-olbion, or a chorographicall description of . . . Great Britain* (XIX).

> Or cheese, which our fat soil to every quarter sends,
> Whose tack the hungry clown and plowman so commends.

If you can remember far enough back in your life, you might recall that you were given 'zwieback' to chew on. Like 'biscuit' it, too, is made up of two words, but this time they are German, not French. The words are *zwei* (two, spelled *zwie* nowadays) and *backen* (to bake). So, whether in time gone by you ate the old sailors' version 'hardtack,' the German *Zweiback,* or the English-French version *biscuit,* you were eating twice-baked dough.

The 'jelly' we put on our biscuits comes from the Latin *gelare* (to freeze) and *gelu* (frost) — related to our 'gelatine' and 'congeal.' The *g* in these two words was retained from the French *gelée* (frost), but in 'jelly' the *g* became a *j.* 'Jelly' was known back in 1479, but it was in a form quite different from what we put on bread and crackers today. In John Lydgate's *Debate between the horse, goose, and sheep* we find

> Of the shepe . . .
> Of whose hede boylled . . .
> Ther cometh a gely and an oynement.

We have discussed previously the origin of the word 'grape' under 'grapefruit,' but we should look at a couple of suggestions from the past regarding its use. Arbuthnot, who discussed virtually every kind of food, had this to say about grapes (*Rules of diet*).

> Grapes, taken in moderate Quantities, help the Appetite.

A cookbook printed c. 1420 had this advice (*Liber Cocorum*).

> Take persole [parsley] . . . grene Grapus, and stofe thy chekyns with wynne.

Shape was the determining factor in the naming of the 'pineapple.' It is the resemblance of the fruit to the shape and appearance of the pine cone, which was called a *pine apple* in Middle English, that caused it to be so named. 'Peach' comes from the Late Latin word for peach, *persica.*

'Pear' is the English version of the Anglo-Saxon *pere,* the French *poire,* and the Italian *pera,* from the Latin *pirum.* An earlier version of the common proverb "You can't tell a book by its cover" is found in John Lydgate's *Minor Poems,* 1430.

> Appeles and peres that semen very gode
> Ful oft tyme are roten by the core.

The 'apricot,' spelled *apricock* by Shakespeare, gets its name from the fact that it ripens early. It is from the Latin *praecos* (premature, early ripe) — from where we get also our 'precocious,' to describe someone whose talents mature earlier than normal. The word 'apricot' was applied to the fruit after its ripening characteristics were noticed, and this fact was known and described in Henry Lyte's translation in 1578 of R. Dodoens' *Niewe herball or historie of plantes* (VI, 40).

> There be two kindes of peaches . . . . The other kindes are soner ripe, wherefore they be called abrecox or aprecox.

The original root of the word 'apple' (Middle English *appel, appil, appell*) is unknown. Like Arbuthnot, Elyot (*Castel,* VII) wrote about virtually every kind of food. Here is his prescription for apples.

> Rough tasted appules are holsome where the stomake is weak.

In the word 'cherry' we have an instance of a word ending in the sound *s* in a foreign language (French *cerise*) and taken over into English, where it assumed a different form. In its original form it was singular, from the Latin *cerasus* (cherry tree, cherry), and it came into English at first as 'cherries' meaning one piece of the fruit. But 'cherries' ends with an *s* which sounded like a plural in English, so the final *s* was dropped and a proper English ending for the singular was added. The result was the word 'cherry' as the singular and 'cherries' as the plural. Others beside Elyot and Arbuthnot wrote about the effects of food on the body. William Langham wrote about cherries in 1579 *(Garden)*.

> The black sowre Cheries do strengthen the stomacke.

Instead of fruits for our afternoon snack we could have 'nuts' (Middle English *note*, Old English *hnutu,* Latin *nux*) even though they are much more caloric. Calories were not a concern of Thomas Fuller in 1642 when he used 'nuts' to illustrate a maxim for living (*The holy state 1642; the profane state 1642*, III, 17).

> Worldly riches, like nuts, teare many clothes in getting them.

The 'walnut' was not native to English, so it was given a name in Anglo-Saxon made up of two words which indicated this fact, *wealh* (foreign) and *hnutu* (nut). The 'filbert' may be an eponym, from Saint Philibert, whose day is August 22, which is in the middle of the nutting season. (Since there are no 'nuts' in May it is hard to understand the first line of the old song which goes "Here we go gathering nuts in May," until we realize that the word 'nuts', in this case, means "knots." There are many knots of flowers in May and that is what people go gathering in the song.) Another explanation of the origin of the word 'filbert' is that it comes from two Old High German words, *filu* (very, many) and *bert* (bright).

Ogden Nash gave us a succinct recipe for the conquest of a woman, "Candy is dandy, but liquor is quicker." Compilers of proverbs in the sixteenth and seventeenth centuries in England used 'nuts' and 'apples' instead of candy and liquor. In 1562 John Heywood (*Prouerbes*) wrote:

> She is lost with an apple and woon with a nut.

Somehow the proverb took a complete about-face (even the sexes shifted roles) in a little under a hundred years. This is how it was written by James Howell in *English proverbs,* 1660.

> He may be gott by an Apple, and lost by a Nutt.

We may like to think that the expression 'to be nuts about' is modern slang, but it is over one hundred years old. In the March 29, 1862, issue of *Punch,* the British humor magazine, the following appeared.

> Johnny and Georgy were nuts on their pet . . . and tabled their money freely.

Elyot and Boorde both wrote about all sorts of nuts and their value to man. In 1533 Elyot (*Castel*) wrote:

> Fylberdes and hasyll nuttes . . . are more stronge in substance than wall nuttes.

In the case of the 'chestnut' we have a choice as to origin. It may have come from the city of Castana in Asia Minor, in which case the tree is named for a place; or it is from the Armenian word *kaskeni* (chestnut tree), a tree which grew in the area, in which case the place is named for the tree. A word of Algonkian origin is the 'pecan.' It is from the Cree *pakan,* Ojibway *pagan,* and Abnaki *pagann,* all words for any hard-shelled nut.

The 'cashew' is from the East Indian word *acajou* from the *acaiaba* tree on which the 'cashew' nuts grow. In the word 'almond' the *l* is an inserted letter, owing to the confusion of the initial letter *a* from the Latin word *amygdala* (almond) with the Arabic definite article *al* in the Spanish and French forms of the word *almendra* and *almandre*. The Arabic form would have been "al amendra" following the Latin form. About their use Boorde (*Dyetary*, XII) had this to say.

> Almons be hote & moyste; it doth comforte the brest.

Last but certainly not least in America is the 'peanut.' It got its name from the fact that the pod or shell has two edible seeds in it that resemble peas.

If you have played some tennis, ridden a bicycle, swum, or simply walked during the afternoon after your snack, you have developed an appetite for dinner, the main meal of the day. It doesn't matter whether we call it dinner or supper, or whether we have it at night during the week and at midday on Sunday, it still remains the main meal. For Chaucer it could serve as a reward for good behavior (Prologue, 799).

> Which of yow that bereth hym best of alle . . .
> Shal haue a soper at oure aller cost.

Boorde in 1542 and Thomas Hunt in 1671 had conflicting advice as to the kind of activity one should engage in after a large meal. Boorde said (*Dyetary*).

> After your supper, make a pause or [ere] you go to bedde.

while a certain Hunt advised:

> After dinner sit a while, after supper walk a mile.

James R. Planché, writing many years later, c. 1860, had another view of possible postsupper activity (*Extravaganza*, III).

> Some tell us after supper walk a mile,
> But we say, after supper dance a measure.

As we can see from the above citations, supper (from Middle English *soper, super*, Old French *soper, souper*, to sup, eat a meal of bread sopped in gravy, Middle Low German *supen*, to sup, sip up) used to be the last meal of the day. Today, depending on locale and social status, the night meal may be called either dinner or supper, but if the main meal is served at noon, it is usually called dinner.

It is the custom in many households to have a preprandial drink (generally with alcohol) before dinner. We use the generic term 'liquor' to describe such drinks. The word 'liquor,' however, was originally used as we use the word 'liquid' today. It is in this sense that the following appeared in *The myroure [mirror] of oure Ladye, containing a devotional treatise on divine service, etc.,* 1450–1530.

> Wyth thre lyquores that ys with wepynge teares, wyth blody swette, and wyth blode.

(Sound familiar? Churchill made it famous during World War II, when he told the English people he had nothing to offer them but "blood, toil, tears, and sweat.") 'Liquor' was still used with the meaning of 'liquid' in 1789 according to William Buchan's *Domestic Medicine*.

> Persons afflicted with low spirits, . . . find more benefit from . . . solid food and generous liquors.

We call the time devoted to the predinner drink the 'cocktail' hour. The word 'cocktail' meant originally, according to *The Dictionary of Rural Sports* of 1870

> Any horse of racing stamp and qualities, but decidedly not thorough-bred, from a known stain in his parentage.

By transference it came to mean one assuming the position of a gentleman, without true gentlemanly breeding. Thackeray wrote of such a one in *The Newcomes*.

> Such a selfish, insolent coxcomb as that, such a cocktail.

How it came to mean a mixed drink is not known, but it was used in that sense by Washington Irving as early as 1809 in *Knickerbocker's History of New York*.

> They lay claim to be the first inventors of those recondite beverages, cock-tail, stone-fence, and sherry-cobbler.

While some like their drinks mixed, others prefer them straight or "neat." The liquors used in these drinks might be whiskey (rye, scotch, or bourbon), vodka, gin, or rum. 'Rum' is a contraction of the Devon (England) word *rumbullion,* meaning great tumult or disturbance. In a manuscript in Trinity College, Dublin, *Description of Barbados,* written about 1651, is this definition.

> The chief fudling [inebriating drink] they make in the island is Rumbullion, alias Kill-Devil . . . made of sugar canes distilled, a hot, hellish and terrible liquor.

Rumbullion became in succession *rumbowling, rumbo,* and then 'rum.' Lord Byron in 1819 had a different view of 'rum' (*Don Juan,* II, 26).

> There's nought, no doubt, so much the spirit calms
> As rum and true religion.

'Whiskey' on the other hand was viewed in an entirely different light by James Maidment in 1715 (*A book of Scotish pasquils* [published or posted lampoons]).

> Whiskie shall put our brains in rage.

The word 'whiskey' (the American spelling; in England and Scotland it is spelled 'whisky' and refers only to what we in America call Scotch or Scotch whiskey) is a contraction of the Gaelic *uisge-beatha* (water of life), which is itself a direct translation of the Latin *aqua vitae* with the same meaning. The Scandinavian countries still use the word *aquavit* to describe strong spirits or brandy. 'Bourbon' is an eponym from Bourbon County in Kentucky, where the liquor is produced.

Along with cocktails we may partake of appetizers, hors d'oeuvres, or canapés. 'Appetite' is from Latin *appetere* (to long after), composed of *ad* (toward) and *petere* (to fly, rush swiftly, seek swiftly — *ad* became *ap* before a following *p*). Whether our 'appetite' is for food or for learning, we rush toward our desire to satisfy it as quickly as possible. The plight of the hungry has always stirred compassion in the hearts of men, as shown in these lines from *Twenty-six political and other poems* (II), c. 1400.

> Whoo that is hungry, and hath no thyng but boonys [bones]
> To staunche his apetyght.

To one replete with food the most elegant dish in the world would have no appeal. Richard Brome in the prologue to his *Demoiselle,* c. 1650, put it this way.

> 'Tis appetite makes dishes, 'tis not cooks.

'Hors d'oeuvres,' literally "outside the work" or "nonessential," is a French phrase taken over without change into English and is another, more elegant way of saying 'appetizers.' 'Hors d'oeuvres' may take almost any form, such as small servings of paté, meat, fish, vegetables, or cheese. In Tobias Smollett's *The Expedition of Humphrey Clinker* of 1771 we find this reference.

I have seen turnips make their appearance, not as a dessert, but by way of 'hors d'oeuvres,' or whets.

'Canapé' is another word used to describe the delicacies served with predinner cocktails and drinks. It used to be a piece of wheat bread with garnishes. By extension it has come to be pieces of bread or toast spread with assorted bits of food.

With our appetites properly whetted with cocktails and appetizers, we can proceed directly to the main course. We can skip the soup since we had some for lunch. For the main course we have a choice of three general categories of food: fish, fowl, or meat. Let us start with fish.

The word 'salmon' is from the Latin *salmo* and the French *saumon* (in the English form the *l* is not pronounced). The name is probably derived from the Latin verb *salire* (to jump, leap), a reference to the habits of the fish as it returns upriver to its original spawning grounds. 'Salmon' have been known and enjoyed for a long time. We find this reference in the fourteenth century *King Alisaunder*

> And of perches, & of salmouns,
> Token & eten grete foysouns [portions].

'Sole,' as in 'filet of sole,' comes by virtue of its shape from the Latin *solea* (which was both the fish called 'sole' and the 'sole' of the foot). *Solea* is from the Latin *solum* (ground), which is the root of our English word 'soil.' The fish is flat and therefore close to the ground. (The word 'sole' for the fish should not be confused with the word 'sole' when it means "alone." There is another Latin word *solus* [alone] which gives us English words like 'desolate,' 'soliloquy,' 'solitary,' and 'solitude.' Modern French, however, distinguishes between *seul*, alone, *sole*, the fish, and *sol*, soil.) In *Babees Book* there is advice about the fish 'sole.'

> Solea is the sole, that is a swete fisshe and holsom for seke [sick] people.

We are constantly being besieged today with claims and counterclaims for the benefits to be derived from foods of all kinds. As we have noticed, this is nothing new. Thomas Flatman praised 'shrimp' ("Belly God," in *Poems and songs*), 1674.

> An ore-charg'd Stomack roasted shrimps will ease.

The word 'shrimp' is a parallel form of 'shrink' and was used in

Middle English in the form *scrimpit* (stature) meaning dwarfish. It is because 'shrimp' first meant small that we use it for persons of short height, rather than mussels, clams, or oysters, which are just as small as shrimp. Shakespeare used it with the connotation of size in *Henry VI, Part I* (act II, scene 3).

> Alas, this is a child, a silly dwarf!
> It cannot be this weak and writhled shrimp
> Should strike terror to his enemies.

Another fish that might be cooked and served at dinner is the 'perch.' The skin of this fish is speckled with dark marks, and that is how it got its name, from the Greek *perknos* (dark, dusky). (When we speak of a bird 'perched' on a wire or rail, however, we are using a different word, which comes from the Latin *pertica*, pole, bar, rod.)

One origin ascribed to the word 'mackerel' is fascinating, though not necessarily true. There is a similarity between 'mackerel' and the French word for it *maquereau*, which has the additional meaning of "panderer." It was popularly believed in France that in the spring the 'mackerel' leads the female shad to their mates. It is, of course, possible that the story may have come from the similarity in names, not the unlikely activity of the mackerel.

The word is, however, from the Low Latin *maquerellus* and was spelled *makerel* in Middle English. That the word *maquerel* did have another meaning long ago is shown in this citation from Caxton's translation of *Caton* in 1483.

> Nyghe his house dwellyd a maquerel or bawde.

Raw 'oysters' could be served at the beginning of the meal or they could be fried, baked in a pie, or cooked in a 'stew' (Middle English *stuwen*) for the main course. The word 'stew' is from the Old French *estuves* (stews, stoves, hot-houses). The word 'oyster' is from the Latin *ostrea* (oyster), which is akin to the Latin *os* (bone) and was applied to the mollusk because of the nature of its home, a shell of bone. *Babees Book* approved of oysters.

> Oysturs in Ceuy [Chives], Oysturs in grauey,
> Your helthe to renewe.

But some of us may feel about oysters as did John Wolcott in 1806 (*Tristia*, V).

Who first an oyster eat, was a bold dog.

'Lobster' is a delicacy which may be enjoyed boiled or broiled, but we are not normally given to flights of poetry to describe it. In 1559 John Marston talked about some food delicacies. (*The scourge of villanie corrected, with the addition of newe satyres*, J, 3).

A Crabs baked guts, a Lobsters butterd thigh.

Gay (*Poems*, II) continued the tradition.

On unadulterate wine we here regale,
And strip the lobster of his scarlet mail.

'Lobster' is from the Anglo-Saxon *lopust,* which may be a corruption of the Latin *locusta* meaning both 'lobster' and 'locust.' According to John Kersey's *Dictionarium Anglo-Brittanicum, or a general English dictionary,* 1715, 'locust' meant

a fish like a lobster, called a long-oister.

The shellfish 'crab' (Middle English *crabbe,* Anglo-Saxon *crabba*) is a word different from the 'crab' of 'crab-apple,' which comes from the Swedish *skrabba* (fruit of the wild apple, also anything poor or weak). The Zodiac sign 'cancer' is from the Latin *cancer* and the Greek *karkinos* (both meaning 'crab'). From the same source is the medical word 'cancer,' a tumor or growth; it was named by the famous Greek physician Galen, who observed that the swollen veins around the growth resembled a crab's limbs.

Another popular fish for our main course is the 'halibut,' a dish which should be eaten with a certain amount of reverence because of the origin of its name. In Middle English there were two words, *holi* (holy) and *butte* (flounder). Because the fish was considered excellent eating for the holiday, it was given its name 'halibut.'

Our next fish got its name from its appearance. Next time you buy 'smelts,' take a good look at their scales. They are smooth and shining. That is what the Anglo-Saxon word *smolt* meant, and that is where 'smelts' got their name. Back in 1655, there was another opinion as to the origin of the word. Boufet and Bennet offered this explanation (*Healths improvement*).

Smelts are so called because they smell so sweet.

That is about as fine an example of folk etymology as you are likely to find anywhere.

'Cod' is an old word having existed in exactly that form back in the fourteenth century. A young codfish split and prepared for cooking is called a 'scrod' or 'schrod,' from the Middle Dutch *schrode* (strip, piece cut off). From this same root we get our word 'shred.'

For some of us the 'snail' is a delicacy, for others it is an abomination. Perhaps the latter are wiser than the former; it may be that they know that the word 'snail' is from the Anglo-Saxon *snaca* (snake, creeping thing).

Having looked at a number of fish dishes as possible main courses for our dinner, it is time now to move on to the bird family. Although we do not serve 'rooster' as a dish, it is worth noting the origin of its name. In Anglo-Saxon the phrase *henne hrost* meant "hen roost"; *roost* then was a perch for a bird. In America *er* was added to 'roost,' and the male fowl got its name.

The rooster's mate is called a 'hen' or a 'chicken.' The Middle English 'hen' had the plural *hennes* and came from the feminine form of the Anglo-Saxon *hana* (cock). 'Chicken' is from a Middle English word, *chiken* (to sing). Whether the sound the 'chicken' makes can be called singing is questionable, but that's what gave it its name.

'Chicken' also figures in a couple of proverbs, well-known for hundreds of years. Stephen Gosson wrote in 1579 that we should not anticipate good fortune (*The ephemerides of Phialo . . . And a short apologie of the Schoole of abuse*).

> I woulde not haue him to counte his Chickens so soone before they be hatcht.

In 1810 the poet Robert Southey wrote his version of another common proverb (*The curse of Kehama*).

> Curses are like young chickens: they always come home to roost.

Contemporary slang uses the phrase, 'She's no chicken,' to refer disparagingly to a female who is no longer young. It is not a new expression; Jonathan Swift said in a poem, "Stella's Birthday," 1720:

> Stella is no chicken.

The traditional Christmas dinner in England is built around the 'goose' (Middle English *gos*, goos). Clumsiness and silliness have often been associated with the 'goose,' probably because of its

EAT YOUR WORDS   131

awkward appearance and motion on land. Thackery said of one of his characters:

(She) called herself a little goose in the simplest manner possible.

Another view of the 'goose' was expressed in Nicholas Udall's translation of *The apophthegius of Erasmus* in 1542.

We say in English, As wise as a gooce, or as wise as her mother's aperen string.

Echoing Udall, this view appeared in *Cornhill Magazine* in 1868.

. . . it being only ignorance of the darkest hue that ventures to portray the goose as deficient in sagacity or intelligence.

'Duck' for the bird and 'duck' for the cloth are two different words with different roots. The word for the bird is descriptive of the plunge by the bird down to the water in search of food, as seen in the Middle English *duke* or *doukem* (to dive, 'duck'). The 'duck' of the cloth is from the Dutch *doek* (linen cloth, towel, canvas).

Finally we shall take a look at our traditional bird, the 'turkey.' When the 'turkey' was discovered in North America and brought back to Europe, it was considered a strange, even a bizarre bird. The bird arrived in England by way of Turkey, an appropriately exotic land, so the English named this odd bird a "turkey cock." The French called it *la poule d' Inde* (the chicken from the Indies), and the name was gradually shortened to *le dindon*.

The Spaniards have two names for the bird. One followed the French and became *gallina de India* (Indian bird). The other name shows greater independence and brings in yet another exotic influence. It is called the *gallina Morisca* in recognition of the tremendous influence the Moors had on Spanish history. Not to be outdone by their French neighbors, the Germans once had their own version of what was exotic and bizarre, calling the bird *Calecutischer Hahn* (Calicut rooster). The English even went so far in their use of the name "turkey" to denote things that were strange as to call maize (the Taino word for corn) "Turkey wheat."

In any word-association test in America, the word 'turkey' might immediately invoke the word 'cranberry' (Low German *kraanbere*). One earlier form is *craneberry*, and it may have gotten its name from an imaginative connection between the long stalk of the plant and the legs and neck of the *crane*. A close second to the 'cranberry' in association with the turkey would be the 'pumpkin.' The original Greek word, *pepon,* meant cooked by the sun, ripe, mellow. The Latin version was *pepo* (large melon, pumpkin). In Old French it became *ponpon* (melon), and as it moved into Old English, it was transformed into *pompion* or *pumpion* and finally changed into a 'pumpkin.' While 'pumpkins' today are quite commonplace, John Stow thought differently of them in the sixteenth century.

All manner of strange fruits, as pomegranates, oranges, pompions.

We have included 'cranberry' and 'pumpkin' here because of their relevance to 'turkey.' Other vegetables will be discussed later on in this chapter.

Enough of fish and fowl! We are a nation of meat eaters, and it is time to focus on meat as the main dish. A common breakfast dish, but one which is served at many a dinner, is 'ham.' As we delve into the origin of this word, we find a dual development from the original Greek *kneme* (the lower part of the leg). In Old French it became *gambe* (leg) — from which we get our modern slang word for legs, 'gams' — and then it became the Modern French word *jambon* (ham). In a parallel development through the Teutonic languages, *kneme* became *hom* in Icelandic, *hamma* in Old High German, *hamme* in Middle English, and 'ham' in modern English. Shakespeare used 'hams' to mean legs in *Hamlet* (act II scene 2).

. . . they [old men] have a plentiful lack of wit, together with most weak hams: . . .

'Lamb' (Middle English *lamb, lomb*) occurs in virtually all of the Teutonic languages in forms like *lam, lamm,* and our modern 'lamb,' but its root is not known at present. We do find the word 'lamb' in the well-known proverb that in 1768 was already part of the language

As well be hanged for a sheep as a lamb.

We may know nothing about the root of the word 'lamb,' but we do know all about 'mutton' and its interesting history. It goes back to a Late Latin word *multo* which meant both sheep and gold coin. It got the latter meaning from the fact that there was a sheep figure stamped on the face of the coin. In Middle English the *motoun* or *motone* meant only a coin of gold, not a sheep. By the time it got to be our modern word 'mutton,' the idea of the gold coin had disappeared and only the idea of the sheep was retained. DuGuez, quoted in *Babees Book,* praised mutton highly.

> The moton boyled is of nature and complexion sanguyne, the whiche, to my jugement, is holsome for your grace.

As late as 1828, Sir Walter Scott was using 'mutton' for a coin (*Fair Maid of Perth,* VI).

> Reckon with my father about that . . . he will pay you gallantly; a French mutton for every hide I have spoiled.

'Veal' is a word that owes its origin to the Indo-European root *wetos* (year). It held its meaning in the Greek *etos* (year), but in Sanskrit *vatsa,* Latin *vitellus,* and French *veau* its meaning shifted to calf or 'veal,' with the sense of a one-year old animal. Chaucer knew all about its quality (The Merchant's Tale, I).

> Bet than olde boef is the tendre veel.

In the word 'veteran' (Latin *vetus,* old, and *vetulus,* little old man) we have the same meaning of "year" as in the original root, but now the sense has shifted to "one of many years" rather than just "one year." 'Steak' (Middle English *steike*) is the ultimate main dish for many of us. It takes its meaning from the way it was originally cooked; a strip of meat was roasted on a stick or 'stake,' from the Icelandic *steikja* (to roast, especially on a spit or peg). The word 'stick' is related, coming from the Anglo-Saxon *sticca* (stick peg or nail).

One of the great erroneous stories of all time connected with origins of food words must be that of the cut of meat called 'sirloin' of beef. In 1655 Thomas Fuller wrote that Henry the Eighth was so taken with the fine dinner one of his nobles had prepared for him that he drew his sword and knighted the 'loin' of beef. Apparently unaware of what Fuller had written, Jonathan Swift penned these lines in 1738 about another king of England (*A complete collection of genteel and ingenious conversation,* II).

> Miss. But, pray, why is it call'd a Sir-loyn?
> Lord Sparkish. Why! . . . our King James First . . . being invited to Dinner by one of his Nobles, and seeing a large Loyn of Beef at his Table, he drew out his Sword, and . . . knighted it.

Not to be outdone by Fuller or Swift, *Cook's Oracles* gave, in 1822, the honor of naming that special cut of meat to still another king of England.

> Sir-loin of Beef. This joint is said to owe its name to King Charles
> the Second, who, dining upon a Loin of Beef, . . . said for its merit it
> should be knighted, and henceforth called Sir-Loin.

All these attributions are delightful examples of folk etymology,
but they are none the less rubbish. Once again we have the problem
of the English taking over a French word as it sounds without
regard to its meaning. The Old French word in question is *surlogne*,
sur meaning on or above. The cut of meat we are discussing is that
part above the 'loin,' but the English heard the French word *sur* as
"sir," and so we now call that portion of the animal the 'sirloin.'

The 'T-bone steak' takes its name from the shape of the bone in
the steak; but 'club steak' is named for the shape of the meat not the
bone. 'Club' is from a number of Swedish, Danish, and Icelandic
words meaning chunk, block, or clump. ['Club,' in the sense of an
association of people, is from the same root with the meaning of a
clump or group of persons. However, the 'club' suit in a deck of
cards is a direct translation of the Spanish *bastos* (cudgel, club),
which was the symbol of the suit.]

'Pork' (Middle English *pork*, French *porc*, and Latin *porculus*, pig)
was, according to Elyot (*Castel*), highly praised by Galen, the Greek
physician.

> Aboue all kyndes of fleshe in nouryshyng the body, Galene most
> commendeth porke.

'Corned beef' is not prepared with corn, but gets its name from
the *grains* of salt that are used in the curing process. The root word
for 'corn' is the Indo-European *garnom* (corn) which developed
along divergent directions. On the one hand it gave us 'corn,' and
on the other 'grain,' through Latin *granum*. In 'corned beef' we
kept the wrong development of *garnom*; we should have kept
'grain.' Of course the whole situation would have been simpler and
made much more sense had we decided to call the meat "salted
beef" instead of 'corned beef', but then we would not have had this
interesting story to tell. In 1572 John Jewel used a phrase that
shows clearly one road taken by *garnom* (*An exposition upon the two
epistles . . . to the Thessalonians*).

> We must vnderstand this authoritie with a corne of salt [L. cum
> grano salis], otherwise it may be vnsauorie.

Today, of course, we say, 'with a grain of salt,' which means exactly the same thing.

This final meat item is not particularly common, but nevertheless provides another example of how an action word, or verb, can become a static word, or noun. The Latin verb *venari* (to hunt) became the noun *venatio,* meaning the hunt and that which is hunted. In Old French a derivative from *venatio* became *venaison* (flesh of edible wild beasts of the chase), which became the English 'venison' (through Middle English *veneison, veneysun*), meaning the edible flesh of the deer.

Meats are often served with 'sauces' and 'gravy.' 'Sauce' is from the French *sauce* (condiment, sauce), which came from the Latin *salsa* (something salted). The root is *sal* (salt), and from this root, via the above noted changes, we get the word 'saucy,' denoting a brash kind of behavior. It was used this way c. 1685 in *Satyr against Hypocrites.*

> Then, full of sawce and zeal, up steps Elnathan.

One of our best known proverbs has to do with 'sauce.' Here is the form in which it was written by Jeremy Collier in 1700 (*Essays upon several moral subjects*).

> That that's Sawce for a Goose is Sawce for a Gander.

Then the pedants took over, and what had been a delightful, meaningful statement in simple language appeared in the August 5, 1905, edition of the *Athenaeum* in London as follows.

> What is sauce for the verb is surely sauce for the verbal substantive.

If you think that's bad, look at this example from Allen Upward in 1900 (*Ebenezer Lobb*).

> It seemed to me as though what was sauce for the insured ought to have been sauce for the annuitant.

'Gravy' takes us back once again to the Latin *granum* (grain). From this word the Romans made an adjective *granatus* (full of grains), an apparent allusion to a grain-thickened broth. In Old French, however, there appears to have been a reading and printing error. The word *grane* (sauce for meat) was misread as *grave,* and it is from this misreading and subsequent misprinting that we got our word 'gravy.' It should have been "grainy" where the grains were little bits of spices floating in the sauce.

Some of the meats described above are available as 'chops' or 'cutlets.' 'Chop' is a later form of the earlier English word *chap* (to cut), from the Middle English *chappen* with the same meaning. The 'chop' in the world of the butcher has been limited to a piece cut from a rib, loin, or shoulder of the animal. The origin of 'cutlet' is quite different from that of 'chop.' In Latin the word *costa* means 'rib.' In Old French *costellette* and modern French *côtelette* we have a double diminutive of the root word *costa*. *Costa* plus *el* plus *ette* makes our modern English word 'cutlet' mean a "little, little rib."

When we do not manage to eat all of the main course at the original meal, the cook has a problem. What to do with the left-overs? One could make 'hash.' The Old French word *hacher* (to hack) and the noun derived from it, *hachis* (minced meat), are related to the modern French word *hache* (axe), which is also the word from which we get our English word 'hatchet.' The cook has to 'cut' up the meat, but he certainly does not need a 'hatchet' to do it.

To vary the leftovers, the cook may shape them into 'patties,' which is a variant on *little pie*. The Greek word *passein* (to sprinkle [salt]) had the idea of a salted mess of food. In Latin it became *pasta* (paste) and in Old French *paste* (pie, pastry), while in modern French it is *pâté*.

The expression 'eat humble pie' fits particularly well in this section on leftovers. We can trace the 'humble' back to the Latin *lumbus* (loin roast) and its diminutive *lumbulus* (little roast). When the word came into Old French, it became *nombles* due to confusion with the French word *nombril* (navel). As it arrived in Middle English, it became *numbles* and got the meaning of the organs nearest the loin, that is, the cheaper meats, the tripe, the intestine, etc. These were baked in a pie for the dock workers in London. They called it at first a *numbles pie*. The "noncing" phenomenon — the dropping of the initial *n* from a word and adding it to the article preceding it — took over, and the pie began to be called *an umbles pie*. Not knowing its origin and not understanding noncing, the upper-class Englishman thought that *an umbles pie* was cockney pronunciation (a singular characteristic of which is dropping the initial *h* of a word), and so he changed it to *a humbles pie*. Since there was no such word as *humbles*, the final *s* was soon dropped, and the phrase 'humble pie' came into being.

Another way to use leftovers is to make 'croquettes' with them. Woe betide the eater who chews on what the cook made if the product of his cooking follows literally the meaning of the French word from which we get 'croquette.' The word is *croquer* (to crackle under the teeth, crunch), but since our 'croquettes' are usually soft as mush, we don't have much to worry about.

Fish, fowl, meat, and game may be the principal dishes of a meal, but they alone do not a dinner make. They are cooked with spices to give them taste, and served with vegetables and grains to round out the meal. The rest of this chapter will be devoted to these items, and we will end our look at food with a discussion of fruits and desserts.

Many years ago, before it was discovered that ice would preserve the freshness of food, spices were used to disguise the taste and smell of food that was on the turn, as well as to enhance its flavor. There are so many spices that their use in cooking is limited only by the ingenuity of the cook.

Although 'vinegar' is actually not a spice, it is used so widely as a flavoring that it properly belongs in this section. The word means "sour wine" and is from two French words, *vin* (wine) and *aigre* (sour, sharp, bitter). Elyot advised caution when using it (*Castel*).

> Olyues . . . doth corroborate [corrupt] the stomake . . . being eaten with vyneger.

But in a translation of Camillus Leonardus' *Mirror of Stones* in 1750 there were some good words for 'vinegar.'

> If it be drenched nine times in vinegar, it makes a fine eye-salve.

That most pungent flavoring, 'garlic,' is also from two words, this time Anglo-Saxon. They are *gar* (spear) and *laec* (leek), and so 'garlic' is really a leek with spear-shaped leaves. Richard Hakluyt mentioned 'garlic' as an aid to healing in his *Voyages* (III).

> Our general was taught by a negro to draw the poyson out of his wound by a clove of garlike, whereby he was cured.

'Soy' sauce was known in early England and was called *sooja*, but it originated in Japan. The Japanese word for it is *shoyu*, describing a sauce made from a bean called *diadzu*. William Dampier wrote in *A new voyage round the world*, 1698:

> . . . Japan, from whence true Soy comes told me that it was made only with Wheat and a sort of Beans mixt with Water and Salt.

'Ketchup,' or 'catsup,' are derived from the Malay word *kechup* (sauce, soy).

'Chives' are related to the onion family, and so it comes as no surprise to find out that the word is from a Latin word for onion, *caepa,* which became the French word *cive* (scallion, unset leek) and finally our 'chives.' Another example of a word with two meanings is 'sage.' The word for the spice is from the Latin *salvia* (sage), which in turn is from another Latin word, *saluus* (in good health, sound). The name was given to the plant because it was supposed to have special healing values. These values were recognized by Robert Sharrock in a letter he wrote April 7, 1668, *To Boyle.*

> I have known sage-bread do much good in drying up watery humours.

(The word 'sage' meaning wise comes from another Latin word, *sapius,* wise.)

'Salt' and 'pepper' are probably the most widely used condiments in cooking. 'Salt' (Middle English *salt,* Anglo-Saxon *sealt,* Latin *sal*) and 'pepper' (Middle English *peper,* Anglo-Saxon *pipor*) go with everything, and the words for them are remarkably similar in many of the related languages of the Indo-European family. 'Pepper' can be traced back to the Sanskrit *pippoli,* which meant a long pepper, or the fruit of the holy fig tree. *The Booke of Precedence* (I) had a warning c. 1430 which is applicable today.

> Ley salt on thi trenchere [plate] with knyfe that be clene; Not to [too] myche, be thou were [aware], for that is not gode.

'Cinnamon' is from a Hebrew word *qinnamon,* a word which may have been borrowed from the Malayan words *kaye manis* (sweet wood). Another spice word made of two parts is 'nutmeg,' from the English word *nut* combined with the Latin word *muscus* (musk). In French it is called *noix muscade* (musk nut), which came into English as *notemuge,* and later 'nutmeg.' There are numerous remedies for the common cold that have been suggested through the years, some so-called scientific and some that might be classified as belonging to the "old-wives" school of thought. One remedy we haven't tried lately was suggested by Boorde (*Dyetary,* XXII).

> Nutmeges be good for them the whiche haue colde in theyr hed.

'Vanilla' with its beans in a pod is another common flavoring and its origin is surprising. The Latin word *vagina* (sheath, husk, pod) traveled into Spanish as *vaina* with the same meanings; the diminutive of *vaina* is *vainilla* (small pod), and it is from this form that we get 'vanilla.' The Native Americans had a recipe for wisdom that was reported by Henry Stubbe in 1662 (*The Indian nectar, or a discourse concerning chocolate,* II).

> They added . . . the Vaynillas [to the chocolate] . . . to strengthen the brain.

Since 'vanilla' ice cream is the number-one flavor in this country, one might well ask, "Why are we not smarter than we appear to be?"

'Mustard' got its name from a word we no longer use, *must,* meaning "new wine" or "vinegar." The word *must* is from the Latin *mustus* (young, fresh, new) and it was the process of mixing the pounded seeds of the mustard plant with *must,* or new wine, that gave the condiment its name. In Old French it was *mostarde,* and it was from this form, not the modern French *moutarde,* that the English word was derived. Fuller (*Holy and Profane,* III, 2) used one of the qualities of mustard to make a literary point.

> Some think their conceits, like mustard, not good except they bite.

'Chili' is from the Spanish *chile* (red pepper) and has no connection with the name of the South American country Chile. 'Pimento' as well as 'pimiento' started with the Latin *pigmentum* (pigment, the juice of plants). Like the use of the Latin *radix* (root) for one special root, 'radish' (see below), this is a case where the original broad meaning of juice of plants in general was narrowed to mean one particular plant, the 'pimento.'

The word 'mint' stems from the Latin *mentha* and the Greek *mintha* (both meaning mint). The other 'mint,' a place where money is coined, is from the Latin *moneta,* "the admonisher," epithet of the goddess Juno, at whose temple in Rome money was manufactured. In 1622 Frances Bacon (*History of Henry VII*) used 'mint' in this latter sense.

> And so (vpon the matter) to set the mint on work, and to giue way to new coines of siluer, which should bee then minted.

Like 'peas' (see below) and 'cherries' (see above) we use the word 'mace' as a plural, but it is properly a singular form, coming from the French *macis.* In 1392 it was used in the plural as 'maces,' but the

English penchant for dropping the final *s* on words in order to create a new singular form, took effect here, and we have the form 'mace' standing for both the singular and plural.

With 'ginger' we have another word formed from two words and, in addition, deriving its name from a resemblance to a shape. The Sanskrit words *crnga* (horn) and *vera* (shape) were combined in the Latin *zingiber* or *gingiber* and the French *gingembre* to give us 'ginger,' a horn-shaped plant. Advice on its use was given by Henry Buttes (*Dyets drie dinner* O, ij) in 1599.

> Greene ginger, condite with hony, warmes olde mens bellyes.

An adverbial form of the word with a different meaning and root, 'gingerly,' probably comes from the Old French *gensor, gentior* (pretty, delicate). Edward Blount used it with this meaning in *The hospital of incurable fooles,* 1600.

> This man is very ginger & dangerous of himselfe.

'Dill' (Middle English *dille, dylle,* Anglo-Saxon *dile*) has its counterpart words in Dutch, Danish, German, Swedish, and other Teutonic-based languages; they are similarly spelled and pronounced. How euphemistic was Michael Drayton in 1612 when he suggested the use of dill for women (*Poly,* III)?

> The wonder-working Dill . . .
> Which curious women use in many a nice disease.

Drayton also refers to certain special powers of 'dill' (*The battaile of Agincourt . . . Nymphidia, the court of fayrie, . . . elegies upon sundry occasions*) in 1627.

> Therewith her Veruine and her dill,
> that hindreth Witches of their will.

It was the sweet smell of the 'thyme' plant that gave it its name. The Greek *thymos* (thyme) is related to the Greek *thyein* (to make fragrant) and the Latin *fumus* (smoke). It is from these roots via French *thym* and Middle English *tym* that we get our modern word 'thyme.' According to William Turner, in 1562, thyme had special qualities, too (*Herbal,* II).

> Thyme hath the poure [power] to driue furth fleme [phlegm].

Incidentally, the *th* is pronounced *t* because the word was borrowed quite early from the French who always pronounce *th* as *t*.

'Rosemary,' from a fanciful connection with sea spray, is named from two Latin words, *ros* (dew) and *marinus* (sea). The Latin name was a combination of these two, *ros marinus,* but when it was carried over into English, it became 'rosemary' because of popular etymology, linking a rose with the Virgin Mary.

'Curry,' a popular spice of Indian origin, is taken from the Tamil word *kari* (relish for rice, sauce). The word 'curry', meaning to groom as a horse, is from the French *courroyer* (to dress leather). There is a phrase in common use, 'to curry favor.' On first glance the phrase doesn't seem to make much sense, but when we discover its origins, we can understand how it came to mean what it does. To "get around" someone or obtain some special objective, we sometimes 'curry favor.' There was a story written in the fourteenth century called *Roman de Fauvel* (Story of Fauvel). Fauvel was a talking horse full of cunning, guile, and fraud. One who treated this horse well by grooming (currying) him in order to get his help in some scheme, was said to *curry Fauvel.* We no longer remember the horse named Fauvel but we still 'curry' favor (Fauvel) when we think it will help us achieve our goal. Richard Taverner made reference to this saying in *Prouerbes or adagies with newe addicions, gathered out of the Chiliades of Erasmus* (fol. 44) of 1539.

> He that will in court dwell, must needes currie fabel . . . Ye shall understand that fabel is an olde Englishe worde, and signified as much as favour doth now a dayes.

'Chutney' is a relish made with fruits, spices, herbs, and pepper, and is also of Indian origin, this time from the Hindi *chatni* with the same meaning. 'Tarragon' started off in Greek as *drakon* (dragon). It went into Arabic as *tarkhun* (dragon-wort) and then into Italian as *targone* and Old French as *targon* and French as *estragon*. The dragon has disappeared but the spice remains.

'Marjoram' added an *r* in its development from the Latin *majorana*. Perhaps 'marjoram' is the miracle ingredient that toothpaste manufacturers have been seeking for so long. At least it would appear so if you believe what you find in Humphrey Lloyd's (or Llwyd's) translation of *The treasure of health conteyning many profitable medycines gathered out of Hypocrates, Galen and Avycen, by one Petrus Hyspanus* XV, E, vb) around 1550.

> Let thy teeth be washed with the decoction of wilde Margerum.

"Variety is the spice of life," they say. Certainly there are enough spices to give variety to almost everything one might want to cook; we have covered many of them. Let us top this section with a dash of 'paprika' — from the Greek *peperi* (pepper).

In addition to a main dish with its flavorings, a well-balanced meal usually includes vegetables. Some that might be served are 'peas,' 'beans,' 'onions,' 'squash,' and 'turnips.'

The vegetable 'pea' underwent the same changes with regard to the letter *s* as did the cherry. In its original form it was *pease* (Latin *pisum*, pea) and its plural in English should have been and was for a while *peases*. Later the *se* of *pease* was dropped from the true singular form and a new singular 'pea' was created with its plural becoming 'peas.' The problem of handling singular and plural was discussed by James Greenwood in *An essay towards a practical English grammar* in 1711.

> Some words are used in both numbers, as Sheep . . . Pease . . . but it is better to say in the Singular "Pea," in the plural "Peas."

Green string 'beans' are frequently served as well as other varieties of the 'bean' family. The word 'bean' (Middle English *bene*, Anglo-Saxon *bean*) has its equivalents in Dutch *boon*, Icelandic *baun*, and German *bohne*. Turner warned against consumption of 'beans' in 1551 (*Herbal*, I).

> Beanes . . . are harde of digestion, and make troblesum dreames.

There are other words in Latin for 'onion' in addition to *cèlpa* mentioned above. One of these words is *unio*, which has three meanings in Latin, two of which are of interest to us in this context of food. One meaning is oneness or unit; the second meaning is a single pearl; the third meaning is a kind of onion. The latter two coalesce in what we now call 'pearl onions.' For some unknown reason Henry Brinklow chose the 'onion' to demonstrate futility (*Complaint of Roderick Mors*) in 1545.

> As moch for that purpose as to lay an vnion to my lytel fynger for the tothe ache.

'Squash' is a peculiarly American vegetable, and the word illustrates the formidable problems encountered by the first English settlers in America with the pronunciation and spelling of Native

American words. 'Squash' developed over a period of sixty-six years from its first appearance in English in 1634 as *isquonterquashes* to *squontersquashes* to 'squash' in 1700.

'Turnip' is another favorite vegetable. The second half of the word, 'nip,' is from the Anglo-Saxon *naep* (turnip), from the Latin *napus* (a kind of turnip). The first half, 'tur,' is most likely from the French *tour* (turn, in a sense of a wheel), and therefore the word 'turnip' seems to mean a "round turnip." Elyot liked 'turnips' and their effect on those who eat them (*Castel*).

> Turnepes beinge welle boyled in water, and after with fatte fleshe, norysheth moche.

There are also those who cherish 'cauliflower,' and they should know that there is a folk etymology and a true origin for the word. Folk etymology has it that the word is made up of an Italian word, *colle* (with the), plus the word *flower*, and that when the word came into English, the *colle* became *cauli*, the whole word meaning "with the flowers." It sounds good but it just isn't so. 'Cauliflower' is really from the Latin *caulis* (cabbage) and *flos* (flower), which became the Italian *cavolfiore*, then our 'cauliflower' — a "cabbage flower" or "cabbage with flowers."

'Corn' on the cob is a very special summertime delicacy. In England the word 'corn' means grain; their word for our corn is 'maize' (Spanish *maiz*, Taino *mahis*, *mahiz*). As we have already seen, there is and never has been any shortage of advice on the value of certain foods to our good health. In 1732 Arbuthnot recommended (*Rules* of diet, 1)

> Beets, emollient, nutritive, and relaxing.

Tobias Venner (*Via Recta*, VI) stated that

> Some Physitians commend the eating of radishes before meate.

'Beet' is the outgrowth of the Latin *beta*, Anglo-Saxon *bete*, and Middle English *beta*. Latin also contributes the root word for 'radish,' and here the expression "root word" is used advisedly because the Latin word is *radix* meaning — "root." It used to go in Old English by the name of *radishe root* to distinguish it from other roots, but the *root* was dropped leaving us with the term 'radish' being used specifically for just one root. As an interesting sidelight, the word 'eradicate,' which is from the same *radix*, literally means to pull out by the root.

In addition to the vegetables already discussed, there are several others that could be served along with our main course. 'Cabbage' stems from the Latin *caput* (head). In the French *caboche* and the early English *cabage* (as spelled by Ben Jonson in *Volpone, the Fox*) there was only one *b*. But present English spelling seems to have been influenced by the Italian *cappocia* (large head). The *p* became *b*, and we now have two *b*'s in 'cabbage.'

'Artichoke' is from an Arabic word, *al harshal* (artichoke), and passed through changes like Spanish *alcachofa* and Middle English *artochocke* before assuming its present form. Another popular vegetable is 'asparagus.' It started off as the Greek word *asparagos*. When it first came into English, it was *sperage*, *sparage*, and *sparagus*. In the sixteenth century, it assumed its present form, but it was not destined to keep it very long. In the eighteenth century, it was called *sparrow-grass* or *sparagrass* out of confusion with the pronunciation. Finally when its origin and history were better known, it reverted to its present form 'asparagus.' The poet Robert Couthey was certain of its spelling. He was quoted in 1801 in *Life and Correspondence* (edited by C. C. Southey).

> Sparagrass (it ought to be spelt so) and artichokes, good with plain butter.

'Carrots' are among the most commonly used vegetables adding flavor to all sorts of dishes. While their flavor was not in doubt, their nutritive value was questioned in 1823 (*Vegetable substances used for the food of man*).

> The quantity of nutritive matter in the whole weight of carrot, being 98 parts in 1000.

The origin of the word may be in the Greek word *kara* (head); perhaps it was some association of the shape of the vegetable with a head that gave it its name. A redhead is frequently called a 'carrot top' today, and hair of that color is usually admired widely. There was an opposing opinion recorded c. 1680 (*The Roxburghe ballads*, VI).

> The Carrot pate be sure you hate,
> For she'l be true to no man.

'Broccoli' follows the familiar path of Latin *brocca* (pointed stick) to Italian *brocco* (shoot or stalk) to *broccolo* (sprout) to its plural and present form 'broccoli.' Both the white and purple 'eggplant' are called that because of the resemblance of the plant's edible fruit to the whole egg in the shell.

'Parsley' comes from the Latin *petroselinum* (rock parsley), leading to the French *persil* and the Middle English *percil,* and finally to our 'parsley.' In 1398 Trevisa (*Bartholomeus, XVII*) referred to 'parsley' as follows:

> Petrosilye hatte Petrosilium and is an herbe that groweth in gardynes with goode smel.

'Celery,' via Italian and French forms, goes back to *selinon,* which was, curiously, the name for — parsley. 'Parsnip' is from the Latin *pastinare* (to dig up) via Middle English *parsnep.*

'Potato' came to English through a different route. It was *patata* or *batata* in Spanish, but its origin was not Latin but from the West Indies, the Arawakan word *batata.* 'Potatoes' were introduced into England in the sixteenth century, and Sir John Hawkins reported on their quality in 1655 (*The [second] voyage made to the coast of Guinea and the Indies of Nova Spania, begun in 1564*).

> These potatoes be the most delicate rootes that may be eaten and doe far exceede our passeneps or carets.

The 'yam' is from West Africa; it was called *inamia* in Benin and *inhame* in Portuguese, and shortened to 'yam' in English.

In addition to vegetables, the dinner might include grains, whether served in soup, separately, or in breads. Let us look at some. 'Barley' is made up of two words, Anglo-Saxon *bere* (corn) and the suffix *lic* (like). Therefore 'barley' is a grainlike corn. 'Rice' was known throughout the ancient world; the word for it in Persian is *wrijet,* in Arabic *aruzz,* in Spanish *arroz,* in Italian *riso,* and in French *riz.* Arbuthnot had something good to say about it in 1742 (*Rules of diet*).

> Rice, nourishing, good in hemorrages.

'Wheat,' too, has similar forms in many languages, and all of them come from the Teutonic root *hweit* (white) indicating the grain was named for its color. The origin of 'oat' is obscure, but it seems to be allied to the Russian *iodro* (grain, gland) and the Norwegian *eitel* (knot, kernel). Both are from the Greek *oidos* (a swelling). Arbuthnot approved of oats (*Rules of diet,* I).

> Oats, cleansing, resolving, and pectoral.

"Bread is basic," say the bakers. 'Bread' comes in a number of shapes and may be made with any number and variety of grains. When served with a thick soup, it can be a complete meal. The dieters are forever vowing to cut down on bread as if that alone were the main contributor to their extra avoirdupois. Doctors are continually warning us to beware of overindulgence in many things besides bread, and the advice given in Thomas Phaer's translation of J. Goeurot's *Regiment of life,* 1544, was to the point.

> Beware of spicery, pastry and bread not very well levened.

Beaumont and Fletcher used the word 'pastry' to describe the place where such delicacies were made (*Woman-Hater,* act I, scene 2).

> Go, run, search, pry in every nook and angle of the kitchens, larders, and pastries.

Similarly we have the 'pantry,' which meant originally the place where 'bread' (Latin *panis,* bread) was baked and then simply where it and related foods were stored.

The man who was in charge of the 'pantry' in earlier times was called the 'pantler.' Shakespeare described his duties in *Henry IV, Part I* (act II, scene 4).

> A good shallow young fellow; a' would have made a good pantler, a' would ha' chipt bread well.

Babees Book had clear advice for one who held the office of 'pantler.'

> In your offyce of the Pantrye, see that your bread be chipped and squared & note how much you spend in a daye.

In addition to the cocktails served before dinner, it is customary for many people to serve 'wine' with dinner. The word 'wine' is from the Latin *vinum* (wine). The harmful or beneficial effects of the "juice of the grape" have been argued for as long as this alcoholic beverage has been known. A somewhat negative view was taken in the *Gesta Romanorum* (XXI), in this translation c. 1440.

> But man contrarious aunswereth,
> The wyne is over myghty, it is not good.

Rather than 'wine', an alcoholic punch might be served during or after dinner. The word 'punch' has several meanings: to perforate, to beat, a beverage, and the character Punch from the Punch and Judy show; all of these have come from different roots. 'Punch,' to perforate, is from the earlier English and French *puncheon* (a kind of awl) and the Latin *punctum* (a pricking, puncture); 'punch,' to beat or bruise, is from the Latin *punire* (to punish); the 'Punch' (a contraction of *punchinello*) of the puppet show is from the Italian *pollecena* (a young turkey-cock); and the drink word 'punch' is from the Hindi word *panch* (five), and one explanation of its use in this connection is that there were five ingredients in the Hindi version of the concoction; they are spirit, water, lemon-juice, sugar, and spices.

One of the better known afterdinner drinks is 'brandy.' The word is from the Dutch *brandewijn* (burnt or distilled wine). The Dutch verb *branden* means to burn or to distill. In a medical work, in 1676, Richard Wiseman recommended 'brandy' as a cure for an all-too-common ailment, the hangover (*Several chirurgical treatises*).

> It has beem a common saying. A hair of the same dog; and thought that brandy-wine is a common relief to such.

After the main course at dinner, we are likely to have 'dessert.' The word is the past participle of the French word *desservir* (to clear the table, take away the plates). Only after this is done will the proper hostess serve the 'dessert.' A cautionary opinion of dessert was offered in a book on health published in 1600 by W. Vaughan (*Directions for health*, II, 9).

> Such eating, which the French call desert, is unnaturall.

But a cookbook written by William King in 1708 disagreed (*The art of cookery in imitation of Horace's art of poetry*).

> 'Tis the dessert that graces all the feast.

Many fruits are served as 'desserts' after dinner. 'Rhubarb' is a sort of eponym since the first part of its name comes from *Rha*, the Scythian name of the Volga; the second part comes from Greek *barbaron* (foreign). Its spelling in Late Latin was *rhubarbarum*. A translation of *Secreta Secretorum* said:

> Get ye reubard . . . withdraws ye fleume fro ye mouth or ye stomake.

Sir Antonie of Guevara, too, knew of the value of 'rhubarb' as a medicinal ingredient, but, as pointed out in 1577 in one of his letters in *Guevara's familiar epistles,* translated by Edward Hallowes, the user had to be prepared to pay a price for its use.

> The patient that doth determine to receiue a little Rheubarb suffereth the bitternesse it leaueth in the throte for the profite it doth him against his feuer.

'Plum' had a change of letter from *r* to *l* in its transition from the Latin *prunum* (plum) to modern times; but 'prune,' the dried 'plum,' kept the original spelling. In early England *plum* meant raisin, and that is why there are no 'plums' in a 'plum pudding.' Stephen Dowell wrote in 1884 on this odd state of affairs (*A history of taxation and taxes in England,* IV).

> The dried grapes which the French term raisins secs, or raisins passés, we term simply raisins when used for eating uncooked, and plums when they form an ingredient in the famous English plum pudding.

The indefatigable Elyot had guiding words for many foods, as we have seen. Here are some on the prune (*Castel*).

> The damaske prune rather bindeth than lowseth.

John Lyly used 'prune' as a verb with a different meaning (*Euphues, anatomy of wit*) in 1579.

> What Vine, if it not be proyned, bringeth foorth Grapes.

And Sir Francis Bacon, writing a short time later, used the same verb in a different context (*Advancement of learning,* II):

> Laws . . . are to be pruned and reformed from time to time.

The verb 'to prune,' however, is from the Middle English *prunen* and Middle French *prognier* (both meaning to trim).

The English are not alone when it comes to altering the spelling and the sounds of a foreign language in carrying a word from one tongue to another. For example, the French version of 'roast beef' is *rosbif,* and the Japanese say *baisu-boru* for 'baseball' and *aisu-kureemu* for 'ice-cream,' and in Spanish our 'home run' ended up as *onrón*. None of these examples is as odd as the move of 'avocado' from Aztec to English. The starting place was the Aztec *ahuatcatl* (testicle), which became the Spanish *avocado*. Its first entry into

English was respectable enough, coming out *avogato,* but the English were not satisfied to leave well enough alone. They soon corrupted the acceptable *avogato* into *alligator,* and finally called the fruit 'alligator pear,' still an alternative term for the fruit we know as the 'avocado.' (The crocodilian 'alligator,' has of course a quite different origin, coming from the Spanish *el lagarto,* the lizard.)

Two fruits which are used in desserts and also for the flavoring of drinks are the 'lemon' and the 'lime.' The etymology of both words suggests that they are one and the same. The fruits were differentiated by the change of the second letter from *i* to *e*. The root words in Malay *limau,* Persian *limu,* Arabic *limah,* and French *limon* all show the second letter to be *i* and further demonstrate that the two words have identical roots. Here is Elyot again, this time on the citrus fruits.

> The juyce of orenges or lymons may be taken after meales in a lyttell quantitie.

Poets find their subjects in many places; James Thompson found inspiration in 1727 in these same fruits (*The seasons. Summer*).

> The lemon and the piercing lime . . .
> Their lighter glories blend.

Oliver Goldsmith used 'lemon' in an unusual way in 1773 (*She stoops to conquer,* act I, scene 2).

> I'll be with you in the squeezing of a lemon.

There is another word 'lime' (Anglo-Saxon *lim,* cement, glue), which used to be placed on trees to catch birds. Shakespeare used it with a slightly different object in *Two Gentlemen of Verona* (act III, scene 2).

> You must lay lime to tangle her desires.

What else shall we have for dessert? The traditional choices are 'pie,' 'cake,' 'pudding,' 'ice cream,' or 'sherbert.' 'Pudding,' whose older sense was probably a "bag," is based on a Teutonic root *pud* (to swell out), which led to the Old English words *puddle* (short, fat) and *poddy* (round, stout in the belly). In Low German the root *pud* became part of *puddle worst* (thick black pudding) and *puddig* (stumpy).

In *Child's Ballads* there is described a supper scene which showed the connection between 'bag' and 'pudding.'

> Then to their supper were they set orderlye, with hot bag-
> puddings, and good apple pyes.

'Currants' are used in puddings, cakes, and cookies. The name
derives from the Corinth isthmus in Greece. Stephen Dowell
(*Taxes,* I) knew that 'currants' was an eponym, but he wasn't sure
what to call them or how to spell the word.

> The impost on tobacco from the royal colony of Virginia
> encountered no serious opposition, but another impost, upon cur-
> rants, currans, corinths, or grapes of Corinth, had not such an
> uninterrupted course.

The word 'cake' in early English meant a small round loaf, and it
comes from the Icelandic and Swedish word *kaka* (cake). The
Teutonic root is *kak* or *kok*, and it is from the latter of these that we
get our word 'cook.' The Arabic verb form *sharika* (he drank) is the
origin of the word 'sherbert,' another example of an action word
becoming a specific object involved in that action. An associated
word from the same root is 'syrup.'

The history of the word 'pie' is long and varied, involving printers, the prayer book, and a probable joke. In the vocabulary of the
printer's trade the word 'pi' or 'pie' means a hopelessly jumbled
mixture of black and white type. The word was originally *magpie*
and was shortened to 'pi.' The use by printers is derived either from
the black-and-white colors of the bird (like the black and white of
the printed page), or from the miscellaneous objects found in the
bird's nest. (The word 'piebald,' used to describe the color of a
horse, is made up of *pie,* short for 'pied' — that is, like the magpie in
color — and *bald,* denoting a white streak.)

Another use of the word 'pie' was as a substitute for the word
'pica,' a Latin word for the book which ordered the manner of
performing the divine service. It probably came to be used this way
because of the black letters on the white paper, which resembled
the colors of the bird. As a pastry the word 'pie' may well be a
medieval joke on the miscellaneous contents of the directory mentioned above; the same mixture of ingredients might be found in a
'pie.'

Shakespeare used the oath "by cock and pie" in both *The Merry
Wives of Windsor* and *Henry IV, Part II.* One interpretation of the
oath has it that it is a euphemism for "by God and the prayer book."

Another authority suggests that it may have to do with a slang meaning of 'cock' as a man of spirit as described by Philip Massinger in 1639 (*The unnaturale combate, a tragedie,* act II, scene 1).

> He has drawn blood of him yet.
> Well done, old cock.

Whatever the real origin may be, it appears to have little or nothing to do with food.

There are many varieties of 'pies' — apple, lemon, mince, banana, to name a few. The list is endless, limited only by the imagination of the baker. Today one doesn't have to bake one's own 'pies'; the woman of the house can buy them at the bakery. But in 1839 Winthrop M. Praed (*Poems,* II) said there wasn't much doubt as to a woman's place — it was in the kitchen.

> And lords made love — and ladies pies.

There seems, however, to be something missing in the equation; if the ladies were in the kitchen making pies, to whom were the lords making love?

If your sweet tooth is not completely satisfied with the desserts offered above, you could have some 'licorice,' 'candy,' or 'chocolate.' 'Licorice' is from two Greek words *glykys* (sweet) and *riza* (root). Chaucer suggested an interesting use of licorice in The Miller's Tale (I, 504).

> But first he cheweth greyn and lycorys to smellen sweete.

Unfortunately for the health of our teeth, 'candy' is almost entirely 'sugar,' from the root word in both Arabic and Persian *gand* (sugar, sugar candy). (We looked earlier at the origin of 'sugar.') In Italian the word for 'sugar' was placed before the word for 'candy' with the resulting expression *zucchero candi* (sugar candy). In the midnineteenth century, the English developed the word 'candy' to refer to fancier bonbon types but kept 'sugar-candy' for boiled sweets or hard 'candy.' Chocolate has been discussed earlier in this chapter.

Such an abundance of food as we have been tasting might properly be called 'manna' from Heaven. There are two explanations given for the origin of 'manna.' The first says that it is from the Hebrew *man hu* ("what is this?"), from the inquiry the Hebrews made when they first saw it on the ground. But this is popular etymology, since *man* is not Hebrew but Aramaic. A second theory is that the sense of *man* is "it is a gift" (cf. Arabic *mann,* meaning beneficience, grace, favor).

Sir John Maundeville wrote of 'manna' in 1400 (*Travels*).

> This manna is clept [called] Bred of Aungels; and it is a white thing, that is fully delicyous, and more swete than Hony or Sugre.

A fitting close to this section on food might be delightful after-dinner grace said at the Christmas feast in the late nineteenth century as quoted in *Bermudian Cookery* (by the Bermuda Junior Service League, 1976).

> The Lord be praised, my tummy's raised
>   An inch above the table
> And I be dammed — but I be crammed
>   As full as I be able.

WORDS ON LOVE AND SEX

If she be my wife Sir? I have wedded
her and Bedded her, what other
Ceremonies would you have?
                              Thomas Killigrew

1. Thoughts About Love

The words of a popular song, some years back, would have us
believe that

Love and marriage, love and marriage,
Go together like a horse and carriage.

The kind of 'love' (Middle English *love*, Anglo-Saxon *lufu*, both
allied to Sanskrit *lubh*, to desire) referred to in the song is highly
romantic, idealized in a multitude of Hollywood movies, popular
novels, and songs. Love "in the real world," however, has many
other aspects; it is much more complex, taking in a far wider
territory than merely its association with marriage. In this chapter
we shall focus on the words used for centuries to describe the many
guises of love, the varied vocabulary of sex and those who engage in
it, as well as those who arrange to sell it to others, and we shall look
at words for marriage, divorce, and childbearing.

The old words for these actions will be examined in their original
meanings, and we shall trace the changes in meaning of some of
these words through the years. While the actions themselves, like
human nature, do not change, there is a continuous introduction of

new words to describe these actions; these too will be examined.

Recorded thoughts about 'love' abound in endless variety; they range from the romantic to the cynical, from the deeply felt to the superficial, from the sweet to the bitter, from comic to tragic.

In 1667 John Milton wrote (*Paradise Lost*, IX, 832):

> So dear I love him,
> That with him all deaths I could endure.

Some years earlier, however, Shakespeare had cast a cynical eye on such beliefs (*As You Like It*, act IV, scene 1).

> . . . men have died from time to time, and worms have eaten them, but not for love.

A fate worse than death was the choice of one who was deeply smitten, as described in John de Trevisa's translation of *Polychronicon*, 1387.

> . . . hadde obleged hym self to the devel
> for the love of a wenche.

To Richard Whitford, in 1537, the deeper the passion the more ephemeral it was (*Work for Householders*).

> Hot love is soon cold.

In 1697 in *The Provok'd Wife* Sir John Vanbrugh aimed still another barb at the condition of 'being in love.'

> When a man is really in love he looks insufferably silly.

Abraham Cowley played with the problem of unrequited love (*Anacreon VII, Gold*).

> A mighty pain to love it is,
> And 'tis a pain that pain to miss;
> But of all pains, the greatest pain
> It is to love, but love in vain.

Of all the emotions aroused by love, 'jealousy' is among the most grievous and most devastating. Chaucer outlined the limits to which a 'jealous' man might go (The Miller's Tale).

> Jalous he was, and heeld hire [her] narwe [narrow] in cage,
> For she was yong and wylde and he was old.

Lawrence Durrell gave a new twist to the old adage (*Justine*) in 1957.

It is not love that is blind, but jealousy.

Shakespeare's *Othello* was truly blinded by his jealousy (act V, scene 2).

> . . . one that lov'd not wisely, but too well . . .

Francis Bacon made the point bluntly in 1625 (*Essays*).

> It is impossible to love and be wise.

Is the love between a man and a woman sufficient in itself to keep them together? Not according to William Caxton and Royall Tyler. Caxton wrote in *Chesse* (III) in 1474 about the one ingredient necessary to preserve love.

> Hereof men say a comyn proverbe in englond, that loue lasteth as longe as the money endurith.

Tyler echoed the sentiment more elegantly in 1790 (*The Contrast*, II).

> The chains of love are never so binding as when the links are made of gold.

'Marriages' based on reasons other than love are the ones that will turn out best, according to J. L. Vives' *Instruction of a Christen woman* (IV, ij), translated by Richard Hyrde, 1540.

> They that mary for love, shall lead their life in sorrow.

What kind of man married for love? According to James Boswell, Samuel Johnson pictured such a man (*The Life of Samuel Johnson, LL. D.*, March 28, 1776).

> It is commonly a weak man who marries for love.

We shall end this section on 'love' with a wish for women. In 1665 Richard Brathwait described the ideal husband from a woman's point of view (*A comment upon the tales of . . . Chaucer*).

> That they may have Husbands Meek, to live with, Young, to love with, and Fresh, to lie with.

Through the ages, men and women have been inventing terms of endearment which they use both to describe and address each other. 'Honeybunch,' 'sugar,' 'turtle dove,' 'my little chickadee' (made famous by W. C. Fields) are just a few. Perhaps the most common are 'dear,' 'darling,' and 'sweetheart.'

'Dear' (Middle English *dere, deere, deore*, Anglo-Saxon *deore, dyre*) had the earlier sense of esteemed or valued, a meaning which, of course, it still has. In Chaucer's The Knight's Tale we find this.

> Ther was no man that Theseus hath so derre.

Around 1435, the word was used with the idea of parental love (*Torrent of Portugal*).

> I have a dowghttyr that ys me dere.

Shakespeare used 'dear' with the meaning of love between a man and a woman (*Coriolanus,* act V, scene 3).

> . . . that kiss I carried from thee, dear . . .

'Darling' is from Middle English *derling* or *durling* and Anglo-Saxon *deorling* (favorite). This latter form is made up of *deor* (dear) plus the diminutive suffixes *l* and *ing*. (We have similar formations in English with 'duckling' and 'gosling'.) 'Darling' was the subject of a proverb quoted by John Heywood (*Prouerbes*).

> It is better to be An olde man's derlyng
> Than a yong mans werlyng [one who is despised or disliked].

It took over three hundred years for the word 'sweetheart' to shift from two words to one. 'Sweet' is from Middle English and Anglo-Saxon *swete,* and 'heart' from Middle English *herte* (pronounced with two syllables) and Anglo-Saxon *heorte*. This usage appeared in the late thirteenth century (*South-English Legendary*).

> Alas . . . that ich [I] scholde . . . a-bide that mi child, mi swete heorte, swych cas [case] schal bi-tide.

By 1596, Thomas Nashe had brought the two words closer together (*Have with you to Saffron-Walden,* III).

> So hath he his Barnabe and Anthony for his minions and sweetharts.

Not too many years later in 1613, Thomas Middleton completed the separation (*Triumphs Truth,* VII).

> O welcome, my triumphant lord, My glory's sweetheart!

2. Attraction and Courtship

At the beginning of this chapter we spoke of 'romantic' love, and now we shall look at some of the words that describe the actors in the game of love and their feelings as they pursue the opposite sex.

The word 'romance' is used to describe the 'love affair' between two people, as in 'romantic love.' Its adjectival form 'romantic' distinguishes an idealized form of love from the more lasting, realistic kind of love that sustains a relationship. *Webster's New World Dictionary* defines 'romance' in its main meaning in this manner: "formerly, a long narrative in verse or prose, orig. written in one of the Romance dialects, about the adventures of knights and other chivalric heroes."

As the dialects developed into separate languages, such tales began to be written in those languages, whereas previously the only written language was Latin. Because the languages were derived from Latin, the language of Rome, the term 'Roman' or 'romance' was applied to these tales of love and 'derring-do' (from Middle English *dorryng don,* daring to do). They were first written in verse in French and then in prose. Gradually such writing spread to other languages. In both modern French and German the word *roman* means a novel.

Eventually the term 'romance' took on the wider meaning it now enjoys. In the late nineteenth century, it was no longer used in English for novels or adventurous tales, but was confined to the meaning of 'love' and matters connected with love. In 1873 William Black wrote (*A princess of Thule,* XXIV):

> Romance goes out of man's head when the hair gets grey.

Oscar Wilde treated 'romance' with his usual barbed touch in *A Woman of No Importance* (act II), 1893, where Mrs. Allonby says:

> Men always want to be a woman's first love. That is their clumsy vanity. We women have a more subtle instinct about things. What we like is to be a man's last romance.

Lovers, whether young or old, may 'sigh' with 'passion' for their loved ones; they may be 'fervent,' 'ardent,' or 'wistful'; they may be 'agog' at the sight of their lovers and be full of 'desire' and 'yearning.' 'Sigh' is from Middle English *sighen* and Anglo-Saxon *sicna* (to sigh). Chaucer associated lovers' sighs with heat and fire (*The parlement of foules*), c. 1381.

> Withyn the temple of syghes hote as fyre
> Whyche syghes engendryd were with desyre.

In his famous speech in Shakespeare's *As You Like It* Jaques says (act II, scene 7)

> . . . and then the lover,
> Sighing like furnace, with a woeful ballad
> Made to his mistress' eyebrow; . . .

'Passion' is not an emotion of equanimity; its root tells us that. It is from the Latin *passio* (suffering), spelled in Middle English *passiun*. We speak of actions taken in the 'heat of passion'; Byron recognized the connection (*Don Juan*, II), in 1824.

> For health and idleness to passion's flame, are oil and gunpowder.

'Ardent' and 'fervent' are also connected with heat. 'Ardent' comes from Old French *ardant* (burning) and Latin *ardere* (to burn). Latin *fervere* (to boil) and Old French *fervent* (hot) are the source of 'fervent.'

A universal symbol of love in the Western world is the figure of 'Cupid' with his darts. The name of the god is from the Latin *cupido* (desire, passion), which also gives us the words 'concupiscence' and 'cupidity.' But the idea of love or lust has completely disappeared from our use of the word 'cupidity'; what is left is desire, but for money, not for love. It still retained its connection with love in 1753 when Samuel Richardson wrote *The history of Sir Charles Grandison*, VI).

> Love, as it is called by boys and girls, shall ever be the subject of my ridicule . . . villanous cupidity!

One smitten with the dart of Cupid 'covets' the object of his affections. This word is also allied to the Latin *cupidus* (desirous, eager) and came into English through the Middle English *coveiten* or *coveten*. The word was used in *The Destruction of Troy*, c. 1400.

> . . . that thou couetus vykyndly to couple with me.

There are also those who love from afar. They may not have the depth of passion in their love, and the more appropriate word for them would be 'wistful.' 'Wistful's' precursor word was *wishful*, a much stronger word as evidenced by Shakespeare's usage in *Henry VI, Part III* (act III, scene 1).

> There be certain women that can kill with their eye-sight whom they look wishfully upon.

The original sense of 'wistful' seems to have been silent or hushed, a meaning it probably got from the old verb *whist* (to keep silence), whose earliest form was as an interjection commanding silence similar to our modern "hsst" or "hush." (The card game 'whist' was first called *whisk*, c. 1529, from the sweeping-up or whisking the cards from the table. About 1709, *whisk* was corrupted into 'whist,' and a new etymology was invented for this new word. It was claimed that it came from the word *whist* — hushed, silent — because of the necessity to be silent in order to play the game properly.) In his novel *Harold, the last of the Saxon kings* Edward Bulwer-Lytton used the word 'wistful' in its modern sense, in 1848.

> The terror that seized the girl as she gazed long and wistful upon the knight.

The lover is 'agog' to see his love, full of eagerness for her company. To achieve his goal, he will try to arrange a meeting with her. These meetings have had various names over the years. Men and women have established times and places for an 'assignation,' a 'rendezvous,' a 'tryst,' or a 'date.' 'Agog' is an adaptation of a French phrase *en gogues* (in mirth), from which came *en gog*, then *a gog*, and finally 'agog.' Francis Beaumont and John Fletcher used just *gog* to denote eagerness in 1614 (*Wit Without Money*).

> You have put me into such a gog of going, I would not stay for all the world.

In 1865 Thomas Carlyle used the word 'agog' as we do today (*Frederick the Great*, V, 8).

> The Eldest, age fourteen, had gone quite agog about my little Girl, age only nine.

'Assignation' is from Old French *assigner* (to assign), Latin *assignare* (to affix a seal, appoint, ascribe), which is made up of two Latin words, *ad* (to) and *signare* (to mark), from *signum* (a mark). John Crowne used the word in 1680 (*The Misery of Civil War*, II).

> 'Twou'd have spoil'd An assignation that I have to-night.

The original meaning of 'rendezvous,' according to Cotgrave, was

> "rendez-vous" — a rendezvous, a place appointed for the assemblie of souldiers.

'Rendez-vous' is literally the French imperative "be there!" (and its root lies in the Latin *reddere,* to give back).

'Tryst' (Old French *tristre, triste,* to ambush, to station to watch while hunting) had the meaning in Middle English of "trust," probably derived from Scandinavian words like Icelandic *treysta* (to trust, rely upon) and Danish *troste*(to trust). Chaucer used it with the former meaning (*Troilus*).

> Lo holde thee at they triste cloos,
> and I Shal wel the deer unto thy bowe dryve.

'Date' (from Latin *dare,* to give) had the idea in classical Latin of marking a place of writing, as in *datum Romae,* meaning "given (i.e., written) at Rome." George Ade used it with its contemporary meaning in *Artie* (VII) in 1896.

> I s'pose the other boy's fillin all my dates?

A lover constantly 'yearns' (Middle English *yernen,* Anglo-Saxon *gyrnan, giernan*) for and 'desires' the company of his love. The word 'desire' (Middle English *desyrne, desiren*) comes from Latin *desiderare* by way of Old French and modern French *désirer.* The Latin *desiderare* meant to miss, regret, or long for and was made up of *de* (from) and *sidus* (a star).

Other words used to express one's desire for another are 'fancy,' 'like,' 'be keen on,' 'itch for,' 'have a yen for,' 'hanker for,' 'long for,' 'languish for,' 'crave,' 'pant for,' and 'pine for.' 'Fancy' is a corruption of the fuller form *fantasy.* It is from the Greek *phantasia,* from which we also get our word 'phantom.' In 1568 Richard Grafton used the *ph* spelling (*A chronicle at large and meere history of the affayres of England,* II).

> She went as simply as she might . . . that the king should not phansie her.

'Like' (Middle English *lyken,* to please) was originally used in the third person as in "it likes me" (it pleases me). In English we now say, "I like it"; the French still use the same construction and say, *cela me plaît* (it pleases me).

The etymology of the word 'keen' (Middle English *kene*, Anglo-Saxon *cene*) in the phrase 'to be keen on' is obscure. It may have had a meaning of knowing or skillful. Fom this idea comes the basic notion of "capable" when applied either to the senses or to materials. We speak of a keen knife, a keen wit, while as a slang word 'keen' means good or excellent, all of which fit the original sense of the word. 'To be keen on' seems, therefore, to mean that the object of one's attention is worthy of that attention.

'Itch' is from Middle English *iken, icchen,* and Anglo-Saxon *giccan, gyccan* (to itch). By extrapolation from its basic meaning of an irritation on the skin which can be assuaged by scratching, it has come to mean as well a restless desire, as in 'an itch to travel' or 'an itch for someone.' 'Yen' in the phrase 'have a yen for' someone, is the Chinese word for opium or smoke and is probably connected to the addictive powers of opium. (The 'yen' of Japanese money is from the Chinese *yuan,* a round thing.) In 1930 William Riley Burnett was using 'yen' with the colloquial meaning of attraction (*Iron Man*).

> He's got . . . a strong yen for your woman.

There is another expression of longing that has a modern colloquial ring to it, but is really quite old. Samuel Butler used 'hanker' (allied to Provincial English *hake,* to wander about, loiter, tease) in *Hudibras,* 1663.

> And felt such bowel-hankerings to see an empire, all of kings.

Two hundred years later, Oliver Wendell Holmes used 'hanker' in the modern sense of longing after another (*The Professor at the Breakfast Table,* IV).

> He . . . seemed to be kinder hankerin' around after that young woman.

The word 'long' in the expression 'to long for' is from Middle English *longen, longien,* and Anglo-Saxon *langian.* (It is not connected with the adjective 'long', meaning extended, not short, which has its roots in Middle English *lang* and Anglo-Saxon *lang.*) 'Long' appeared with our modern connotation in *The Destruction of Troy,* c. 1400.

> A fell arow . . . of loue . . . Made him langwys [languish] in Loue & Longynges grete.

One who 'languishes' after another is usually described as without energy for the everyday tasks of life, as drooping about the house. The description is accurate since the word is from the Latin *languere* (to be tired or weak) and *languescere* (to become tired or weak). In French it took the form *languir* (to languish, pine), and in Middle English it was *languishen* with the same meanings. The word appeared with its contemporary meaning in the *Cursor Manuscript*, c. 1300.

> I languis al for the [thee].

The word is used in John Dryden's translation of *The Workes of Virgil, containing his pastorals, georgics and Aeneis* (III), 1697.

> With two fair Eyes his Mistress burns his Breast,
> He looks, and languishes, and leaves his Rest.

'Crave' (Middle English *craven*, Anglo-Saxon *crafian*) is more intense than 'to long for.' 'Pant for' implies an active role on the part of the lover. The word 'pant' is related to 'fancy' deriving from the same root, the Greek *phantasia* (fantasy). 'Pine for' may be said to be at the opposite pole from 'pant for.' It implies inactivity and private torment. It was borrowed from Latin *poena* (pain, punishment) and reached English by way of Anglo-Saxon *pin* (pain) and Middle English *pinen* (to torment). Its sense is clear in Shakespeare's *Romeo and Juliet* (act V, scene 3).

> . . . the new-made bridegroom, . . .
> For whom, and not for Tybalt, Juliet pined.

What makes men and women long for each other? Perhaps it is that they have been 'titillated' or 'tantalized,' and have thereby become 'infatuated,' 'enchanted,' or even 'bewitched.' In any or all of these states they may have been 'enticed,' 'allured,' 'attracted,' or 'tempted.' 'Titillate' (Latin *titillatus*, tickled) literally means "to tickle," and it was so used by Tobias Venner in 1620 (*Via recta*, VI).

> It . . . exciteth the appetite, by corrugating the mouth of the stomacke, and titillating the pallate.

Since the sensation of being tickled is pleasurable, the meaning of the word was extended to anything which causes pleasure, such as the sight or thought of a loved one.

'Tantalize' is an eponym taken from the name of a king in Greek mythology, *Tantalus*. He was a son of Zeus and defied his father; his punishment in the lower regions was to suffer eternal hunger and thirst. He stood in water up to his chin, but whenever he tried to drink it, the water receded; similarly, fruit on branches over his head moved away when he reached for it. In 1849 Charlotte Brontë has a character in *Shirley* (XXIX) treat his "victim" in like fashion.

> I will tantalize her; keep her with me, expecting, doubting.

After having been titillated and tantalized, some become 'infatuated,' a sorry condition as evidenced by the root of the word. It is from the Latin *fatuus* (foolish), and it is from this root that we get our word 'fatuous.' In 1751 Samuel Johnson lumped together two unlikely categories in an issue of *Rambler, #160.*

> Authors and lovers always suffer some infatuation from which only absence can set them free.

One sometimes wonders at what is supposed to be the profound wisdom of country folk as expressed in their proverbs. Match the above statment of Johnson's with the well-known proverb "Absence makes the heart grow fonder." Where lies the truth?

Some lovers may be so infatuated that they feel they are under a spell of 'enchantment' (Latin *in* plus *cantare,* to sing). The prefix *in* tends to intensify the meaning; we find this same effect in the word 'incantation,' meaning to repeat a 'chant' (of the same root) with magical effect. There is a feeling of benevolence attached to the word 'enchantment,' but the word 'bewitched' has a malevolent ring to it. It is from the Anglo-Saxon *be* or *bi* plus *wiccian* (to be a witch, use witchcraft). Robert Burton conveyed the sinister feeling attached to 'bewitched' in *The Anatomy of Melancholy,* 1621.

> Love doth bewitch and strangely change us.

If the object of one's affections is not aroused, one must take steps. One may 'entice,' another word in our lexicon that has a relationship to fire or heat. It is from Latin *in* plus *titio* (firebrand) and could be read as "to add fuel to the fire." To 'lure' someone is to set oneself up as bait, for that was the meaning of the French word *loerre,* a falconer's lure or bait. John Dryden prescribed the elements necessary to 'attract' a man (*Eleonore; a panegyrical poem*) in 1692.

> A wife . . .
> Made to attract his eyes, and keep his heart.

The word 'attract' is from the Latin *ad* (toward) and *trahere* (to draw, pull). Perhaps in order to 'attract' one must first 'allure,' and then, having attracted attention, one must 'tempt.' 'Tempt' is from Late Latin *temptare* or *tentare* (to test, touch, urge). In Middle English the verb was *tempten*. Oscar Wilde commented at least twice on the problem of 'temptation.' In *The Picture of Dorian Gray* (ch. 2) he wrote, in 1891:

> The only way to get rid of a temptation is to yield to it.

While in *Lady Windemere's Fan* (act I) he said, in 1892:

> I can resist everything except temptation.

Wilde's sentiment is echoed in the contemporary bumper sticker which says, "If it feels good, do it."

After all the titillating and tempting, the object of pursuit may still be 'coy,' a word with a rather pedestrian origin compared with its current meaning. It is from the Latin *quietus* (quiet, still) and came into English through Old French *coi, quei,* and *cooit,* all with the same meaning as their Latin root. Being quiet may be a cloak for a shy and retiring nature, and from there it is but a step to pretending to be shy and retiring, hence the current meaning of 'coy.' In *Venus and Adonis* (line 96) Shakespeare caught the essence of the word.

> "O, pity," gan she cry, "flint-hearted boy!
> 'Tis but a kiss I beg: why are thou coy?"

Andrew Marvell (1621 – 68) was impatient, too; he wrote a poem, "To his coy mistress," which starts

> Had we but world enough and time,
> This coyness, lady, were no crime.

He berates her for wasting precious time and sums up his feelings with these two well-known lines.

> The grave's a fine and private place,
> But none I think do there embrace.

In the beginning of a relationship one may 'trifle with,' 'dally with,' 'flirt with,' or 'cast sheep's eyes at' another. Any of these activities may lead to more serious matters like 'courting' or 'wooing.' 'Trifling' (Middle English *trufle, tryfyl,* and Old French *trufle,* mockery, raillery) was the subject of advice from John Gay (*The coquet mother and the coquet daughter*) in 1727.

> She who trifles with all
> Is less likely to fall
> Than she who trifles with but one.

'Dally with' is a virtual synonym for 'trifle with.' It is from Old French *dallier* (to chaff, jest at) and was spelled *dalien* in Middle English. In The Doctor's Tale Chaucer spoke of public opportunities for dallying, c. 1386.

> . . . at festes, reuels, and at daunces,
> That ben occasiouns of daliaunces.

But in *The Roxburghe Ballads* (VII) of 1685 'dallying' was a much more private affair.

> I have a Chamber here of my own,
> Where we may kiss and dally alone.

'Flirt' (Middle English *flurt*, to mock, scorn) had earlier meanings of to jump and to jerk lightly away. William Spurstowe used it that way in 1666 (*The spiritual chymist*).

> As weak as the Grasshoppers who give only a small flirt upwards, and then fall down to the Earth again.

We generally think of females as being the 'flirts,' but John Gay applied the word to a man in *Distressed Wife*, in 1732.

> A flirt, One who gives himself all the airs of making love in public.

In 1889 Mrs. Margaret Oliphant put the word in its modern perspective in *A Poor Gentleman* (XXXVII).

> Or if, perhaps, it was only a passing folly, a foolish little flirtation, nothing serious at all?

Presumably because sheep's eyes were so clear and innocent looking, the phrase 'casting sheep's eyes' implied something of promise behind them. It could be a dangerous practice, said John Heywood in *Edward IV, Part I*, in 1599.

> Go to Nell; no more sheep's eyes; ye may be caught, I tell ye; these be liquorish lads.

The sublety of Heywood's warning became blunt, albeit euphemistic, in Samuel Lover's *Handy Andy; a tale of Irish life* (II), 1842.

Tom's all ram's horns, and the widow is all sheep's eyes.

'Woo' (Middle English *wo, wowe, wowen*, Anglo-Saxon *woh*, bent, crooked) has the literal sense of to bend or to incline. The desired effect of 'wooing' is to incline someone else toward oneself. Robert Burton did not approve of long engagements (*Anatomy*, III).

> Blessed is the wooing
> That is not long a'-doing.

In his *Proverbs* John Ray reserved to the young the right to woo.

> To wo is a pleasure in a young man, a fault in an old.

'Court' is from the Latin *cohors* (courtyard, enclosure). It is, of course, also used without reference to love in the sense of "to seek favor." The whole game of love is summed up by William Warner (*The first and second parts of Albion's England, reuised and corrected*, VI, 31) in 1589.

> With rufull lookes, sighes . . . and
> Fooleries more than few I courted her.

3. Words on Sex

'Ribald,' 'risqué,' 'obscene,' and 'erotic' are some of the words used to describe preoccupation with, discussion of, or thoughts on sex. 'Ribald' (Middle English *ribaud*, Old French *ribald, ribaud* (ruffian, low licentious fellow) is from the Latin *ribalda* (prostitute). It had a broader meaning in 1599 than it does today, as shown in Francis Thynne's *Animaduersions vppon the annotacions and corrections of some imperfections of impressiones of Chaucers workes*.

> He is called "Roye des Ribauldez" whiche is "the kinge of Ribaldes, or Harlottes," or euill or wicked persons.

By 1835 the word 'ribald' had taken on its modern meaning, as seen in this line from Washington Irving's *A Tour on the Prairies* (X).

> Peals of laughter were mingled with loud ribald jokes.

'Risqué' is a form of the French verb *risquer* (to risk, hazard) with the meaning in English of bold or daring, usually with immoral or sexual overtones. The etymology of 'obscene' is doubtful; it comes from the Latin *obscenus* (repulsive, foul) and may be connected with the Latin *caenum* (filth). 'Erotic' has its root in the Greek *erotikos* (relating to love), from *eros* (desire). Walter Charleton had a dim view of 'erotic' (*The Ephesian and Cimmarian matrons; two notable examples of the power of love and wit,* II, pref.) in 1668.

> That Erotic passion is allowed by all learned men to be a species of Melancholy.

William H. Van Buren and Edward L. Keyes went a step further in 1874 (*A practical treatise on the surgical diseases of the genito-urinary organs*).

> Erotomania is a species of insanity.

Words which would be considered ribald, risqué, obscene, and erotic have as their central theme sex and sexual activity. They express a great variety and a range of sensitivity and intensity. 'Sensual,' however, is a more inclusive term. It deals with all the senses and appetites, not merely with sex. It comes from the Latin *sensus* (feeling) and the Late Latin *sensualis* (endowed with feeling). It was used in its broadest sense by Robert Fabyan (*The new chronycles of Englande and of Fraunce*).

> He was gyuen to all sensuall luste of his body.

Preachers and philosophers over the ages have wondered why men seem to prefer evil over good. Richard Hooker outlined the problem in *Sermons* c. 1600.

> The greatest part of men are such as prefer . . . that good which is sensual before whatsoever is most divine.

Before going to words in the essentially sexual category (eight of which incidentally begin with the letter *l*), it might be wise to note Isaac Watts' point, made in 1734 in his *Logick: or the right use of reason in the enquiry after truth* (I, 4).

> Words that were once chaste, by frequent use grow obscene and uncleanly.

'Lewd' is such a word. It is from the Middle English *lewed* and the Anglo-Saxon *laewede* (lay, of the laity) with the sense of untaught or ignorant as opposed to a learned clergy. This is how Chaucer used 'lewd' (Prologue, 502), c. 1385.

> For if a preest be foul, on whom we truste,
> No wonder is a lewed man to ruste.

("To ruste" had the meaning in Chaucer's time of to deteriorate, to become degenerate or spoil.) 'Lewd' picked up the additional meanings of bad, evil, or vile as time went by; it appears with this sense in 1481 in *The Paston Letters* (III).

> Plese zow . . . to forgeve me, and also my wyffe of owr leude offence that we have not don ower dute.

Henry Smith, a preacher, gave the word its modern significance in 1591 (*Sermons*).

> If harlots intice thee to leaudnesse . . . flie from them.

'Loose woman' is a cliché; one almost never hears the word 'loose' attached to a man; but this was not always so, according to Robert Henryson (*The morall fabillis of Esope,* III), c. 1480.

> He was sa lous, and sa lecherous.

Addison wrote in the *Spectator* #262:

> I have shown . . . I have avoided all such Thoughts, as are loose, obscene, or immoral.

'Licentious' is another word that had an innocent beginning. It is from the Latin *licentia* which had the original meaning of liberty, freedom. Following Watts' logic, it gradually developed the sense of unbridled and eventually dissolute and lascivious. By 1555 its meaning had been clearly established, as shown by Richard Eden (*Decades,* tr. 53).

> Dissolute lyunge, licentious talke, & such other vicious behauours.

'Lubricious' is a word that maintained three meanings for many years; today it has but one, obscene and uncleanly. It is from the Latin *lubricaus* (slippery) and was used by Pliny in Holland's translation of *Historie,* (II).

> The same liquor is easie to diuide into drops, and as apt again by the lubricitie thereof, to run into an humor.

Long before this, however, the word had taken on its modern meaning, as seen in Caxton's translation of *Vitas Patrum* (I), 1491.

> The poore doughter was two yere liuynge in lubrycyte and lecherye.

Meanwhile the meaning of slippery had developed into one of

instability or shiftiness, and 'lubricity' was used with this implication by Miall *(Nonconformist,* II).

> The speech, in their judgment, exhibits more of the lubricity of the clever tactician than of the serious designs of the minister.

The last four words in the "starting with the letter *l* category" are 'libidinous,' 'lascivious,' 'lecherous,' and 'lustful.' They are honest words in the sense that their current meanings conform to their origins. 'Libidinous' traces its roots back through Latin *libidinosus* (eager, lustful, arbitrary) to Latin *libido* (lust, pleasure). In an issue of the *Spectator* (#90, 1711) Addison adapted the adage "A leopard does not change its spots" and applied it to human development.

> A lewd Youth . . . advances by Degrees into a libidinous old man.

Like libidinous, 'lascivious' goes back for its roots to two Latin words *lasciviousus* (lustful) and *lascivus* (sportive, lustful). In Langeley's translation of *Vergil* (III, 9) there is horror at a local custom.

> Meene & Women were permitted moste lasciuiously to bath together.

Launcelot became the object of some biting words in Sir Thomas Malory's *Morte d'Arthur* (XVIII, 2), 1470 – 85. One of those words is 'lecher' (Middle English *lecher, lechour,* and Old French *lecheor, lecheur, lechier,* to lick, live in gluttony or debauchery).

> Launcelot now I well vnderstande that thou are a fals recreaunt knyghte and a comyn lecheoure, and louest and holdest other ladyes.

The last word in this series is 'lustful' (Middle English and Anglo-Saxon *lust,* pleasure, which is allied to the Sanskrit *lash,* desire). In Holland's translation of Camden's *Britain* (I), 1610, we find

> That King plied getting children so lustfully, as that hee was father of thirteen Bastards.

Three other adjectives that belong in this group of words are 'wanton,' 'smutty,' and 'salacious.' The first two have one thing in common; they adhere closely to the line laid out by Watts. Their roots are ordinary and innocent, but they have developed meanings that are anything but innocent and pure.

'Wanton' is a combination of two Middle English words, *wan,* a prefix meaning lacking or wanting, and *towen,* from the Anglo-Saxon *togen* or *toen* (to educate, bring up). It was spelled *wantoun* and *wantowen* in Middle English. Its true sense, therefore, is unrestrained, not taken in hand by a master or teacher, and thus 'licentious' or free from rules. In 1638 John Ford used the word as we would today (*The Lady's Triall,* act I, scene 2)

> A wanton mistress is a common sewer.

'Smutty' (Middle English *smutt, smoot,* dirt), although sounding very modern, was known back in the seventeenth century with our present-day meaning. Pepys assumed the role of literary critic when he wrote in his famous *Diary* on June 20, 1668:

> I saw this new play my wife saw yesterday, and do not like it, it being very smutty.

A note familiar to us today sounded in the *Spectator* of December 4, 1886.

> The public must have titles, or smut, or murder, and wishes in its heart always to have two of them together.

'Salacious' comes from the Latin word *salax,* meaning lustful, licentious, 'salacious,' and never seems to have had any other meaning in English. Thomas Brown, in 1704, wrote his *Satire Against Women* (I) and in it penned the following.

> Let every man thou seest give new desires
> And not one quench the rank salacious fires.

'Debauch' (*debosh* in Middle English and *desbaucher* in Old French, of obscure etymology) has changed its meaning over the years. It may be from a combination of Latin *dis* (away) and Old High German *balco* or *balcho* along with Old French *bauche,* words that were connected with building operations, but whose exact meaning is not clear. It may also be allied to Old French *deboucher* (to rough down timber, leading to the idea of "to destroy" and finally "to corrupt"). It appears to have had the sense of "to take away the frame of a building" or "to leave it [the building] incomplete"; it may be from these meanings that it got its earliest sense — "to entice away from duty." In 1595 Sir Roger Williams wrote (*The actions of the lowe countries,* 5)

> That Count Egmont would be deboshed from them by the
> Spanish . . .

In his *Dictionary* Cotgrave gave the word greater range.

> "Desbaucher," to debosh . . . seduce, mislead; make lewd, bring to
> disorder, draw from goodnesse.

One hundred years later, Steele used the word as we would today
(*Spectator* #151, 1711).

> A young lewd Fellow . . . who would . . . debauch your Sister, or lie
> with your Wife.

We will wind up this section with the words 'concupiscence,'
'prurience,' and 'pornography.' We have already looked at the
origin of 'concupiscence,' when talking about 'Cupid.' Its meaning
of lustful desire was made clear as early as 1386 in Chaucer's
Parson's Tale.

> The fuyr [fire] of fleisschly concupiscence.

According to the *Sermons* of Hooker you weren't allowed even to
think about desire.

> We know even secret concupiscence to be sin.

From its Latin root *pruriens* (itching) our English word 'prurient'
developed a meaning that is much narrower in scope; today it
means only lustful or lascivious. In a landmark decision on censor-
ship, *Roth* v. *United States* and *Alberts* v. *California,* 1957, the majority
opinion of the Supreme Court confirmed this meaning of 'pru-
rient': "Obscene material is material which deals with sex in a
manner appealing to prurient interests."

The meaning of 'pornography' is crystal clear from its origins. It
is from two Greek words, *porne* (harlot) and *graphe* (writing), which
were combined to mean writing about the activities of harlots.
There have always been cries of alarm from those concerned with
the effect of such writings on our moral standards. This was true in
1880, and it was true in 1957, and it is still true. In the *Guardian* of
October 27, 1880, there appeared the following.

> The excesses of the [French] press designated as "pornographic"
> . . . have . . . become such as to compel the authorities to adopt
> strong measures against them.

4. Sex in Action

Up to now, our words have had to do with talk of, thoughts about, and writings on love and sex. Here are some words that have to do with action. The first actions between two partners are generally the 'kiss' and the 'hug.' 'Kiss' is from Middle English *cos, cus, kisse,* and Anglo-Saxon *coss.* 'Hug' is a word of uncertain origin; it is perhaps from the Icelandic *hugga,* but with a change of sense because that word means to soothe, to comfort.

In 1589 George Puttenham described different 'kissing' customs (*The arte of English poesie,* III, 24).

> With vs the wemen giue their mouth to be kissed, in other places their cheek, in many places their hand.

One of the early uses of 'hug' in a sexual context occurred in Pope's *January and May* in 1705.

> He hugg'd her close, and kiss'd her o'er and o'er.

This next group of words is primarily colloquial and covers touching, up to but not including actual sexual intercourse. 'Pet,' 'neck,' 'spoon,' and 'smooch' are, for the most part, twentieth-century words. 'Pet' (of uncertain origin, maybe from Middle French *peton,* little fool) was used in 1846 by Douglas Jerrold in *Mrs. Caudle's curtain lectures* (XXXVI) with a rather different meaning.

> Get another wife to study you an pet you up as I've done.

One of the characters in Harry Marks' *Plastic Age,* 1924, used 'pet' in its modern sense.

> "Say, this kid was the hottest little devil I ever met. Pet? My God!"

An issue of the *Literary Digest* in 1957 distinguishes between 'petting' and our next word 'necking.'

> ... the fiancé holds petting privileges (petting is necking with territorial concessions).

That 'necking' stops short of sexual intercourse is clearly implied in this citation from Philip Wylie's *Finnley Wren,* 1937.

> I thought . . . that at least you'd want to neck me.

Groucho Marx saw through the euphemism that was 'necking.'

Whoever named it necking was a poor judge of anatomy.

One might assume from the foregoing that 'necking' is a modern word, but it has been in the language for over one hundred years. In 1842 Zachariah Allnut wrote in his *Diary*:

> I came rather suddenly upon a man who unceremoniously put his arms round a young lady, and . . . said . . . "I was only a'necking on her a little bit, Sir."

'To spoon' meaning to kiss or fondle was in common use around 1900. But it had a different meaning back in 1863; the phrase 'to be spoons with' was slang for 'to be sentimentally in love with.' This is how it was used in a parody on *Enoch Arden* appearing in the *Melbourne Punch* in that year.

> Philip Ray and Enoch Arden, Both were 'spoons' on Annie Lee.

Another word which is considered to be modern slang was in use in the late sixteenth century. 'Smooch' (Middle English *smouch,* to kiss, buss) appeared in *English Tripe-Wife* in 1595.

> Kisse and smowtch the Widdow neuer so much . . .

Cotgrave defined the French *baiseur* as a "kisser, smoutcher, smacker." (Caution: In modern French it is an "offensive" term, meaning strictly someone who is engaged in sexual intercourse.)

In the current vernacular, 'to make out' means to neck heavily or passionately. According to some, however, it has the connotation of sexual intercourse and is virtually a synonym of "to go all the way," a phrase which was in use some twenty or thirty years ago.

When petting, necking, smooching, or other such activities are not satisfying a need, the partners are indeed likely to "go all the way." There are polite words or phrases for this act, such as 'sexual intercourse' (Latin *inter,* between, and *currere,* to run), 'having sex,' 'coitus,' 'copulation,' the legal term 'carnal knowledge,' and the biblical terms 'to know' and 'to lie with.'

'Sex' (Middle English *sex,* Old French *sexe,* and Latin *sexus,* probably from the Latin verb *secare,* to cut, divide) is, in addition to its use as a delineator of male and female, the word that describes 'intercourse' between the two sexes.

The richness and variety of thoughts about sex defy description; here are two particularly choice ones. In *A Memoir of the Reverend*

Sydney Smith by Lady Holland, published in 1855, his daughter quotes him as saying:

> As the French say, there are three sexes — men, women, and clergymen.

Mark Twain was puzzled.

> Of all the delights of this world man cares most for sexual intercourse, yet he has left it out of his heaven.

'Coition' or 'coitus' had two meanings in the seventeenth century, but only one has survived to our day. It comes from the Latin, *co-* (together, with) and *ire* (to go), and from this combination came the following meaning used by Thomas Blount (*Glossographia*).

> "Coition," an assembly, confederacy or commotion.

A few years earlier, Sir Thomas Browne used the word with its modern connotation (*Religio Medici*, II), 1642.

> I would be content . . . that there were any way to perpetuate the world without this triviall and vulgar way of coition.

There are two other words in this group that, like 'coition,' had two meanings simultaneously; they are 'carnal' and 'copulate.' 'Carnal' is from the Latin *carnalis* (fleshly) and appeared in Burton's *Anatomy* (III, 4; II, 1) with the meaning of nonspiritual.

> Meer carnalists, fleshly minded men.

Shakespeare used the word with its sexual connotation in *Othello* (act I, scene 3).

> . . . our carnal stings, our unbitted lusts . . .

The word 'copulate' is also from the Latin, this time from the word *copulare* (to link, couple). In 1669 it appeared in *The court of the gentiles* by Theophilus Gale (I, 3) with that root meaning.

> Things of themselves most opposite, were copulated and linked together.

Ephraim Pagitt, writing twenty-four years before Gale, employed the word with its sexual connection which still obtains (*Heresiography; or, a description of the hereticks and sectaries of these latter times*).

> Marriage, which is a lawful copulation of a man and a woman.

'Fornication,' meaning unlawful sexual intercourse, has a very interesting root. It is from the Latin *fornicare* (to go to a brothel). This verb got its meaning from the fact that brothels were often located under a *fornix* (arch, vault, basement). Such vaults were often used as a place convenient for intercourse, and for this reason *fornix* came later on to mean 'brothel.' Robert Manning of Brunne defined 'fornication' in 1303 *(Handlyng synne,* 7352).

> "Fornycacyoun" (ys), whan two vnweddyde haue mysdoun [misdone, a euphemism for "had sexual intercourse"].

Samuel Johnson was quoted on the subject (Boswell's *Life,* April 5, 1776).

> All men will naturally commit fornication, as well as men will naturally steal.

Two other euphemisms for sexual intercourse, 'to lie with' and 'to know,' come from the Bible. 'To know' (Middle English *knowen,* Anglo-Saxon *cnawan;* probably allied to Latin *noscere* or *gnoscere,* to know) was used by George Joye in 1535; he explained the euphemism he was employing *(An apology made to satisfy, if it may be, W. Tindale).*

> Before she knew [that is] slept with hir howsbonde.

Malory used 'to lie with' ('to lie' from Middle English *leye, lighe, lygge*) to outline one of the moral strictures imposed by King Arthur on his men *(Morte,* V, 12).

> That none of his lyege men shold defoule ne [nor] lygge by [lie with] no lady.

We shall now look at some of the slang, vernacular, colloquial, or, some might say, downright obscene words which are much more commonly used today than some of the more polite words we have just described. Here is a short, but by no means complete list. 'Fuck,' 'bunny fuck,' 'bang,' 'ball,' 'hump,' 'lay,' and 'screw.' It is very difficult to establish origins and roots for most of these words because they have been taboo words and therefore books, even dictionaries, would not list them, making it impossible to establish either their etymologies or their early uses. Suffice it to say that there is no doubt whatsoever about their current meanings.

There has been much research done on the word 'fuck,' but there is still no unanimity among scholars as to its origin. Two of the more likely sources are French *foutre* and Latin *futuere,* both with the meaning of sexual intercourse; even more probable is the connection with the German *ficken* (to strike, move back and forth, copulate) with its meaning of 'to copulate' dating from the sixteenth century. The word 'fuck' itself goes back to at least 1234. A 'bunny fuck' is a quick, hurried act of sexual intercourse. To 'bang' (Icelandic *banga* and Danish *banke,* to beat) has been traced in its meaning of 'have intercourse' to the German *ficken* mentioned above. Another synonym is 'ball' — having a good time with sex.

Still another synonym is 'hump,' which was common in the late eighteenth century. To 'hump' has survived and became a part of Joe E. Lewis's routine at the Copacabana night club in New York.

> I miss the circus. I miss watching the elephant's trunk and the camels hump.

Along with 'hump,' two other words are in common use today, 'lay' and 'screw.' 'Lay' may have taken its meaning literally from laying a woman down for sexual purposes. James T. Farrell wrote in 1930:

> Both agreed that the two girls looked like swell lays. . . .

In 1812 James Hardy defined the word 'screw' (*A new and comprehensive vocabulary of the flash language*).

> To screw a place is to enter it by false keys . . . Any robbery effected by such means is termed a screw.

In the 1811 edition of Grose's *Dictionary of the Vulgar Tongue* (see Bibliography) 'to screw' is defined as "to copulate." It has been suggested that 'screw's' meaning of sexual intercourse came from this idea of stealing; that is, to steal sex from a woman is 'to screw' her. The word 'screw' with this connotation has been well-known and in wide use from the beginning of the nineteenth century.

One of the possible results of a woman's having been 'laid' or 'screwed' (it is interesting to note here the male orientation in our society, the man as the active agent in sexual pursuit, the woman as the passive recipient) is 'pregnancy.' The most common slang phrase for this condition since the nineteen twenties has been 'knocked up.' However, 'to knock' a woman goes back to at least the early nineteenth century as it is listed in Grose's *Dictionary of the Vulgar Tongue*, 1796, with the meaning of "to have carnal knowledge of her."

To describe the violent act on the part of a man in forcing a woman to have sex with him, generally under threat of bodily harm, there are several words; among them are 'rape,' 'seduce,' 'violate,' 'defile,' and 'ravish.' 'To rape' is from the Latin *rapere* (to snatch), which meaning is evident in the word 'rapacious' (taking by force, plundering, greedy) but which has no sexual connotation whatsoever. It is only in the word 'rape' that this connection exists. Thomas Heywood commented on the unchanging nature of human beings (*The hierarchie of the blessed angells*), in 1635.

> There's nothing new, Menippus; as before,
> They rape, extort, forswear.

'Seduce' springs innocently enough from the Latin *ducere* (to lead), with the prefix *se* (apart), but it garnered some violent meanings on its way to and through the English language. One may be 'seduced' into evil ways by the temptations of money or power. Samuel Richardson warned women against another kind of temptation (*Clarissa*), 1747–48.

> A woman who is above flattery and despises all praise but that which flows from the approbation of her own heart, is, morally speaking, out of reach of seduction.

'Violate,' unlike 'seduce,' lives up to its origins. It is from the Latin *violare*, which comes from *vis* (force). Severe penalties have been decreed for centuries for the crime of 'rape' or 'violation,' but they have not succeeded in stemming the practice. John Bouchier Lord Berners reported one such attempt (*The boke of duke Huon of Burdeux*, CXIII), c. 1530.

> He made it to be cryed in euere strete that no man shulde be so hardy on payne of dethe to vyolat any woman, or deflowere any mayd.

Among the many meanings of 'flower' (Middle English *flowre, flour, flur*, French *fleur*, from Latin *flos*) is the idea of a jewel, a precious possession, as used by Henry Brinklow (*The lamentacyon of a christen agaynst the cytye of London*) in 1545.

> London beyng one of the flowers of the worlde as touchinge worldlye riches.

Another meaning, that which concerns us here, is that of virginity — hence 'to deflower' and 'defloration.' John Gower wrote (*Confessio,* II):

> O Pallas noble quene . . .
> Help, that I lese nought my flour.

For another maid, as reported by Fabyan (*Chronicles,* VII), there was no help.

> The whiche . . he deflowered of hyr vyrgynytie.

Like 'violate, 'defile' is true to its roots; it is from a combination of the Latin prefix *de* and the English base *foul,* and was spelled in Middle English *defoulen* (to tread down, oppress, outrage, violate). One characteristic of a female saint was the avoidance of the corrupt touch of men, according to a report in 1400 (*Coventry mysteries*).

> She wold not be defylyde
> With spot or wem [stain of sin] of man.

'Ravish' is from the same root as 'rape' and has the same meaning. The actions of a man accused of this crime were described in 1436 (*Rolls of Parliament,* IV).

> [He] flesshly knewe and ravysshed ye said Isabell.

But what of those who, for whatever reason, do not participate in sexual intercourse? They have their words, too. Many have wondered at the attraction of 'chastity' (from Old French *chaste,* Latin *castus,* chaste, morally pure) for so many men and women through the ages. Anatole France wrote:

> Of all sexual aberrations, chastity is the strangest.

According to the narrator of Chaucer's The Tale of the Wife of Bath there are factors other than choice that influence chastity.

> Filth and old age, I'm sure will agree
> Are powerful wardens upon chastitye.

Ambrose Bierce poked wry fun at those who practice 'abstinence' (Latin *ab,* away, and *tenere,* to hold) in *The Devil's Dictionary,* 1906.

> Abstainer, n. A weak person who yields to the temptation of denying himself a pleasure.

The law reserves sex for the married; society for the most part does as it pleases. The root of 'celibacy' is consonant with the law; it is from the Latin *caelebs* (single, unmarried). Samuel Johnson, in 1759, had a dim view of the practice of 'celibacy' (*Rasselas*, 26).

> Marriage has many pains, but celibacy has no pleasures.

There is a state between those who "do" and those who "don't"; it is called 'continence' (Latin *continere,* to contain). Here is Elyot's definition (*The boke named The gouernour,* I, 21), 1531.

> Continence, which is a meane between Chastitie and inordinate luste.

Jeremy Taylor had a different definition in 1667 (*The rule and exercises of holy living,* I, 3).

> Chastity is either abstinence or continence; abstinence is that of virgins or widows; continence, of married persons.

"Illegal" sex may be enjoyed anywhere, but in order to provide a reasonably comfortable, private location for one kind of it, certain houses have been established, called 'whorehouses.' There have been other names for them in our past such as 'brothel,' 'bordello,' 'stew,' 'bagnio,' 'hothouse,' and 'bawdy house.' 'Whore' (Middle English *hore, heore, hoore, whoor*) may be allied to Gothic *hors* (adulterer) and Old Frisian *hora* (to fornicate). There have always been all kinds of double standards, but this one described by John Gay in 1727 is unusual (*The Beggar's Opera,* I, 4).

> Gamesters and Highwaymen are generally very good to their Whores, but they are very Devils to their Wives.

" 'Tain't what you do, it's the way that cha do it," according to a song popular some years ago. Bishop George Berkeley agreed (*Alciphron, or the minute philosopher,* II), in 1732.

> To cheat, whore, betray, get drunk, do all these things decently, this is true wisdom, and elegance of taste.

'Brothel' is the shortened form of its antecedent 'brothel-house,' which itself replaced 'bordel' and 'bordel-house.' The Middle English *brothel* referred to a person of low character. Two other forms of the word were *brethel* (wretch) and *bretheling* (beggarly fellow). All of these came from Anglo-Saxon *abreodan* (to ruin, destroy). The word *brothel* became confused with the Middle English *bordel* and the Old French *bordel,* a diminutive of *borde* (hut, cot, shed made of boards). Gower used 'brothel' in its original meaning, referring to a person (*Confessio,* III).

> Quod Achab thanne, There is one,
> A brothel, which Micheas hight [who is called Micheas].

By the time of Shakespeare's *King Lear,* the word had taken on its present meaning (act I, scene 4).

> . . . Epicurism and lust
> Makes it more like a tavern or a brothel
> Than a graced palace.

Chaucer used the early form 'bordel' (The Parson's Tale).

> Harlottis, that haunten bordels of these foule wommen.

(Note the word *harlottis;* as we shall see later, and as is apparent from this context, the word 4efers to men.) In 1794 Thomas J. Mathias used the word in its present form (*The pursuits of literature, or what you will, a satirical poem*).

> The stews and bordellos of Grecian and Roman antiquity.

The word 'stews' in the above citation is from Late Latin *exstufare* (to steam, smoke), which is a combination of *ex* and Greek *typhos* (steam, smoke). It took on the meaning of bordello because of the frequent use of the public hot-air baths for immoral purposes, called 'stews' in the vernacular of the day. Alexander Pope wrote about 'stews' (*Satires and epistles of Horace imitated,* I, 6), 1732.

> Shall we every decency confound?
> Through taverns, stews and bagnios take our round?

Like 'stew,' the word 'bagnio' meant a bath; it is from Latin *balneum* and Italian *bagno* with the same meaning. But the same reason that gave 'stew' its meaning of bordello gave this meaning to 'bagnio.' So wrote Philip Massinger (*Parliament,* act II, scene 2).

> To be sold to a brothel,
> Or a common bagnio.

'Hothouse' was another word for a bathing house with hot baths, and it, too, like stew and bagnio, became a synonym for whorehouse. A publication in 1511 had this word about 'hothouses' (*Churche of yvell men,* A, IV).

> Bordelles, tauernes, sellers, and hote houses dissolute, there as is commyted so many horryble synnes.

The last word in this group is 'bawdyhouse.' 'Bawd' is of uncertain origin. It is a contraction of Middle English *bawdstrot,* and one authority suggests that its roots may be Old High German *bald* (bold, gay, lively) and Middle High German *strotzen* (to strut about). However, there are unanswered questions. What was the bridge from these meanings of *bawdstrot* or *bawd* to the meaning of procurer, as in Chaucer's The Friar's Tale?

> He was A theef, and eek a somnour and a baude.

(*Somnour* is from Old English *samnian* and Middle English *somner,* a summoner, or what we would call today a process-server.) But by 1541, the sex of 'bawd' had changed (*Henry VIII*).

> That baude the lady Jane Rochford, by whose meanes Culpepper came thither.

The person who presides over such houses, whatever their names, is a woman who goes under the general title of 'madam' (Middle English and modern French *madame,* Middle French *ma dame,* from Latin *mea domina,* all meaning "my lady"). The word has been in use with this meaning for hundreds of years. Thomas Heywood wrote in 1624 (*The captives, or, the lost recovered,* act IV, scene 1)

> Naye, make his honest and chast wyfe no better then a madam makarell [procurer].

In 1954 W. Henry wrote about a 'madam' in *Death of a Legend.*

> Presently the door swung open. . . .This was "Big Mary" Binistrone, a Madam of the old school.

There are those who engage in sexual intercourse, and, as we have seen, there are those who do not. There are also some who engage in it to excess, unable to control their drives. There are words for these people too. A common word reserved for women in this category is 'nymphomania' (Latin and Greek *nympha,* bride, and *mania,* madness); it is a fairly recent word. The following appeared in a medical work published in 1899 (*A system of medicine: by many writers,* edited by Thomas C. Allbutt, VIII).

> The furious nymphomaniac who embraces every man she can get at.

The equivalent condition for men is the lesser known word 'satyriasis,' from the Greek *satyros* (a sylvan god, companion of Bacchus, literally a "sower"). The word was in use in 1657 when

William Coles wrote *Adam in Eden; or natures paradise* (CCLXXX).

> Being put into Plaisters and applyed to the Reines, it helpeth the
> Satyriasis or continuall standing of the Yard.

5. The Male of the Species

We will look now at four categories of men: those who engage in sex
for pleasure and/or a sense of power over women, those who do it
for money, those who collect money for providing partners for
men to do it with, and finally some who engage in sexual practices
that are different from those that have hitherto been considered by
society to be "normal."

In the first group one might find the eponyms 'Don Juan,'
'Casanova,' and 'Lothario,' and the words 'gay dog,' 'gay deceiver,'
'libertine,' 'stud,' or 'wolf.' 'Don Juan' was a figure in Spanish
legend, a dissolute nobleman and seducer of women, the central
figure of many poems, plays, and operas. 'Casanova,' Giovanni
Giacomo Casanova (1725 – 98), was an Italian adventurer, edu-
cated for the priesthood, who was by turns diplomat, preacher,
abbé, alchemist, cabalist gambler, violin player, and, in all these
occupations, a constant seducer of women. He wrote his superbly
styled *Mémoirs,* in 12 volumes, a record of his rogueries and innum-
erable amours.

There was a young rake and seducer of women named 'Lothario'
in Nicholas Towe's *The fair penitent, a tragedy* of 1703. The name was
borrowed by Lytton and made universally known in 1849 in *The
Caxtons, a family picture* (VXVIII, 6).

> No woman could have been more flattered and courted by
> Lotharios and lady-killers than Lady Castleton has been.

The word 'gay' has a very special meaning today, but it used to be
only a synonym of merry and happy. Edward Peacock used it in the
sense from which we get the association with 'dog' and 'deceiver'
(*Narcissa Brendon,* I).

> This elder Narcissa had led a gay and wild life while beauty lasted.

'Libertine' (from Latin *liber,* free) was, according to Skeat (see
Bibliography), "applied at first to certain heretical sects, and in-

tended to mark the licentious 'liberty' of their creed." In 1593 Garbriel Harvey put the word in today's perspective (*Pierce's super-rogation, or a new prayse of the old asse*).

> The whole brood of venereous Libertines, that knowe no reason but appetite, no Lawe but Luste.

'Stud' (Middle English *stod*, Anglo-Saxon *stood,* a collection of breeding horses and mares) was short for 'stud-horse,' that is, stallion. While it is not possible to trace any direct etymology, it is obvious how the term 'stud' has come to applied to a particular kind of man. The connection between 'wolf' (Middle English *wolf,* Anglo-Saxon *wulf,* with a sense of to tear or render) and the lady-killer 'wolf' is somewhat more tenuous; this usage may have evolved around 1930, and had become part of the standard vocabulary by 1945.

Adjectives used to describe such men as we have just discussed are 'goatish,' 'randy,' and 'ruttish.' 'Goatish' (from Middle English *goot, gote,* Anglo-Saxon *got*) appeared in Shakespeare's *King Lear* (act I, scene 2) in a way that leaves no doubt as to its meaning.

> . . . an admirable evasion of whore-master man, to lay his goatish disposition to the charge of a star!

'Randy,' the etymology of which is not clear, means sexually warm and lecherous; but it earlier meant having a rude, aggressive manner, as shown in this usage by Sir Walter Scott (*Old Mortality,* XXVII).

> It was him and his randie mother began a' the mischief in this house.

However, there was a dialectal usage of 'randy' in the mid-nineteenth century, with the meaning of wanton, lustful, or lewd, and it is from this offbeat usage that we get our modern meaning of the word. 'Rut' (Middle English *rutyen,* Old French *ruit,* Latin *rugitus,* roaring, as of a deer in 'rut') is also found in one of Shakespeare's plays, *All's Well That Ends Well* (act IV, scene 3).

> . . . that is an advertisement to a proper maid in Florence, one Diana, to take heed of the allurement of one Count Rousillon, a foolish idle boy, but, for all that very ruttish.

There are those who have felt the need for potions, foods, or substances of some kind to arouse or increase sexual desire. The word for these items is 'aphrodisiacs' (Greek *Aphrodite,* the goddess of love, from *afros,* foam, so-called because the goddess was supposed to have sprung from the foam of the ocean). Here are three food notes for the sex-starved gourmet. John Lindley wrote *An introduction to the natural system of botany* in 1830 with this suggestion.

> The nut . . . is eatable and aphrodisiac.

In Africa and other parts of the world powdered rhinoceros horn is still considered an 'aphrodisiac.' In 1874 Mordecai C. Cooke removed one item from the preferred list (*Fungi; their nature, influence and uses*).

> Truffles are no longer regarded as aphrodisiacs.

The second category of men discussed here had to do with those who engage in sex for money. Our modern vocabulary is deficient in words to describe a male prostitute. The title of a movie, *Midnight Cowboy,* serves as a descriptive term for such men, but it appears to be one of the very few words or phrases available. There are more colorful words from our past which deserve their place in today's lexicon.

'Gigolo,' a word from the nineteen-twenties, had more the connotation of a paid evening escort and/or dancing partner than sexual object. It has enjoyed a revival with a new twist in the movie *American Gigolo;* the male lead is indeed a male prostitute. The word 'gigolo' is from Middle English *giglet* or *giggelot* (wanton woman) and is connected with Middle English *gigge* (flighty girl). That it once referred to a girl is clear from this advice given c. 1430, "How the good wyf taught hir doughtir," in *Babees Book*).

> Go not to the wrastelinge . . as it were a strumpet or a giggelot.

By the early twentieth century, 'gigolo' referred to a man. The *Daily Express* of October 24, 1927, had this news item.

> The Riviera 'wake-up' . . . Well known mannequins, dance partners, gigolos and barmen . . have once more returned to their place in the sun.

There are available from our literary past two fine synonyms for male prostitute; they are 'sellary' (Latin *sellarius,* from *sella,* seat, couch) and 'spintry' (Latin *spintria*), the latter defined in *Mrs. Byrne's Dictionary* (see Bibliography) as "a male whore." Ben Jonson used both words in 1603 (*Sejanus, his fall,* act IV, scene 5).

> Ravish'd hence, like captives, and, in sight of their most grieved parents dealt away, unto his spintries, sellaries, and slaves.

The word 'spintry' was also used as a synonym for whorehouse by Clement Walker in 1649 (*Relations and observations historicall and politick, upon the parliament begun 1640; divided into two books. I. The mystery of the two junto's; II. The history of independence*, II).

> Their New erected Sodomes and Spintries at the Mulbury-garden.

The most common word today for the man who sells someone else's sexual services is 'pimp'; other names are 'procurer,' 'mackerel,' 'panderer,' 'fancy man,' and 'whoremonger'. Most authorities acknowledge that the origin of 'pimp' is unknown but several possibilities have been advanced. It may be from the Middle French *pimperneau* (knave, rascal varlet) or Old French *pimpernel* (small eel), or it may be connected with Middle French *pimper* (to render elegant). Whatever its origin, it has been in use for a long time. Pepys wrote in his *Diary* (June 10, 1666):

> The Duke of York is wholly given up to his new mistress . . . Mr. Brouncker, it seems, was the pimp to bring it about.

'Procurer' (Latin *pro*, in behalf of, and *curare*, to take care of) has been applied to women as well as men. Robert South wrote of such women in 1716 *(Sermons preached upon several occasions*, II).

> Strumpets in their youth turn procurers in their age.

'Mackerel,' in this context, is an obsolete word whose origin is also obscure. In Chapter V we have seen its possible connection to the French *maquereau*, and have speculated how the sexual connotation may have come about. The French and English words both appear in this citation from John Lydgate's translation of *Pilgrimage*;

> 'Glotonye': Yiff thow me calle . . . Lyk as I am, a Bocheresse, Or in ffrench . . . I am callyd a Makerel, Whos offyce . . . Ys in ynglysshe bauderye [panderer].

'Panderer' is from Middle English *Pandare*, Latin *Pandarus*, the name of the man who procured for Troilus. In later years, it became an eponym meaning a procurer, and was used as such by Boccaccio, Chaucer, and Shakespeare. It appeared in a translation by Sir Thomas North in 1579 (Plutarch's *Lives of the noble Grecians and Romanes*).

> He that was the Pandor to procure her.

A 'fancy man' lives on the earnings of a prostitute. Some authorities think that 'fancy' is related to *the fancy,* a cant term for the boxing world, in use around 1810. The December 6, 1890, issue of the *Spectator, #825,* carried this item.

> They will bear from the "fancy-man" any usage, however brutal.

(Cant terms are defined by *Webster's New World Dictionary as*

> **1.** whining, singsong speech, esp. as used by beggars   **2.** the secret slang of beggars, thieves, etc.; argot   **3.** the special words and phrases used by those in a certain sect, occupation, etc.; jargon . . .)

The treatment that whores receive from their pimps today is not any different from that received from 'fancy men' almost one hundred years ago. The British have two other slang words for 'pimp,' 'ponce' and 'bully.' The etymology of both is obscure; 'ponce' may be from *pounce,* and 'bully' may be from Dutch *boel* (lover, of either sex). It is proposed that this notion of "lover" may be responsible for the meaning of a protector of a prostitute. The *Clerkenwell News* of January 27, 1872, equated these words.

> Prostitutes, or their "ponces" or bullies.

Partridge, in his dictionary of slang (see Bibliography), dates 'bully' back to c. 1690. He quotes Farmer and Henley's *Slang and its Analogues,* 1874, on the subject of the social position of 'ponces.'

> Low-class East-end thieves even will "draw the line" at ponces, and object to their presence in the boozing-kens!

The last in our series of words about men who profit from the sale of sex is 'whoremonger.' 'Monger' (Middle English *mangere,* dealer, from Latin *mango,* pushy salesman, slave dealer) was a common suffix in England to denote a dealer in all kinds of goods. William Roy and J. Barlow used the word in 1528 (*Rede me and be nott wrothe, For I saye no thinge but trothe*).

> Lycknest thou to whoarmongers
> A colage of clarckes and scolears?

Perhaps 'pimps' and the like got that way because they are 'misogynists' (Greek *misos,* hatred, and *gyne,* woman). It is doubtful that a pimp would acknowledge even the limited worth of a woman as outlined by Richard Whitlock in *Zwootomia or observations on the present manners of the English,* 1654.

The hardest task is to persuade the erroneous obstinate misogynist, or woman hater, that any discourse acknowledging their worth can go beyond poetry.

The word chosen by this next and last category of men (or women) to describe themselves is 'gay,' in the sense of homosexual. There seems to be no universally accepted view of the etymology of this meaning. The word 'gay' itself is from the Old French *gai* (merry), and that is what it has meant for hundreds of years. Grose in 1811 (*Dictionary*) defines "gaying instrument" as "the penis." Incidentally, the 'homo' part of the word 'homosexual' is from the Greek *homos* (one and the same); it has no connection with the Latin *homo* (human being, man, person). Havelock Ellis talked about the word in 1897 (*Studies of Psychology*, I).

Burton's climatic theory of homosexuality. Note: "Homosexual" is a barbarously hybrid word, and I claim no responsibility for it.

A frequently used term for homosexual is 'deviate,' with the sense of 'gone astray' (Latin *de*, from, and *via*, road). Sir Simonds D'Ewes wrote about King James in 1625 (*The journals of all the parliaments during the reign of Queen Elizabeth*).

He had his vices and deviations.

Some derogatory and offensive vernacular words for homosexual are 'queer,' 'nancy,' 'nancy-boy,' 'fag,' 'fairy,' 'pansy,' and 'queen.' In this context the word 'queer' is a modern term, but the word is an old one; it comes from the Low German *queer* (across) and *quere* (obliquity). It is a cant word; with its modern meaning, 'queer' appeared in Dr. Rose Franzblau's column "Human Relations" in 1956.

. . . some girls said that I was queer and that she shouldn't be friendly with me.

A word used in England for homosexual that never made it to the United States is 'nancy' or 'nancy-boy.' Hugh Walpole, in 1933, wrote about one who wasn't (*Vanessa*).

But he isn't one of those, you know, not a bit nancy.

'Fag' has had several meanings. For example, it was another word for cigarette in the early twentieth century. There is a World War I song that goes ". . . while you've a lucifer [match] to light your fag . . ." By the nineteen thirties it was no longer used for a cigarette and had taken on the meaning of homosexual. Budd Schulberg wrote in 1941, in *What Makes Sammy Run:*

> He had the body of a wrestler and the face of a fag.

One suggestion as to the reason why 'fag' became a synonym for homosexual is that in the early part of the century men smoked pipes and cigars, and smoking cigarettes or 'fags' was considered unmanly. Another explanation goes back to the public schools in England (in America called private schools) where the term 'fag' was applied to the servant of the students at Oxford and Cambridge with the implication of sexual activity between student and servant.

'Fairy' has a respectable ancestry (Middle English *faerie, fairye*, enchantment) coming from the Late Latin *fata* (fairy) and the Latin *fata* (fate). It appeared with its modern meaning in F. Lonsdale's *Spring Cleaning* (II), 1925.

> MONA.   I say, what's the fairy's name?
> RICHARD.   Happily for the moment I have forgotten it.

Some authorities date 'pansy' from the 1930s but there seems to be no etymology which would explain its use as a synonym for homosexual. Its origin is in the Middle French *pensée* (thought), from Latin *pensare* (to weigh, think). Because there is no apparent clue in either of these roots, it may lie in the meaning of 'pansy' as a flower, conveying a sense of daintiness. The last in our series of synonyms for homosexual is 'queen,' again with no etymology for this special meaning.

'Sodomy,' 'buggery,' and 'pederasty' describe sexual intercourse between men. 'Sodomy,' an eponym from the infamous town of *Sodom* in the Bible, has been in use for hundreds of years. Here is an example from the *Cursor Manuscript*, c. 1300.

> Vnkindli sin and sodomite, Austin cals [calls] al suilk [such] delite, that es not tuix [between] womman and man.

Sir Peter Gretton quotes Sir Winston Churchill on the subject of 'sodomy' *(Former Naval Person)*.

> Don't talk to me about naval tradition. It's nothing but rum, sodomy, and the lash.

An abbreviated form of this sentiment is known as "rum, buggery, and the lash." Two naval catch-phrases from the nineteenth century in the same vein are

> Rum, bum, and bacca.

and

> Ashore it's wine, women, and song;
> Aboard it's rum, bum, and concertina.

Samuel Purchase defined the word in *Pilgrimage,* 1613, by the use of another of our words.

> They are addicted to sodomie or buggerie.

'Buggery' is a term used in law in England; it comes from the Middle Latin *bulgarus* (Bulgarian, a heretic, sodomite). The last of our words is 'pederasty,' which comes from Greek *pais* (boy, child) and *erastes* (lover). Purchase discussed this word also.

> He telleth of their paederastie, that they buy Boyes at an hundred or two hundred duckats, and mew [confine] them vp for their filthie lust.

6. The Female of the Species

The male-oriented, male-dominated nature of our society becomes apparent when we look at the words for women in their roles as participants in sexual activity. The words for men that we have discussed show them as active pursuers and dominators of women in their personal pursuit of sex, and as directors and managers in the activity of selling sex to other men. The words for women will show that they are objects, recipients of men's favors in one-to-one sex, subject to men's control in selling their own bodies to male buyers. Even the word 'female' is an accommodation to man. It comes from the Middle English *femele,* Old French *femelle,* and Latin *femella,* a diminutive of *femina* (woman), and its spelling was changed along the way to make it appear to be the other part of "male." 'Virgin' (Latin *virgo,*) when used in the sexual context, is today nearly always connected with women, but even that word was once used for men. Edward Webber wrote in 1590 (*The rare and most wonderfull things which E. Webber hath seene in his travails*).

> Before the sepulcher of Christ there is masse said euerie day, and
> none may say the masse there but a man that is a pure virgin.

The words for women engaged in conspicuous sexual activity
indicate that they might be divided into several categories. There
are those who have sexual relations for pleasure, not money, and
are promiscuous, not tied to one man. There are those who do it for
pleasure and/or reward, and who are restricted to one partner
only, at least for a certain period of time. There are those who do it
for money and/or reward, and who do not discriminate among
partners. There are those who arrange the sale of sex and also
manage the locale where it is sold. And finally there are those who
have relations with their own sex.

While there have undoubtedly always been women who have
been promiscuous and have distributed their sexual favors without
regard to payment, it is only very recently that words to describe
them have come into the language; words like 'jailbait,' 'tramp,'
'piece,' and 'broad' are among the more common ones.

'Promiscuous' (Latin *pro* and *miscere,* to mix) had for many years
the innocuous meaning of mixed. By 1865, when John McLennan
wrote *Primitive Marriage,* it had taken on a sexual connotation
(VIII).

> Promiscuity in the connexion of the sexes.

The *Dictionary of American Slang* (see Bibliography) explains 'jail
bait' as

> a sexually attractive girl who has not reached the legal age of
> consent.

The same source defines 'tramp':

> A promiscuous girl or woman, regardless of social class, marital
> status, or intelligence.

'Piece' is a harmless word from Late Latin *petium* (piece of land),
but a clue as to its modern meaning may be found in this line from
Robert Burton's *Anatomy* (I, 2).

> A waspish cholerick slut, a crazed peece.

When used in a sexual context, the word means 'piece of ass,'
according to the *Dictionary of American Slang.* Calder Willingham
used the word in a similar phrase with a similar meaning (*End as a
Man,* 1947).

> This kid . . . never had a piece of tail.

In Grose's *Dictionary*, 1796 and 1811, this definition of 'piece' appears.

> A wench. A damned good or bad piece; a girl who is more or less active and skilful in the amorous congress.

In another edition of his dictionary Grose lists 'tail.'

> Mother, how many tails have you in your cab? how many girls have you in your nanny house?

There was apparently a difference of opinion as to the meaning of the word 'broad' in the 1920s and 1930s. This is how the columnist Damon Runyon used it in 1932 (as quoted in the *Dictionary of American Slang*).

> He refers to Miss Perry as a broad, meaning no harm whatever, for this is the way many of the boys speak of the dolls.

But L. B. N. Gnaedinger, writing in the March 1926 issue of the *American Mercury*, gave the word not only a somewhat different meaning but an etymology as well.

> *Broad* is usually applied by New Yorkers to women who, it is hoped or believed, are of uncertain morals. It is derived from *bawd*.

The next four words describe the women in our second category. 'Concubine,' 'courtesan,' 'mistress,' and 'moll' usually designate those women who sell theselves to but one man, or a very selective few men at one time. The roots of 'concubine' point clearly to ity meaning; it is from two Latin words *con* (with) and *cubare* (to lie). Sir Thomas More tried to pinpoint the precise status of concubines in 1515 (*The history of kyng Richard the third unfinished*, II).

> As she wist her selfe to [too] simple to by hys wyfe, so thought she her selfe to good to be hys Concubine.

But William Broome distinguished between concubinage and another type of sexual activity.

> Adultery was punished with death by the ancient heathens; concubinage was permitted.

'Courtesan' (French *courtisane*, lady or waiting woman of the court, Italian *cortegiana* or *cortesana*, the feminine of *cortegiane*, courtier, all of which are derived from Italian *cortese.* courteous, and *corte,* court) may be called a high-class whore. That is how Abraham Fleming made this distinction in 1576 (*A panoplie of epistles*).

> His misdemeanours . . . with courtesans and common strumpets.

Edward Sharpham drew a similar distinction in 1607 (*The fleire,* D, ij).

> Your whore is for euery rascall, but your Curtizan is for your Courtier.

The word 'mistress,' whose most common meaning today is that of a sexual substitute for a wife or a girlfriend of a married man, also has honorable roots. The Middle English form was *maistresse,* from the same word in Old French meaning mistress of a household, dame, or lady. Stephen Hawes used it with an innocent meaning in *The pastime of pleasure* (XVIII) in 1509.

> You are my lady, you are my masteres [mistress],
> Whome I shall serve with all my gentylnes.

But by 1631, when John Donne published his *Sermons,* the word had taken on its new meaning, that of kept woman (LXIV).

> Those women, who the Kings were to take for their Wives, and not for Mistresses (which is but a later name for concubines) . . .

'Moll' is usually coupled with the word 'gangster,' in the writings of Damon Runyon and others in the 1920s and 1930s. It is, however, an old word, used as a synonym for 'doxy' in 1611 by Thomas Middleton and Thomas Dekker in *The Roaring Girle, or Moll Cut Purse.*

> OPENWORK. Doxy, moll, what's that?
> MOLL. His wench.

We have already seen that the language is very short of words for the male prostitute, either because there have not been very many, or because men refused to accept their existence and therefore did not invent words for them. This is not the case with women; we will examine no less than twenty words that men have created for our third category, the female prostitutes, women that sell sex for money.

The word 'prostitute' is from the Late Latin *prostituere* (to offer for sale, expose publicly), which comes from two other Latin words, *pro* (forth) and *statuere* (to place, set). Jehan Palsgrave used it as a verb in 1530 (*Lesclarcissement*).

> I prostytute, as a comen woman dothe her self in a bordell house, "je prostitue."

There has been a complete turnabout in meaning for the word 'harlot' from the time when Chaucer used it in the General Prologue to the Canterbury Tales (I) with its common Middle English meaning.

> He was a gentil harlot and a kynde;
> A bettre felawe shulde men noght fynde.

In Old French the word was *herlot* or *arlot* (vagabond, army or camp follower), derived from two Old High German words, *heri* or *hari* (army) and *lot* (loiterer). The Cornish language borrowed the English word unchanged, but gave it the meaning of rogue, and then came up with a new word, *harlutry* (corruption). In 1604 the word was still used in English to refer to men. Thomas Dekker wrote a play called *The Honest Whore* in 1604 in which he used it with the then common derogatory meaning of a rough fellow (act III, scene 3).

> . . . but for a Harlot to turne honest, is one of Hercules labours: It was more easie for him in one night to make fifty queanes, than to make one of them honest agen in fifty yeeres. . .

(Note that the phrase "to make" in the above citation means to create, that is, to pimp for, and not to have sex with, as it often does today. Also note that the word *quean* — to be discussed later — should not be confused with the 'queen' already described as another word for a male homosexual.) By 1930, when D. H. Lawrence wrote *Pornography and Obscenity,* there was no question as to the meaning of 'harlot.'

> If a woman hasn't got a tiny streak of a harlot in her, she's a dry stick as a rule.

'Whore,' spelled *hore* in 1530, is perhaps the most common term in this group. It is from the Icelandic *hora* (adulteress), the feminine form of *hori* (adulterer), a much narrower meaning than was common in England at the time. According to Skeat, the word may have come from Latin *carus* (dear, beloved) and, if so, originally meant merely "lover"; but as we have seen several times with other words, meanings do become severely distorted. (Anyway, *carus* and 'whore' have a common Indo-European root.) Even though the word was almost universally applied to women by the time of Shakespeare, he used it in *Troilus and Cressida* (act V, scene 1) for a man.

> THERSITES. Thou are thought to be Achilles' male Varlot.
> PATROCLUS. What's that?
> THERSITES. Why his masculine whore.

'Trollop' (Middle English *trolop, trallop*) is another of those words with two meanings that persisted side by side for many years. In 1742 Henry Fielding seems to be using the word in its modern connotation, that of 'whore' (*The history of the adventures of Joseph Andrews,* I, 8).

> That impudent trollop, who is with child by you.

But in 1887, when Augustus Jessop wrote *Arcady* (VII), it was still being used with the sense of an untidy or slovenly woman, just as it had been in early English.

> The husband of a dirty trollop who can neither cook nor sew.

Modern dictionaries define a 'tart' (which once was a term of endearment) as a prostitute or woman of loose morals. The *Oxford English Dictionary* says specifically that 'tart' was "applied [originally endearingly] to a girl or a woman of immoral character." The women reported on by the *Daily News* of February 5, 1894, described their activities euphemistically but with no hint of endearment.

> Some of the women described themselves as "Tarts" . . . and said that they got their living in the best way they could.

Skeat says the word 'baggage,' when it is used as a synonym for prostitute, is a peculiar use of the word which normally meant luggage. It was probably influenced by the French *bagasse,* which meant, according to Cotgrave,

> a baggage, quean, jyll, punke, flirt.

There is an Italian word, *bagascia* (worthless woman), from which its meaning of whore may have been derived. Skeat's conclusion is that the etymology is doubtful, but that it may be derived from the Old French *bague* (a bundle). Whatever its origin, its meaning was in no way doubtful in 1601, as seen in Robert Johnson's translation of G. Botero's *The worlde, or an historicall description of the most famous kingdomes and commonweales therein*.

> Every common soldior carrying with him his she-baggage.

'Quean' and 'queen' are very closely related; in Old English they were both spelled *cwen,* and both referred to either gender. As to the difference between the two words 'quean' and 'queen,' Skeat offers this.

> The best passage to illustrate this word is in *Piers Plowman* where the author says that in the grave all are alike; you cannot there tell a knight from a knave, or a "queen" from a "quean."

But the meaning of 'quean' is best illustrated in *The Times Whistle,* 1616.

> Flavia, because her meanes are somewhat scant,
> Doth sell her body to relieve her want,
> Yet scornes to be reputed as a quean.

'Jill,' or *jyll,* the third term given by Cotgrave above, had several forms, one of which was *gill,* an abbreviation of *Gillian* (a girl's name), from the feminine *Juliana* of the Roman *Julius* or *Julianus*. *Jilt* or *gilt* (the *g* in all these forms is pronounced like the *g* in "gem") were cant words in the midseventeenth century, meaning harlot or strumpet. Bishop White Kennett used one of the forms in 1683 (*Witt against wisdom, or a panegyrick upon folly [from Erasmus]*).

> He whose wife is a common jilt . . . and yet swears she is as chast as an untouch'd virgin.

Cotgrave's word number four, 'punk,' or *punke,* was a slang word which may have been imported from the German *punken-diek,* the name of a dike in Bremen with houses on it that were notorious for the activities that took place inside. In 1607 Thomas Middleton offered several synonyms for 'punk' (*Michaelmas Terme,* III, E).

> I may grace her with the name of a Curtizan, a Backslider, a Prostitution, or such a Toy, but when all comes to al tis but a plaine Pung.

Cotgrave's fifth term is 'flirt' whose etymology we have discussed earlier; it seems to be one word that has defied the deterioration of meaning that we have noticed in many other words. In 1600 Nicholas Breton used it as meaning a woman of loose character (*Pasquils' fooles-cappe*).

> Call'd a Foolish flirt . . .
> When all the world is witnesse to her shame.

Today, of course, its meaning is limited to one who trifles or toys with another's affections.

There are two versions offered for the origin of 'strumpet.' There was the Old French word *strupe* (concubinage), which came from Latin *stuprum* (immorality, violation, dishonor); the English language may have added an *m*, to make 'strumpet.' A second possibility is the Middle Dutch *strompe* or the Norwegian *strumpe,* both of which meant stumbling; therefore a 'strumpet' would be one who trips, or falls, or takes a false step. In any event, Steele preferred to call a spade a spade, in *Spectator #268.*

> An innocent Creature who would start at the Name of a Strumpet, may think it pretty to be called a Mistress.

Although originally having the meaning of a woman of slovenly appearance or habit, 'slut' came to the modern meaning of whore as early as 1580, when Nicholas Breton wrote *Flourish upon Fancie* (I).

> To haunt the Tauernes late . . . and swap eech slut vpon the lippes, that in the darke he meetes.

(While not specific, the implication is clear that the women who are found in taverns at night are whores.)

'Trull' is another word in the group. It is the feminine form of the German *Trolle* or *Trulle* allied to Middle Dutch *drol* (pleasant man, merry man, jester) and Icelandic *troll* (merry elf). 'Trull's' original sense, therefore, was merely that of a merry or droll companion. However, 'trulls' were anything but that, according to Robert Greene in 1592 (*A disputation betweene a hee conny-catcher and a she conny-catcher*).

> These common truls . . . walke abroad as stales [decoys] to draw men into hell.

'Doxy' was a cant term for mistress, paramour, or prostitute. Its origin is uncertain, but it is probably from Middle Dutch *docke* (doll). In 1530 the word was used in the play *Hyckescorner* (in *A selection of old plays,* edited by William C. Hazlitt and Robert Dodsley, I).

> Of the stews I am made controller . . .
> There shall no man play doccy there . . .
> Without they have leave of me.

'Harridan' (a possible variant of Middle French *haridelle*, a lean, ill-favored jade, that is, a worn-out horse) is of unknown origin; its meaning was crystal clear in this dictionary entry of 1700: "Harridan," one that is half Whore, half Bawd.

'Wench' (Middle English *wenche*) was a common word in early English without any pejorative sense; it meant simply a young girl. According to Skeat, "The orig. sense was simply 'infant,' without respect of sex, but, as the word also implies 'weak' or 'tender,' it was naturally soon restricted to the weaker sex." In 1377, however, the word also meant whore (William Langland, *Plowman*, B, XIX).

> Wenches of the stuwes.

Cyprus was famous in ancient times for the worship of Aphrodite or Venus, the goddess of love. From this island came the eponym 'Cyprian' meaning licentious or lewd. An issue of the *Saturday Review* of 1859 (VIII) deplored the presence of streetwalkers.

> The Cyprian patrol which occupies our streets in force every night.

A more recent synonym for whore is 'chippy,' meaning a flirtatious and promiscuous woman, also a young prostitute. Louis Armstrong used the word in his autobiography, *Satchmo, My Life in New Orleans.*

> Around the honky-tonks on Liberty and Perdido life was the same as in Storyville except the chippies were cheaper.

Another word in this category is 'floozie' or 'floozy,' a girl or woman of loose morals — perhaps a variant of the name Flossie, a nickname for Florence. Last in this group of synonyms for prostitute is the 'call girl,' one who is available only by appointment; she doesn't walk the streets.

Earlier in this chapter, in the section on whorehouses, we discussed the women of our fourth category, the 'madams,' who manage such houses; they are often aged prostitutes themselves who have graduated to management.

The fifth and last category comprises women who have sexual relations with their own sex. The most common term for such women has been and still is 'lesbian,' although it is gradually being replaced by 'homosexual' and 'gay.' 'Lesbian' is an eponym from the Isle of *Lesbos* off the coast of Greece. History tells us that the poet Sappho and her followers there engaged in homosexual practices, hence the word 'lesbian' came into being. Shortened forms for 'lesbian' are 'les' and 'lesbo.' In 1956 Joe E. Lewis sang at the Copacabana.

> John and Mary, John and Mary,
> Mary is a les and John is a fairy.

We have discussed earlier the word 'gay,' when talking about men. The *Sunday Times* of July 19, 1868, shows this usage, referring to a woman's immoral life.

> As soon as ever a woman has ostensibly lost her reputation, we, with a grim inappositeness, call her "gay."

A no longer popular synonym for 'lesbian' is 'Sapphist,' from *Sappho,* who was famous for the few love lyrics that have survived and which celebrate female homosexual love.

The female who takes on the male role in homosexual activity is called 'butch' or 'dike.' *The American Heritage Dictionary* defines 'butch' as

> *Slang.* A female homosexual with mannish or aggressive traits. [From *butch,* a haircut usually associated with young ruffians, from *Butch,* a pet name for a young boy.]

The San Francisco *News* of September 1, 1954, had this description of a 'butch.'

> Then some of the girls began wearing mannish clothing. They called themselves "Butches."

The *New Statesman* of March 26, 1965, further clarified the word.

> This rejection of the female role is very common among the "butch" type of lesbian.

The origin of 'dike,' or 'dyke,' is uncertain; it may have been derived from hermaphro*dite*.

7. Marriage or . . .

It is fitting now that we return to the heterosexual (Greek *heteros*, the other, different) relationship that is more likely to result in engagement, marriage, or other long-term shared living.

Let's talk first about an innovation in heterosexual relationships, a life-style that simulates marriage but without marriage's legal commitment. Such arrangements have, of course, existed in the past, but they have not been as widespread. They have been described with the word 'cohabitation' (Latin *co-*, *cum*, with, and *habitare*, to live), an old, formal word for living together without benefit of clergy or justice of the peace. The word was used by Sir Thomas More, as quoted in Samuel Fisher's *The testimony of truth exalted by the collected labours of S. Fisher* in 1530.

> He should . . . make it a matter of great conscience to cohabit with her, being not his lawfull wife.

'Common-law marriage' is a phrase which also describes such a relationship. Some current phrases which describe a relationship 'without benefit of clergy' are 'shacking up,' 'living together,' 'having an affair,' and 'meaningful relationship.'

'Shack' is probably from a Mexican word *jacal*, from the Aztec *xacalli* (wooden hut). A change in public attitude toward today's 'living together' (a literal translation of *cohabitation*) is exemplified by the following exchange. When asked if her daughter were married, a friend chose not to use the expression "to shack up with someone"; instead she said casually, "No, she is not married, but I have a sin-in-law." Although the phrase 'having an affair' has a modern ring to it, it goes back at least to 1702 when Sir Richard Steele wrote *The funeral, or grief a-la-mode, a comedy* (I).

> To marry a Woman after an Affair with her.

There are those couples, however, who are ready for a firm commitment to marriage. The first step in this procedure is to get 'engaged,' 'pledge' or 'plight' one's 'troth,' become 'betrothed,' 'publish the banns,' or become 'affianced.'

The use of the word 'engaged' to denote a mutual promise to marry is fairly recent; previously, as indicated by its origin (French *engager*, from *en*, in, and *gage*, pledge, plight), it was used to mean bound by a pledge to do some act or other. Dickens wrote a letter to a friend in 1859 (*Letters*, II).

> Much excited and pleased by your account of your daughter's engagement.

'Betroth' (Middle English *bitreuthien* — prefix *be* plus *treowthe* or *treuthe,* truth, troth) was in early use. In 1303 Robert Manning (*Handlyng*) wrote:

> Thou shal not betrouthe a womman with hande the whylys here [her] husbande ys lyvande.

It soon became shortened to 'troth' which was used with 'pledge' (Middle English *plegge,* hostage, Old French *plege,* surety, pledge) or with 'plight' (Middle English and Anglo-Saxon *pliht* or *pligt*). 'Pledge' appeared in Sheridan's *The Rivals* (act II, scene 1), in 1775.

> My vows are pledged to her.

The original meaning of 'plight' was danger, and we still use it in that sense. Over the years it underwent a gradation of meaning from danger to responsibility (for handling that danger) to concern or care. It is as a variant of these later meanings that it was used with 'troth' to mean a promise to wed. Here is Trevisa's use in 1398 (*Bartholomeus,* VI, 13).

> In contract of wedding [he] plighteth his trowith and obligeth hym selfe to lede his life with his wyfe and pay here dettes.

In order to allow for possible objections to a proposed marriage, the 'banns' (allied to Sanskrit *bhan,* to speak) were published (Latin *publicare,* to make public). *The Book of Common Prayer* described the procedure.

> Matrimony, the bannes must be asked three seueral Soondaies [Sundays].

'Affianced' — along with our modern words 'fiancé' and 'fiancée' — is from an Old French word *affier* (to trust in), which comes from the Latin *fidus* (faithful) and *fides* (trust, faith). Once the couple has decided to become engaged, monetary arrangements should be made expeditiously, according to a translation of John Perkins' *Profitable booke, treating of the lawes of England* (V), of 1528.

> Endowment ought to bee made immediately after affiance made betwixt them at the Church doore.

Now that the couple is engaged, a wedding is likely to follow soon. Until the day of the ceremony, the male participant in the wedding is still a 'bachelor' (Middle English *bacheler*). In 1755 Samuel Johnson proposed in his *Dictionary* (see Bibliography) that the word most probably came from two Latin words, *bacca* (berry) and *laurus* (bay tree). The idea behind this conclusion was that 'bachelors' were young and of good hope like the berries in the laurel. But most authorities hold that it is simply from Old French *bacheler*, from the Late Latin *baccalaris* or *baccalarius* (with many meanings, including farm servant); some evidence for this view may be seen in the *Cursor Manuscript.*

> He was a borli [burly] bachelere,
> In al that werld had he na pere [peer].

Although used today exclusively for males, 'bachelor' once applied to women as well; Ben Jonson wrote about one (*The magnetick lady, or humors reconcild*) in 1632.

> We do not trust your uncle; he would keep you a bachelor still, by keeping of your portion; and keep you not alone without a husband, but in a sickness.

Both Jonathan Swift and William Makepeace Thackeray extolled the life of a 'bachelor.' Swift wrote in 1738 (*A complete collection of genteel and ingenious conversation*).

> Bachelor's fare; bread and cheese and kisses.

Thackeray was even more explicit about the advantages of 'bachelorhood' (*The Newcomes*, II, 2).

> I can fancy nothing more cruel after a long lazy life of bachelorhood than to have to sit day after day with a dull handsome woman opposite.

'Old maid' and 'spinster' are probably the female equivalent of 'bachelor,' but these words are not used much today. They carry a negative connotation which is not apparent in the word 'bachelor.' 'Spinster' meant one who spins, as we have seen above. In the early seventeenth century, it became a legal term, according to John Minsheu (*The guide into tongues, etc.*), 1617.

> A Spinster, a terme, or an addition in our Common Law, onely added in Obligations, Euidences, and Writings, vnto maids vnmarried.

'Spinster' is defined in the *Oxford English Dictionary* as

> A woman still unmarried; especially one beyond the usual age for marriage, an old maid.

In a contemporary attempt to remedy the lack of an appropriate nonjudgmental term for the female equivalent of bachelor we use the phrase 'single woman,' and the adjectives 'single' (Middle English *sengle,* Latin *singulus* (single) or 'unmarried.'

During the period of the engagement, the betrothed ones prepare for the wedding. The bride puts the final touches on her 'trousseau' (which we discussed in Chapter IV) and, if the wedding is to be a formal church affair, the bride and groom select their attendants.

In other times, and even today in other cultures, the family of the bride must offer a 'dowry' (Middle English *dowary, dowrie,* Old French *douaire,* Late Latin *dotarium,* from Latin *dotare* , to endow) to the groom. In 1530 Palsgrave (*Lesclarcissement*) suggested that there was a way out of this requirement.

> She that is good an fayre nede none other dowrie.

The 'dowry' became the husband's property and was normally not returnable except in circumstances described by John Milton in 1644 in his translation of *The judgement of M. Bucer concerning divorce.*

> That the Husband wrongfully divorcing his Wife, should give back her dowry.

In addition to her dowry the wife might take along her 'paraphernalia' (Greek *para,* beside, and *pherne,* dowery); this was her personal property, so defined in the *Oxford English Dictionary.*

> Those articles of personal property which the law allows a married woman to keep and, to a certain extent, deal with on her own.

In a letter in *The autobiography and correspondence of Mrs. Mary Delany* (Series 11, II) of 1774 this point was emphasized.

> The law restored them to her as her own paraphanalia.

Once the preliminaries of planning are over and the day of the wedding is at hand, the participants assemble. The female attendants at a formal wedding are called 'maid of honor' (if single) and 'matron of honor' (if married) and 'bridesmaid'; the males are called 'usher' and 'best man.' The word 'maid' (Middle English *mayde*, a shortened form of *maiden-girl*, virgin) was once used for a man in the sense of male virgin, according to Trevisa in *Higden* (I).

> a preost that is clene mayde [maid].

By 1586, when Mary Herbert, Countess of Pembroke, wrote about a forthcoming wedding, theword was limited to females.

> Her maides of honor shall on her attend.

In 1794 William Eden Auckland used the modern form when he wrote to a correspondent (*Journal and correspondence*, III).

> It is proposed to one of your sisters to be bridesmaid at the royal marriage.

An 'usher' was once a doorkeeper at a church or public hall whose function was to show people to their seats and guard the door. The word's roots show this to be an appropriate meaning; it is from the Middle English *uschere* and Old French *ussier* or *huissier*, both of which are derived from the Latin *ostium* (door), the root of which is *os* (mouth). Its use to describe a member of a wedding party is quite recent. In an issue of *Outing,* an American magazine published in 1895, the following appears.

> He sent the lady a beautiful Colport cup and saucer, . . . at the same time breathing a prayer that Elliott would not ask him to be usher.

The phrase 'best man' may be of Scottish origin as indicated by Eliza Action in *St. Johnstoun* (III), 1823.

> The two bridegrooms entered, accompanied each by his friend, or best man, as this person is called in Scotland.

In the days when a man raided a town or family to seize a bride, he had assistance. Charles Darwin discussed this practice in the *Descent of Man* (II, 20), 1871.

> In our own marriages the best man seems originally to have been the chief abettor of the bridegroom in the act of capture.

'Groomsman' has been used for both 'usher' and 'best man.' In using the word with the meaning of attendants, Samuel Lysons shed a different light on a common current practice (*Claudia and Pudens*), 1861.

> Then came the ceremony of carrying the brides over the threshold by the groomsmen.

According to the March 2, 1889, issue of *John Bull,* the 'groomsman' was the equivalent of our 'best man.'

> The bridegroom was attended by his brother . . . as groomsman.

The principal participants in the wedding ceremony are, of course, the 'bride' and 'groom.' 'Bride' (Middle English *bryde, brude,* Anglo-Saxon *bryd*) refers today only to the female, but it was not always so. In his translation of a work of G. de S. Du Bartas, Josuah Sylvester wrote in 1598

> Sweet Daughter dear . . . Isis blesse thee and thy Bride, With golden fruit.

Whether the 'bride' be male or female, Chaucer had explicit directions for the wedding night.

> The nyght is come, the bryd shal go to bedde.

The 'bride' is frequently referred to as 'blushing' (Middle English *bluschen, blusshen,* to glow).

A 'groom' was originally a 'lad,' 'boy,' 'male child,' or 'servant-in-waiting.' Its origin is uncertain, but it seems to be from Old French *gromet* (servant, valet, groom). With the meaning of 'lad' it was used in *The lay of havelock the Dane,* c. 1300.

> Ich [I] am now no grom; Ich am wel waxen [grown].

The word appeared in John Bale's *The Vocacyon of J. B.,* 1553, with a meaning it still has today.

> An horse grome of his came unto my court one daye.

Shakespeare associated the word with the wedding ceremony in *Othello* (act II, scene 3).

> . . . Friends all but now, even now,
> In quarter, and in terms like bride and groom
> Devesting them for bed . . .

The meaning of the word 'bridegroom,' which did not appear in English until the sixteenth century, is not clear, but it probably meant a "bride-lad," that is, a young man who was a 'bride.' Miles Coverdale used the word in its modern sense in 1535 (*The second*

tome or volume of the Paraphrase of Erasmus upon the Newe Testament,
XVI).

> The daughters shal mourne, hauinge no brydegromes.

A newly married man or, more properly, a confirmed bachelor
who finally marries, is called a 'benedict,' an eponym based on a
character named Benedick in Shakespeare's *Much Ado about Nothing.* George P. R. James spoke in *Henry Masterton,* 1850, of one who
finally gave up the struggle and got married.

> Having abandoned all his old misogyny and his professions of
> single independence, Coelebs has become a benedick.

Frequently the participants in a wedding ceremony find themselves there because of the efforts of another, a 'matchmaker.' The
word 'match' is from Middle English *macche, mache* (companion,
mate) and Anglo-Saxon *moecca* (comrade, companion, spouse).
R. S. Surtees wrote of such a woman (*Ask Mamma,* IX) in 1858.

> As well try to restrain a cat from mousing as a woman from
> matchmaking.

Whether through the efforts of a 'matchmaker' or efforts of their
own, the couple is ready to participate in the 'wedding,' 'nuptials,'
'hymen,' or 'espousal,' or, put differently, is ready to be 'tied' or
'spliced.' The word 'wed' (Middle English *wedden,* Anglo-Saxon
weddian, to pledge, engage, and *wed,* a pledge) describes the legal
action of binding two people together in matrimony. The parson in
Thomas Killigrew's *The Parson's Wedding* (act IV, scene 1), 1663, has
an explosive answer to a question.

> If she be my wife Sir? I have wedded her and Bedded her, what
> other Ceremonies would you have?

'Nuptials' is a poetic word for 'wedding'; it is related to the word
'nubile' (Latin *nubilis,* from *nubere,* to marry), which means "being
of marriageable age." A related Latin word is *nupta* (bride). The
adjective 'nuptial' was used by Shakespeare in *A Midsummer Night's
Dream* (act I, scene 1).

> Now, fair Hippolyta, our nuptial hour
> Draws on apace.

'Nuptial' (Latin *nuptialis*) is still in use today, but 'hymen' as a
synonym for 'wedding' is not. It would be appropriate, for it comes

from *Hymen,* the Roman god of marriage. Philip Massinger used the word in 1624 (*Works, Renegado*) as just such a synonym.

> Owe we our thanks for gracing thus our hymen?

'Espousal' comes from the French word *épouser* (to marry), the Old French *espouser* (to marry) and *espouse* (spouse, wife). It ultimately traces back to Latin *sponsum* or *sponsa,* from the verb *spondere* (to promise), from which we get our word 'sponsor.' When 'espousal' first came into English, it retained the meaning of marriage. In 1622 Sir Francis Bacon wrote (*The historie of the raigne of king Henry the seventh*).

> The ambassador . . . put his leg . . . between the espousal sheets.

But by 1726 the meaning of the word had changed. John Ayliffe wrote (*Parergon juris canonici Anglicani*).

> I shall here . . . define Espousals to be a mutual Promise of a future Marriage.

'Tie,' used with the meaning of binding together in marriage, has, along with 'splice,' the ring of modern vernacular, if not actual slang. But 'tie' (Middle English *tyen, teyen*) was used in 1894 by Sir John D. Astley (*Fifty years of my life,* I).

> A comelier couple parson has seldom . . . tied up.

'Splice' (Middle Dutch *splissen,* to splice, and Dutch *splitsen,* to split — one had to split the ends of a rope before splicing them together) goes back even further than 'tie' when used with the same meaning. In 1830 John Galt wrote (*Lawrie Todd, or the settlers in the woods,* II).

> She ben't five-and-twenty — she'll make a heavenly splice!

By 1853 a distinction had been established between 'married' and 'spliced.' Charlotte Brontë drew it in *Villette* (XL).

> Alfred and I intended to be married in this way almost from the first; we never meant to be spliced in the humdrum way of other people.

Those who are wed are in a state of 'matrimony' or 'marriage.' The Latin word *mater* (mother) is the root of the Latin *matrimonium* (marriage), from which we get the word 'matrimony.' Oliver

Goldsmith reported on certain activities which have absorbed women for ages (*The Vicar of Wakefield*, II), 1766.

> Exhorting the married men to temperance, and the bachelors
> to matrimony.

Although we have noted the derivation of 'matrimony' as having a female base in *mater*, we can see further evidence of the dominance of the male in our society in the roots of the word 'marriage.' It is from the Middle English *marier* (to marry) and the Latin *maritare* (to give or take a woman in marriage). From the Latin *mas* (male), came *maritus* (husband — *mari* in modern French) and *marita*, which could be read as "provided with a husband," or "joined to a male."

There are a number of thoughts on 'marriage' which are worth sharing. Arthur Young was extraordinarily prescient; his conclusion, in 1767, reflects the thinking of many young people today (*Farmer's Letters to People*).

> Marriage will ever flourish, when there is no danger of children
> proving an incumbrance.

Mary Wollstonecraft wrote an odd description of seduction in *A Vindication of the Rights of Woman* (chapter 3), 1792.

> When a man seduces a woman, it should, I think, be termed a
> *left-handed* marriage.

William Congreve used a theatrical reference point in his discussion of marriage in 1693 (*The old bachelor*).

> Courtship to marriage, as a very witty prologue to a very dull Play.

In *The Devil's Dictionary* Ambrose Bierce offers a puzzle.

> Marriage: The state or condition of a community consisting of a
> master, a mistress, and two slaves, making in all, two.

In *Maxims for Revolutionists — Marriage*, 1903, Shaw wrote of the convenience of the married state.

> Marriage is popular because it combines the maximum of tempta-
> tion with the maximum of opportunity.

In 1670 John Ray told of some disadvantages (*Proverbs*).

> Who marrieth for love without money hath good nights and sorry
> days.

Being either single *or* married had its problems according to Burton (*Anatomy*) — paraphrasing what Socrates had said.

> One was never married, and that's his hell; another is, and that's his plague.

Waiting to get married until you are older poses some problems, said Thomas Nashe in 1589 (*The anatomie of absurditie,* I).

> . . . he that marrieth late marrieth euil . . .

But John Clark went a step further in 1639.

> It is good to marry late, or never.

Here are three contemporary thoughts on marriage. Helen Rowland offers an epigram.

> Love, the quest; marriage, the conquest; divorce, the inquest.

Cleveland Amory, like Lord Chesterfield, had advice for his sons.

> Today, he admits, he gave his sons just one piece of advice. "Never confuse 'I love you' with 'I want to marry you.'"

And finally, Jane Fonda expresses a view which some may consider cynical, but which, in view of the sharply rising divorce rate, seems to represent the view of an ever-growing number of Americans.

> God, for two people to be able to live together for the rest of their lives is almost unnatural.

Should the couple not stay together, but divorce and remarry, Oscar Wilde offers some reasons for the move in *The Picture of Dorian Gray,* 1891.

> When a woman marries again, it is because she detested her first husband. When a man marries again, it is because he adored his first wife. Women try their luck; men risk theirs.

A custom which still exists at weddings is the singing of the wedding song, the name for which is 'epithalamium' (Greek *epi,* at, upon, and *thalamos,* bridal chamber). Spenser wrote a poem call *Epithalamion* in 1595. The act which seals the vows uttered during the wedding ceremony is the 'kiss' (which we discussed earlier). An old proverb says:

> Kissing don't last; cookery do!

Most wedded couples wish they could spend on their 'honeymoon' the amount of time that is implied in the roots of the word. 'Honey' (Middle English *huni,* Anglo-Saxon *hunig*) may be allied to Greek *knekos* (yellow) and Sanskrit *kanaka* (gold); 'moon' (Middle English *mone,* Anglo-Saxon *mona*) is related to Sanskrit *mens* ('month,' 'moon' — giving us both words). The 'honeymoon' is, therefore, a "sweet month," and it was used this way by Charles Leslie in *The Snake in the Grass* in 1696.

> In their Haste, and their Honey-Month while they were New-fangl'd.

8. The Married Couple

Upon completion of the wedding, the two participants take on new sobriquets; they are henceforth to be called 'husband,' 'wife,' 'spouse,' 'mate,' 'yokemate,' and 'helpmeet.' 'Husband' (Middle English *husbonde,* Anglo-Saxon *husbonda*) is from the Icelandic *husbondi* (master of the house). Chaucer wrote of a persistent woman (General Prologue, I)

> Sche was a worthy woman al hire lyfe,
> Housebondes at chirche dore sche hadde fyfe.

John Heywood (*Prouerbes*) quotes an English proverb with tongue-in-cheek praise of a 'wife.'

> A good wife makth a good husbande, (they saie).

'Spouse' is used for either sex; the word is of the same family as 'espouse,' whose roots we have traced above. Here is a poetic proposal from c. 1430 (John Lydgate, *Miniature Poems*).

> To you, dere herte, my veray trouthe
> I plihte As to my spouse.

'Mate' (Low German and Dutch *maat,* companion) is allied to the Gothic *mat,* the base of *mats,* meat, and has the sense of "one who eats with you." As long ago as 1676, Gavriel Towerson warned men to stop acting like male chauvinists (*An explication of the decalogue*).

> Lest . . . men should think it enough to assume a mate . . . without any obligation upon themselves.

Charles Dudley Warner, in 1888, added his bit to those other men who complained about the matchmaking propensities of some women (*Their Pilgrimage*).

> Do women never think of anything but mating people who happen to be thrown together?

Nicholas Harpsfield wrote c. 1555 of one woman who was not very kind to her 'yokemate' (Middle English *yok*, Anglo-Saxon *geoc*, *ioc*) in *A treatise on the pretended divorce between Henry VIII and Catharine of Aragon*.

> [She] all to beat her yokemate with a washbutte.

Our last word in this group of names for marriage partners is 'helpmeet' (Middle English *helpen, holpan*, plus *mete*, to measure). The 'meet' part of the word means fitting or suitable, and the word 'helpmeet' was coined due to a mistaken notion of the phrase *an help meet* (help suitable for) in Genesis 2:18–20, where God decides to create companionship for Adam. (The passage refers to all kinds of animals and birds, not a mate.) In 1673 Dryden was still using the original form of the word (*Marriage a la Mode*, IV, 1).

> If ever woman was a help-meet for man, my Spouse is so.

But by 1722, when Daniel Defoe wrote *Religious Courtship*, he was using the new form and was at the same time preaching equality between the wedded pair (II, 1).

> A woman is to be a helpmate, and a man is to be the same.

Different cultures have produced several kinds of marital relationships over the years. 'Monogamy' (Greek *monos*, one, alone, solo, and *gamos*, marriage) describes a state of matrimony with but one husband and one wife. 'Bigamy' (Latin prefix *bi*, two) involves one of one sex married to two of the other sex at the same time. 'Polygamy' (Greek *poly*, many, much) carries this state a step further — one person married to several of the other sex at the same time. 'Polygyny' (Greek *gyne*, female) and 'polyandry' (Greek *andros*, man) are more specific, the former describes one man married to several women, while the latter is the opposite, one woman married to several men, and all simultaneously. Sir Henry J. S. Maine indicated that the Christian churches had caused confusion in the world of marriage with their concept of morality (*Lectures on the Early History of Institutions*), 1875.

The monogamy of the modern and western world is, in fact, the monogamy of the Romans, from which the license of divorce has been expelled by Christian morality.

Lord Byron offered this thought on 'polygamy' (*Don Juan,* VI, 12).

Polygamy may well be held in dread, not only as a sin, but as a bore.

William Cosmo Monkhouse (1840 – 1901) covered several states of matrimony in *Limericks*.

> There was an old party of Lyme,
> Who married three wives at one time.
> When asked, "Why the third?"
> He replied, "One's absurd,
> And Bigamy, sir, is a crime!"

Edward Clodd, on the other hand, pointed out the logical sequence of events leading to one of the above states of matrimony (*Myths and Dreams,* I, 6), 1885.

> The custom of female infanticide . . . rendering women scarce, led at once to polyandry.

Whatever form marriage may take, one possible end to it is 'divorce' (Old French *divorce,* Latin *divortium,* separation, divorce, from *divertere,* to turn away). To Langland (*Plowman,* B, II) divorce was a moral problem.

> Owre synne to suffre, as . . . deuorses.

In 1873 Will Carleton put a different face on the matter of divorce (*Betsey and I Are Out*).

> Draw up the papers, lawyer, and make 'em good and stout,
> For things are running crossways, and Betsey and I are out.

A way of life for those who can no longer live together as husband and wife but for various reasons do not wish to divorce, is 'separation' (Middle English *separaten,* from Latin *se,* apart, plus *parare* (to arrange, provide). The word 'separation' has been used with this meaning for a long time; witness Shakespeare's use in *Henry VIII* (act II, scene 1).

> . . . Did you not of late days hear
> A buzzing of a separation
> Between the king and Katharine?

Those who remain married may seek sexual adventures

elsewhere. The technical name for this kind of activity is 'conjugal infidelity' (Latin *conjugialis,* pertaining to marriage, from *con,* with, plus *jugum,* yoke; and Latin *in,* not, plus *fides,* trust, faith). The title of a book by "Catamore," published 1700, outlines the problems arising from such extramarital behavior: *Conjugium Languens; or, the Natural, Civil and Religious Mischiefs arising from conjugal infidelity and impunity.* A delightful word from years past for an unfaithful spouse may be found in Shakespeare's *The Winter's Tale* (act II, scene 1).

> ... that she's
> A bed-swerver, even as bad as those
> That vulgars give bold'st titles.

Another word for this kind of behavior is 'adultery' (Latin *adulterare,* to commit adultery, corrupt, falsify, from *ad* plus *alterare,* to change). Arthur Hugh Clough (1819–61) saw no point in the practice of adultery (*The Latest Decalogue*).

> Do not adultery commit;
> Advantage rarely comes of it.

H. L. Mencken had his view of adultery in 1920 (*A Book of Burlesques*).

> It is
> Democracy applied to love.

For the wife who is deceived by her husband, there is sympathy and understanding; for the husband who is deceived by his wife, there is an opprobrious term, 'cuckold' (Middle English *kokewold, cokold, cokewolde,* all of which come from the Middle French *coucou* and the Latin *cuculus,* cuckoo bird, perhaps from the bird's habit of laying its eggs in another bird's nest). A translation of the *Gesta Romanorum* (XCII), 1440, defines a 'cuckold' and uses a euphemism in the process.

> Thy false monke hathe a-way my wife, and made me a Cokewolde.

A more reprehensible type of sexual activity is 'incest' (Middle English *incest,* French *inceste,* from Latin *in,* not, plus *castus,* pure, chaste) — sexual relations between persons too closely related to be legally married. A fifteenth-century publication describes the limits of kinship for marriage and uses another interesting euphemism for intercourse (*Jacob's well, an english treatise on the cleansing of man's conscience*), c. 1440.

> Neyther may be weddyd to otheres kyn, in-to the fyfte degre, ne medle wyth hem; for this bei don, it is incest.

9. Children, Legal and Otherwise

The purpose of marriage is to bring forth children; at least that is what the Bible and many writers have said over the centuries. Two words which mean bring forth or 'create' children are 'procreation' and 'propagation.' 'Procreation' (from Latin *pro* and *creare*, to create) had an additional purpose in the eyes of Thomas De Hoccleve c. 1412 (*The regement of princes*).

> Procreacioun Of children is, vn-to goddes honour.

Using the other word, 'propagation' (from Latin *propagare*, to attend, produce), Thomas Nabbes, in 1640, put child production on a more mundane level (*The bride, a comedy,* act I, scene 1).

> T'increase and propagate was the best end of marriage.

In order to have children, a woman must be 'fertile' (Latin *fertilis,* fruitful). However, as James Matthews Duncan pointed out in 1889, she cannot be 'fertile' with a 'sterile' (Latin *sterilis,* barren) partner (*Clinical Lectures on the Diseases of Women,* XXVI).

> A woman may be sterile with this man and fecund with another.

The word 'fecund' is from Middle English *fecounde,* Old French *fecondite,* and Latin *fecundus* (fruitful). In a translation of a sermon of Hugh Latimer a fruitful father is described in 1537 (*2nd sermon before convocation,* I).

> He was so fecund a father, and had gotten so many children.

If the man and woman are both 'fertile,' the chances are good that the woman will 'conceive' (Middle English *conceiven, conceuen,* from Latin *concipere,* namely, *con,* with, and *capere* (to seize, hold). Having conceived, the woman is 'pregnant' (from Latin *prae,* before, and *gnare,* to bear) or, to use a more elegant word of the past, 'enceinte' (a French word taken over into English with no change in spelling). 'Pregnant' was defined by John Florio (*Dictionary*), 1598.

Pregnanza, greatnes with child, pregnancie, a being great with childe or with yoong.

John Milton described one inevitable consequence of pregnancy in 1667 (*Paradise Lost,* II).

My womb,
Pregnant by thee, and now excessive grown.

The word 'enceinte' is from the Latin *incinctus* (girded), and the sense seems to be of pressure against the waist or girdle. Not all women show their pregnancy like the one mentioned by Milton; to provide for such an eventuality, a provision was inserted in the *Will of G. Taylard,* 1599.

Yf my wife be pryvyment insented wt a manchilde.

Sir Henry Finch elaborated on the phrase *pryvyment insented* in 1613 (*Law, or, a discourse thereof, in foure bookes*).

His wife priuement inseint (that is, so with childe as it is not discerned).

Once pregnant, there is a waiting period, the period of 'gestation' (Latin *gestare,* to bear, carry), which lasts about nine months. The ancients used the moon for measurement, as Helkiah Crooke pointed out in 1615 *(A description of the body of man).*

You shall reconcile Hippocrates to himselfe, if you say, that the end of the tenth moneth is the absolute and longest limit of gestation.

A common term for the end of the gestation period is 'confinement' (French *confiner,* to confine, bind up, from Latin *cum,* with, and *finis,* end, boundary), the time of childbirth. At this time, a woman may be described as nearing 'parturition' (from Latin *parturire,* to give birth, be ready to produce, from *parere,* to appear, related to our 'parent'). Sir Thomas Browne discussed the requirements for 'parturition' in 1646 (*Pseudodoxia epidemica or enquiries into very many received tenents*).

The conformation of parts is necessarily required . . . also unto the parturition or very birth it selfe.

The phrase 'lying-in' appeared as early as 1440 (*Promptorium*).

Lyynge yn, of chylde bedde, . . .

'Birth' (Middle English *birthe,* Anglo-Saxon *beran,* to bear, allied to

Sanskrit *bhrtis,* nourishment) is a very old word, used in the *Cursor Manuscript.*

> Quen Anna was cummen to time of birth . . . .

Immediately prior to birth a woman goes into 'labor' (Middle English *labour,* Latin *labor,* toil or 'travail' — *travail,* labor). In his *Epithalamium,* Spenser spoke of 'labor.'

> Sith of wemen's labours thou hast charge,
> And generation goodly dost enlarge.

An all too common result of 'travail' is tragedy, as in Robert of Gloucester's *Metrical Chronicle* of 1297.

> Vor in travail of his beringe is [his] moder [mother] was verst [first] ded.

An incredibly long 'travail' (with an interesting spelling) is described in "Queen Jeanie" in *Child's Ballads,* VII).

> Queen Jeanie travel'd six weeks and more,
> Till women and midwives had quite gi'en her o'er.

A 'birth' with a happy outcome was described in 1530 by Lord Berners *(History).*

> Florence was brought a bed, and had a fayre sonne.

A birth with results not entirely satisfactory to the father was reported in 1620 in John Pyper's translation of Honoré d'Urfé's *History of Astrea* (I, 6).

> His wife lay downe, but it was of a daughter.

For most women in the confinement period the moment of birth, the 'delivery,' reflects their feelings as indicated by the root of the word; it is from the Latin *deliberare,* to 'deliberate,' but with the later meaning "to set free."

Originally the only assistant at childbirth was the 'midwife.' The *mid* of 'midwife' has nothing to do with "middle"; it is from the Anglo-Saxon and Middle English *mid* which meant simply "with." The general sense of the word 'midwife' is one who is with the woman in labor, assisting her in her delivery. In 1303 there were no doctors at a birth, only midwives (Robert Manning, *Handlyng.*)

> The prest askede the mydwyffe, if hyt were cristenede whan hyt hade lyffe.

All through the nineteenth century, the doctors and teachers in medical schools concerned with birth were connected with the term 'midwifery.' John A. McCulloch wrote of such professors in 1845 (*A descriptive and statistical account of the British empire*, II).

> The professors of Pathology . . . Midwifery, and Clinical Medicine, receive no fixed salaries.

Oliver Wendell Holmes wrote, in 1883, of doctors who specialized (*Medical Essays*).

> A general practitioner, in large midwifery practice.

The word 'obstetric' is from the Latin *obstetrix* (midwife), made up of the two Latin words *ob* (near, beside) and *stare* (to stand). It means one who stands near or beside the woman in labor. The term was used around 1645 by James Howell but had to be explained (*Epistolae Ho-Elianae: familiar letters domestic and forren*, III, 9).

> He doth the obstetritious Office of a Midwife.

In 1819 the two words still had to be associated (*The Pantalogia; comprehending a complete series of essays, treatises and systems alphabetically arranged; with a general dictionary of arts, sciences, and words*).

> "Obstetrics," the doctrines or practice of midwifery . . . Employed in a larger signification than midwifery in its usual sense.

And in 1828 Ryan was apologizing for the use of 'obstetrician.'

> It may be necessary to say a few words apologetic, for my adoption of the word obstetrician.

By 1867 a new discipline of medicine was being established, that of 'gynecology' (Greek *gyne*, woman). Here is a definition written in that year *(Publications of the New Sydenham Society. A biennial retrospect of medicine, surgery and their allied sciences)*.

> Gynecology; embracing the Physiology and Pathology of the non-pregnant state.

By combining the Greek words for woman *(gyne)* and man *(andros)*, a strange word was created in 1684 by Increase Mather (*The Academy*, February 3).

> Gynecandrical Dancing, or that which is commonly called Mixt or Promiscuous Dancing of Men and Women together.

'Abortion' (from Latin *aboriri,* to fail, miscarry) and 'miscarriage' (from Latin *mis,* wrong, and English "to carry" — which is derived from Latin *carrus,* cart) used to be virtual synonyms, both words signifying the failure of a woman to carry to full term and have a live baby. They were used interchangeably by John Arbuthnot and Alexander Pope but given a twist that could come only from a man secure in a man's world (*Memoirs of Martinus Scriblerus*) c. 1714.

> His wife miscarried; but as the abortion proved only a female foetus, he comforted himself.

The live products of a womb are called 'offspring' (from Middle English *springen,* Anglo-Saxon *springan*). Those that are born to a legally married couple are 'legitimate' (from Latin *lex,* law). Depending on their ages and sex, 'offspring' are called 'baby,' 'infant,' 'child,' 'son,' 'daughter,' 'boy,' 'girl,' and 'bairn.' 'Baby' is a diminutive of 'babe' (Middle English *babe, bab, baban,* probably formed from the sound *ba* that an infant makes). Gower in *Confessio* (I) used the original form in

> How this babe all bloody cried . . .

and a plural of the diminutive in

> The yonge babies crieden alle.

In 1533 the plural was given a different spelling in John Bellenden's translation of Livy's *History of Rome* (V).

> We bere na armoure agains babbyis.

By Shakespeare's time, the modern form was established (*The Winter's Tale,* act II, scene 1).

> You'll kiss me hard, and speak to me as if I were a baby still — I love you better.

'Infant' has an appropriate root, it is from the Latin 'in' (not) and 'fans' (speaking).

'Child' (Middle English *cild, child,* allied to Gothic *kilthei,* the womb) has no sex connotation today, but it used to mean a female child. Even as late as 1876 we still find, regionally (*Notes and Queries,* April 26),

> A country woman [in Shropshire] said to me, apropos of a baby, "Is it a lad or a child?"

Shakespeare used it in the same way (*The Winter's Tale*, act III, scene 3).

> Mercy on's, a barne; a very pretty barne! A boy or a child, I wonder?

But "Childe Harold to the dark tower came," in Byron's *Childe Harold's Pilgrimage*, 1812.

'Son' comes from Middle English *sone* (with two syllables) from Anglo-Saxon *sunu*, and is allied to Sanskrit *sunu* (son) from the root verb *su* (to beget, bring forth, bear). 'Daughter' had many different spellings in its time; it is from Middle English *doghter, doughter*, Anglo-Saxon *dohtor*. Here are two other spellings from *Wells Wills*, 1531.

> To my dahtorrs a kow.

And

> To their eldest dafters.

By 1539, when Cranmer translated the Bible, the modern spelling was used (Matthew 9:18).

> My daughter is even now diseased [deceased].

The origin of 'boy' is obscure. It was used at one time in a derogatory sense, due to its being allied to Dutch *boef* (knave, villain) and Icelandic *bofi* (knave, rogue). 'Girl' was formerly used for either sex; this citation from 1290 spelled it *gurles*, which meant both boys and girls.

> And suche gret [great] prece [press] of gurles and men; comen hire al-a-boute.

In 1546 it was restricted to females in Heywood's *Prouerbes*.

> The boy thy husband, and thou the girle, his wife.

The word 'barne,' or 'bairn,' used by Shakespeare above for a child or a baby, is still in use in some parts of England. Abraham de la Pryme spelled it differently in his *Diary* in 1687.

> No one scarce believes that she [the queen] is realy with barn.

And as late as 1867, Edward A. Freeman wrote in *The history of the Norman Conquest*, I, 6).

> Harthacnut too . . . was at least a kingly bairn.

We come now to those children born out of wedlock, today called 'illegitimate' (from Latin *in,* not, and *lex,* law). We will look first at some of the words used in prior times to describe these children. In the seventeenth century, the expressions 'natural' child and 'by-blow' were synonymous. Philip Massinger wrote of one in 1632 (*The maid of honour (A tragi-comedy),* act I, scene 1).

> The natural brother of the king — a by-blow.

A poetic term for 'illegitimate' children is 'babe of love,' or 'love child.' George Crabbe described one in 1807 (*The Parish Register,* I).

> Recorded next a Babe of love, I trace,
> Of many loves, the Mother's fresh disgrace!

The last two words in this group are 'bantling' and 'bastard.' 'Bantling' is from the German *bankling* (an illegitimate child), where *bank* means "bench." A child conceived on a bench rather than in the marriage bed was called therefore a 'bantling.' Washington Irving used the word in *Knickerbocker's History of New York* (48), 1809.

> A tender virgin, accidentally and unaccountably enriched with a bantling.

The etymology of the word 'bastard' is much disputed. One theory has it that it came from the Late Latin *bastum* (pack-saddle) and therefore meant a child conceived on a saddle. The French have the phrase *fils de bast,* meaning a nobleman's illegitimate but ac-knowledged son, or — according to that theory, a "pack-saddle son." In 1951 Truman Capote played on the word in delightful fashion.

> Big Eddie Stover was legally born a bastard; the other two [men] made the grade on their own.

The Hebrew word for 'bastard' is 'mamzer', currently in vogue as a slang word for a detestable person. The word was taken over into Late Latin and appeared in the Vulgate translation of the Bible with the meaning of 'illegitimate' (Deuteronomy, XXIII). In 1562 Ninian Winzet wrote about 'mamzers' in *Certain Tractates, etc.* (Works, I).

> Thair suld nocht be sa mony ... scabbit [scabby] Moabites, Amonities, and sclanderous Mamzeres ... maid [made] preistis.

We have defined, dated, and discussed a large number of words dealing with young love, attraction and wooing, sex in thought and action, men and women involved in sexual activity, engagement, and marriage, and the conception and birth of children. We have made no judgments and drawn no conclusions; we have sought for no moral; we have tried only to describe. Perhaps all of us would wish to keep throughout our lives the kind of love described by John Dryden in this stanza from *Tyrannic Love*, 1669.

> Ah, how sweet it is to love,
> Ah, how gay is young desire!
> And what pleasing pains we prove
> When we first approach Love's fire.
> > Pains of Love be sweeter far
> > Than all other pleasures are.

ALL THE WORDS ON STAGE

What juggling was there upon the boardes!
What thrusting of knyves through many a nose!
What bearynge of formes! what holding of swordes!
What puttynge of botkyns throughe legge and hose!
Thomas Ingeland

"All the world's a stage," wrote Shakespeare (*As You Like It,* act II, scene 7), but according to Richard Edwards, 1567, the idea was not original with him (*The excellent comedie of two the most faithfullest friends, Damon and Pithias*).

Pythagoras said, that this world was like a stage
Whereon many play their parts.

There seems to be something special about the stage, something that excites, alarms, enchants, amuses, and, sad to say, sometimes bores us. How does one define 'show' in a way to capture that elusive essence that draws us to the theater? A hit song from *Annie Get Your Gun* manages to do this very well. "There's No Business like Show Business" was a show stopper and still stirs the adrenalin no matter how many times one hears it. An early use of 'show' (Middle English *schewe*) is found in *A survey of London* by John Stow, in 1598.

Two publique houses for the acting and shewe of Comedies, Tragedies, and Histories.

An older word for a place where 'shows' (mostly with music) were presented is 'odeum' or 'odeon' (Latin *odeum*, Greek *odeion*, music hall, from Greek *ode*, song, 'ode'). An item in the *London Gazette* of 1682, #1726, referred to such a place.

> To this succeeded a Suit of Vocal and Instrumental Musick from the Odeum or Musick Gallery.

Today we go to the 'theater' to see an assortment of presentations, including plays, opera, ballet, burlesque, and others. We shall examine each of them later on in this chapter. The word 'theater' (Middle English *teatre,* French *theatre*) is from the Latin *theatrum* and Greek *theatron* (a place for *seeing* shows). By contrast, the word for the *people* in the 'theater,' the 'audience,' indicates the 'theater' is a place for *hearing* shows, since the word 'audience' is from Latin *audientia* (attention, hearing) and *audire* (to hear). The news summaries of December 31, 1952, quoted Tallulah Bankhead on the subject of audiences.

> If you really want to help the American theater, don't be an actress, darling, be an audience.

In 1577 John Northbrooke had thoughts about the theater (*A treatise wherein dicing, dauncing etc. are reproved*).

> Those places . . . which are made vp and builded for suche Plaies and Enterludes, as the Theatre and Curtaine is.

The theater was not a socially acceptable place in 1633, according to William Prynne (*Histrio-mastix; the Players scourge or actors tragedie*).

> It hath evermore been the notorious badge of prostituted strumpets and the lewdest Harlots, to ramble abroad to plays, to Playhouses; whither no honest, chaste or sober Girls or Women, but only branded whores and infamous Adulteresses, did usually resort in ancient times.

(Unfortunately for Mr. Prynne, Queen Henrietta Maria was taking part in the rehearsal of a ballet at the time, and this statment was construed as an attack upon her. Prynne was imprisoned, fined, and pilloried, lost both his ears, was deprived of his Oxford degree and forbidden to practice his profession. He was in disgrace for eight years, but at the meeting of the Long Parliament in 1640 he was reinstated as a citizen with full rights and voted reparations which were paid by his former persecutors.)

As we approach the theater, we see displayed on the 'marquee,' a roof-like structure projecting over an entrance of a theater or other building, the name of the attraction now showing along with the names of the performers. The word 'marquee' is from the French *marquise* (tent). Because of its ending with the sound of z it appeared to the English to be a plural, so they made the word into an English singular by changing the *se* to *ee*.

In order to gain admittance to the performance, one must buy a 'ticket' (Middle French *etiquet*, little note, bill, ticket; *etiquet* is the masculine form of *etiquette*, ticket, and comes from the German *stecken*, to stick, put, fix, set). It originally had the meaning of a notice stuck up on the wall or gate of a court of justice, signifying the seizure of an inheritance or any other matter which was of legal concern. The following notice appeared in *The Register of the Privy Council* of *Scotland* (I) in 1567.

> At the occasioun of sum tikketis affixt on the Tolbuyth dur [door] of Edinburgh, be [by] his letter sent to hir Majestie, [he] had desyrit James Erll Bothwell, and certaine specifiit in the saidis tikketis, to be apprehendit.

By 1845 the word had taken on one of its current meanings, a piece of paper authorizing admission to a show. Thomas Hood wrote in *Double Knock*

> Sure he has brought me tickets for the play.

We have already looked at the origin of the word 'usher.' He originally had charge of a door and merely admitted people to the hall. John Gower (*Confessio*) spoke of an 'usher.'

> That dore can noon [no] ussher shette.

By the midnineteenth century, an 'usher' had taken on the responsibility of conducting people to their seats. Dickens wrote of an 'usher' in a letter on January 3, 1868, but the word must have just begun to be used with this new meaning, and so Dickens felt the need to define it.

> He met one of the "ushers" (who show people to their seats) coming in with Kelly.

The 'usher' is likely to hand you a 'program' as he (or more likely she) leads you to your seat. The word is from French *programme*, Latin *programma*, and Greek *programma* (public notice in writing), from Greek *pro* (before, publicly) and *graphein* (to write). The 'program' was originally designed as a prospectus for coming events; in an 1823 issue of *New Monthly Magazine* (VII, 2) the following appeared.

> Anticipating the amusement of the month, by a regular program (that is a nice new word imported from France, to supply the hacknied common-place of a "bill of the play") — a regular program, I say, on the second page of your coloured cover.

Today, of course, the 'program' lists the specifics about the event you are to witness that very day, along with comments about the theatrical world, biographies of the performers, and invitations from the advertisers to buy their products. As we walk down the aisle to our seats, we see the various parts of the interior of the theater, the 'auditorium,' the 'parquet,' the 'orchestra,' the 'balcony,' the 'mezzanine,' the 'gallery,' the 'boxes,' and the 'loges.' The 'audience' is seated in the 'auditorium,' a word from the same roots, but it may not necessarily be attentive according to Thomas Moore in *Lalla Rookh, an oriental romance (The veiled prophet of Khorassan, Paradise and the peri, The fire-worshippers, Nourmahal)* of 1817.

> He here looked round, and discovered that most of his audience were asleep.

Ephraim Chambers defined 'auditorium' in his *Cyclopaedia; or an universal dictionary,* 1717 – 51, in a different setting.

> Auditory, auditorium . . . was that part of the church where the "audientes" stood to hear, and be instructed.

By the end of the nineteenth century, the word had taken on its current meaning, the hall in the building where the performance takes place. The *Daily News* of September 12, 1881, had this item.

> Every part of the auditorium, the boxes, the upper circle, and gallery.

The word 'orchestra' (Latin and Greek *orchestra,* literally a "place for dancing") referred in ancient times to two places: one, where the chorus sang and danced, and two, where the musicians sat and played. The latter usage was still current in 1724 as evidenced in this definition from *A short explication of such foreign words as are made use of in musick books.*

> "Orchestra," is that Part of the Theatre, where the Musicians sit with their instruments to perform.

At about the same time, in 1720, John Gay used the word to refer to the group of players of the instruments (*To W. Pultency, from Poems on several occasions*).

> But hark! the full orchestra strike the strings.

In 1880 Vernon Lee (Violet Page) described what then was, and still would be, an unusual sight in Italy (*Studies of the eighteenth century in Italy*, III, 2).

> The singular effect produced by the sight of an orchestra entirely composed of women.

We still retain this meaning for the word, and we have expanded it, to include the main floor of the hall. There was another word in the nineteenth century for the main floor of the hall, the 'parquet' (French *parquet,* a wooden floor — a meaning it still has today), from French *parc* (park, hence small enclosure). The *Oxford English Dictionary* (see Bibliography) defines 'parquet' as "Part of the auditorium of a theatre, the front part of the ground-floor nearest the orchestra, or sometimes the whole of it." Washington Irving was lyrical in his description of a 'parquet' in 1848 (*Life and letters,* IV).

> Ladies . . . with their gay dresses, make what is the parquette in other theatres look like a bed of roses.

In many theaters, depending upon their size, there may be one or two balconies above the main floor. The front part of the first balcony is generally referred to as the 'mezzanine' (French *mezzanine,* Italian *mezzanino,* a diminutive of *mezzano,* middle, and all derived from Latin *medius,* median, middle). The original meaning of 'mezzanine,' however, was quite opposite. It was a floor beneath the stage, so-called because it was halfway between the basement and the stage, from which the short scenes and traps were worked. George Augustus Sala described it in 1859 (*Gaslight and Daylight,* II).

> Work underneath the stage, on the umbrageous mezzonine floor.

In *Chester Forgets Himself* P. G. Wodehouse (1881 – 1975) used the word with humorous effect to describe what we call today a beer-belly.

> The lunches of fifty-seven years had caused his chest to slip down to the mezzanine floor.

Above and behind the mezzanine is the 'balcony' (Italian *balcone*, outjutting, possibly derived from Middle German *balcho* or *palcho*, scaffold). Until about 1825, the pronunciation of the word followed the Italian with the emphasis on the second syllable, "bal-*co*-ny."

'Gallery' may refer to the highest part of the 'balcony,' if there is only one, or it may denote the second 'balcony' or merely its highest part. It may also describe a narrow band of seats all around the theater at the level of either 'balcony.' The word is from Old French *gallerie, galerie* ("long roome to walk in" — Cotgrave) and from Late Latin *galeria* (gallery, portico). The origin of the word is uncertain, although it has been suggested that it comes from the Greek *kalon* (wood, timber).

Today that highest section of the topmost balcony is often referred to as the 'peanut gallery.' It may have been Dickens who provided the inspiration for this phrase in 1839 in *The Life and Adventures of Nicholas Nickleby*, XXIV). He wrote:

> The people were cracking nuts in the gallery.

On either side of the main floor or orchestra there are often small enclosures called either 'boxes' or 'loges.' 'Loge' (Middle English *lodge*) had the meaning of a booth or stall in the mideighteenth century. Lord Chesterfield wrote of such enclosures in a letter dated April 25, 1749, indicating their foreign origin. It is interesting to note in this citation that all words are now Anglicized and are part of our standard vocabulary.

> The several "loges" are to be shops for toys, "limonades," "glacés," and other "raffraichissements."

The other word for these small enclosures in the theater is 'box' (Middle English *box*, Anglo-Saxon *box*, Late Latin *buxis*, Latin *buxum*, anything made of boxwood, and Latin *buxus*, box-tree, all from Greek *puxos*, box-tree). In *The City-Madame, a comedie*, by William Massinger, the host's party has been to the theater in

> The private box ta'en up at a new play
> For me and my retinue.

A common synonym for stage in centuries past was 'boards' (Middle English *bord*, table, Anglo-Saxon *bord*, board). Thomas Ingeland described some of the activities that went on across the boards in 1560 (quoted by Joseph A. Strutt in *The Sports and Pastimes of the People of England,* 1801).

> What juggling was there upon the boardes!
> What thrusting of knyves through many a nose!
> What bearynge of formes! what holding of swordes!
> What puttynge of botkyns throughe legge and hose!

James Boswell quoted the famous actor David Garrick as critic of another actor (*Life of Johnson*).

> The most vulgar ruffian that ever went upon the boards.

Our main word for the area where the action takes place is the 'stage' (Middle English *stage,* Old French *estage,* story of a house, stage, loft, Italian *staggio,* a prop, all allied to Latin *stare* to stand). Richard Eden equated 'stage' with 'theater' in his translation of *A Treatyse of the Newe India,* 1553.

> The Romaynes ... were wont to put them [Rhinoceros and Elephants] together vpon the theatre or stage for a spectacle.

The 'stage' was not only the place where actors performed; it was also a place for certain people to sit during the performance. Ben Jonson set the scene, in 1626 (*The staple of newes*); his comments on why some people go to the theater are still pertinent today.

> MIRTH. Pray you help us to some stools here.
> PROLOGUE. Where, on the stage, ladies?
> MIRTH. Yes, on the stage; we are persons of quality, I assure you, and women of-fashion, and come to see and be seen.

The 'proscenium' (Greek *proskenion*) was, in ancient times, the place where the action took place, the 'stage' itself. Today it means a different location; it now refers to the space between the arch or framework which holds the curtain and the orchestra pit. The modern meaning is made clear in this note from *The Director; a weekly literary journal* (I), 1807.

> This equivocal proscenium, as it were, dove-tails the house with the stage.

The signal that the show is about to begin is the raising of the 'curtain' (Middle English *cortin, curtin,* Old French *cortine, curtine,* Late Latin *cortina,* small court, small enclosures, croft, rampart, or 'curtain' of a castle, from Latin *cors,* court). In 1709 Sir Richard Steele wrote in the *Tatler,* #193.

> I have . . . been bred up behind the Curtain, and been a Prompter
> from the time of the Restoration.

With the rising of the 'curtain' we see the stage and the 'scenery'
(from Latin *scaena,* Greek *skene,* tent, stage, scene, sheltered place).
The word 'scene' is also used to denote a portion of an act. In 1682
Sir George Wheler used the word 'scene' to mean the stage itself (*A
journey into Greece,* V).

> The scene is oblong, jetting out six Paces more forward in the Front
> than the Seats of the Spectators.

Almost one hundred years previously, however, Thomas Kyd had
used 'scene' with an entirely different meaning; in 1592 he equated
'scene' with performance (*The Spanish Tragedie,* act IV, scene 4).

> To die for a day for fashioning our Scene . . .
> And in a minute starting vp againe,
> Reuiue to please too morrowes audience.

Before electricity, the stage was lighted up with lanterns for
footlights, and the spotlight was created by heating lime in an
oxyhydrogen flame. The actor who was to make an important
speech moved to the spot where the light from the burning lime
shone so that he could be seen more easily. Thus today we still say of
one in the public eye that he is in the 'limelight.' A comparison was
made by John Tyndall in 1860 (*The Glaciers of the Alps,* VI).

> The naked eye can detect no difference in brightness between the
> electric light and the lime light.

We have set the physical scene for a performance, but before any
kind of show can begin, several functions are involved: money-
raising, producing, managing, directing, and publicizing. We shall
look at the creative and artistic functions later. Nothing in show
business, or anything else for that matter, starts without an idea;
and the idea, however startling or original it may be, can make no
progress without money.

In earlier days, creative people sought 'patrons' (Middle English
patron, Latin *patronus,* protector, from *pater,* father). Most resident
organizations that sponsor the arts still look for 'patrons' ("fathers"
of a performance), as well as public sources of money for the
creative arts. Francis Bacon decried the need for 'patrons' in 1605
(*The Advancement of Learning,* I, 3).

> Books such as are worthy the name of books ought to have no
> patrons but truth and reason.

Samuel Johnson was constantly rebuffed and insulted by his 'patron' until he began to be successful, at which time the 'patron'
rushed forward to claim some of the glory. Mr. Johnson had the
last word in his *Dictionary of the English language* (see Bibliography),
1755.

> Patron . . . commonly a wretch who supports with insolence, and is
> paid with flattery.

A synonym for patron is 'backer' (from Middle English *bak,*
Anglo-Saxon *baec*). Charles Dickens, in 1839, ddscribed an altogether too common situation *(Nicholas Nickleby,* I).

> When fortune is low and backers scarce.

A modern word for one who puts up money for such ventures is
'angel' (Anglo-Saxon *aengel, engel,* Old French *angele,* Latin *angelus,*
Greek *angelos,* literally "messenger," later an 'angel').

The man who brings everything and everyone together is the
'producer' (from Latin *pro,* forward, and *ducere,* to lead). Synonyms
for 'producer' are 'impresario' (Italian *impresario,* stage-manager,
from *impresa,* enterprise, attempt) and 'manager' (from Middle
French *manege,* the managing of a horse, Italian *maneggio,* business,
handling, *maneggiare,* to handle, and *mano,* hand, all from Latin
manus, hand). In his *Letter to Sir H. Mann* of December 5, 1746,
Horace Walpole wrote:

> We have operas . . . the Prince and Lord Middlesex "Impresarii."

In a publication with the delightful title *The Oxford sausage; or,
select poetical pieces, written by the most celebrated wits of the university of
Oxford,* 1764, the following appears.

> Some who of old could Tastes and Fashions guide, Controul the
> Manager and awe the Play'r.

The *Standard* of December 31, 1864, reported a struggle.

> There is a stringent competition going forward amidst musical
> managers as to who shall produce her [a singer].

The word 'director' (from Latin *directus,* straight, and *dirigere,* to
straighten, direct) has had the meaning of what we would call today

the general manager. Sir George Grove described one such individual in 1890 (*A Dictionary of Music and Musicians*).

> The theatre was turned permanently into an opera-house . . . The director was Mr. Frederick Beale.

The more common meaning today of 'director' is the one who is in control of the action, spacing, timing, and general pace of the performers in the production.

While the show is being readied for performance, there are individuals hard at work to find a place where the show can be put on. They are called 'booking agents.' 'Book' and 'booking' are common Teutonic words (from Middle English *boke, booc, booke*) and may be etymologically connected with the name of the beech tree (Old English *boc, bece,* Old Norse *bok*) because inscriptions might have been first made on tablets of beech wood. The *Pall Mall Gazette* of August 5, 1884, reported a happy situation.

> The number of bookings was much larger than . . . last year.

To many churches over the years the stage has been an immoral place, one to be shunned. In 1900 the *Official Year Book of the Church of England* took note of this fact and reported a new attitude.

> The Church and Stage Guild . . . is a Society
> for getting rid of the prejudices of religious
> people against the stage.

'Guild' is from Middle English *gilde,* Anglo-Saxon *gildan* (to pay, whence the modern English word 'yield'). (The Dutch *guilder,* the unit of money, is from a different root, deriving from *gulden,* golden.)

In discussing a variety of shows, we will look first at some words which are broadly descriptive: 'spectacle,' 'extravaganza,' 'carnival,' 'tableau,' 'charade,' 'pageant.' They delineate presentations with no particular theme or emphasis, as opposed to words like 'tragedy' and 'comedy' which immediately convey a clear message.

'Spectacle' (French *spectacle,* Latin *spectaculum,* a show, from Latin *spectare,* to see) is an old word. It was used before 1340 by Richard Rolle of Hampole (*The psalter; or psalms of David, and certain canticles, with a translation and exposition in English,* XXXIX).

> Hoppynge & daunceynge of tumblers and herlotis [harlots], and other spectakils.

Joseph Jefferson (1829– 1905) reported an interesting joint effort (*Autobiography,* III).

> In the winter season the circus used to amalgamate with a dramatic company, and make a joint appearance in equestrian spectacle.

Conveying a sense of greater elaborateness in presentation is the 'extravaganza,' an Italian word from Latin *extra* (outside, beyond) and *vagare* (to wander). Thomas J. Mathias mentioned one in 1794 (*The pursuits of literature, or what you will, a satirical poem*).

> Author of the pleasant Extravaganza on the Courage of Sir John Falstafff.

While a 'spectacle' or an 'extravaganza' might take place in a theater or open-air arena, the 'carnival' is usually so large that it takes place on the streets of the city or town. 'Carnavale' is from the French *carnaval* (Shrovetide) and the Italian *carnevale* (originally the eve of Ash Wednesday, later the last three days before Lent). *Carnevale* in turn is from Late Latin *carnilevaria,* from Latin *caro* (flesh) and *levare* (to remove), and therefore means taking the meataway, that is, fasting. Popular etymology made further a connection with Latin *vale* (farewell), and simply understood 'carnival' as "farewell to flesh." It is celebrated, especially among Latin cultures, as a last fling before the onset of austere Lent — a literal farewell to meat, and other hedonistic pleasures, for six weeks.

The etymologist Skeat (see Bibliography) has this to add.

> As *carnelevamen* might also mean "solace of the flesh," the word was often completely misunderstood and misapplied; and the sense was altered from "a time of fasting" to "a time of feasting."

The Mardi Gras Carnival in New Orleans is a purely lay festival, without religious significance, an opportunity to gratify all the senses. 'Mardi Gras' is the French equivalent of Shrove Tuesday, the latter so-called because it was the day of shrift or confession before the beginning of the great fast. 'Mardi Gras' means "fat Tuesday" and got its name from the custom of parading a fat ox through the streets on that day. Today it is famous for its lavish costumes and elaborate floats. In England the day was called at one time Pancake Tuesday, and the eating of pancakes survives as a social custom today.

In a 'tableau' (originally 'tableau vivant,' living picture) the participants were silent and motionless. The word 'tableau' is from the French *tableau* (picture, writing boards) and *table* (table), from Latin *tabula* (plank, board, table). Thomas Moore used the original term in *Lalla Rookh* (preface).

> The different stories. . . were represented in "Tableaux Vivans" and songs.

Americans play 'Charades,' a parlor guessing game, but the English act out the clues in scenes or tableaux. In 1848 Thackeray wrote (*Vanity Fair*, II, 16):

> The performers disappeared to get ready for the second charade-tableau.

The word 'charade' is from the French *charade* and Provençal *charrado* (talk) and the verb *charra* (to talk). It may be related to the Spanish *charrada* (speech or action of a clown), from the Spanish and Portuguese word *charro* (churl, peasant).

A performance similar to the 'tableau' or 'charade' is the 'pageant.' The word is from Middle English *pagyn, padgin, pagent,* which is the Anglicized version of the Late Latin *pagina* (a 'page,' but also a scaffold, stage, slab of marble, plank of wood), from Latin *pangere* (to fasten, fix). 'Pageant' has had two meanings; one is the stage on which the scene is exhibited, and the other is the scene displayed on the stage. The latter meaning seems to have appeared first. John Wyclif wrote c. 1380 (*Works*):

> He that can best pleie a pagyn of the devil . . . schal haue most thank of pore & riche.

For the meaning that describes a stage which moves from place to place, we go to *York plays, The plays performed by the crafts or mysteries of York on the day of Corpus Christi.*

> In 1500, the cartwryghts [are] to make iiij [4] new wheles to the pagiaunt.

Before we begin to discuss particular types of shows, we ought to look at an art form which served as precursor to many of them, the 'commedia dell' arte' — a medieval Italian comedy for which the general plot was written out, but in which the actors could improvise the dialogue. Popular, recurring characters included the Captain, the Doctor, the Clown, Harlequin, Columbine, and Pantaloon. Some of these became prototypes of the Punch and Judy show.

Direct descendants of the 'commedia dell' arte' are the 'pantomime,' 'peepshow,' and 'puppet show.' The word 'pantomime' is from the Latin *pantomimus* (actor of many parts in one play), from Greek *panto* (all) and *mimos* (imitator). George Puttenham described this genre in 1589 (*The arte of English poesie*, I, 11).

> Betweene the actes, when the players went to make ready for another, there was just silence, and the people waxt weary; then came in these maner of conterfaite vices, they were called "Pantomimi," and all that had before bene sayd . . . they gave a crosse construction to it very ridiculously.

'Peepshow' (from Middle English *pepe, peepe*) may be allied to the English "peek," but its origin is obscure. Last of this group is the 'puppet show,' known and loved the world over. The word 'puppet' (Middle English *popet*) is from the Middle French and Old French *poupette* (little baby, puppet), derived in diminutive form from the Latin *pupa* (doll, girl). Theophilus Gale described 'puppet shows' in 1667 in *The court of the gentiles* (IV).

> They are but as your "Automata," those artificial Machines or Images called Puppits.

One of the members of the cast of the 'puppet show' is the 'marionette,' from French *marionnette,* a diminutive of the name *Marion,* from *Marie* (Mary). William Browne described a 'marionette' in 1613 in *Britannia's pastorals* (III).

> A little spruce elfe then (just of the sett Of the French dancer or such marionett).

We leave 'puppet' dancers or 'marionettes' on strings in order to see human dancers on feet; we go to the 'ballet' (French *ballet*, little dance, Italian *balleto*, a diminutive of *ballo*, dance, from *ballare*, to dance). John Dryden was one of the first to use the word, in 1667, (*Of dramatick poesie, an essay,* I).

> Not a Balette, or Masque, but a play.

The composer and arranger of a 'ballet' is called a 'choreographer' (from Greek *choria*, dancing, and *graphe*, writing). Charles Burney defined the art in 1789 (*A general history of Music*).

> In Choreography an art invented about two hundred years ago to delineate the figures and steps of the dances.

The theatrical experience which combines voice, music, and dance in splendid spectacle is the 'opera' (Italian *opera*, work, hence a performance, from Latin *opera*, works) described eloquently by Thomas Blount in 1656 (*Glossographia*).

> "Opera" . . . In Italy it signifies a Tragedy, Tragi-comedy, Comedy or Pastoral, which (being the studied work of a Poet) is not acted after the vulgar manner, but performed by Voyces in that way, which the Italians term Recitative, being likewise adorned with Scenes by Perspective, and extra-ordinary advantages by Musick.

Today we consider the music as the most important part of opera, but it was not always thus. Consider Samuel Richardson's view c. 1740 (*Pamela, or virtue rewarded*, IV).

> If the libretto, as they call it, is not approved, the Opera . . . will be condemned.

'Libretto' is a diminutive of the Italian *libro* (book), from the Latin *liber* (book). The 'prima donna' (literally the "first lady" in Italian) has the reputation of being difficult to deal with because of her mercurial temperament. The term 'prima donna' is also used figuratively for all sorts of people, male and female, in and out of the opera, who show this characteristic behavior. J. A. Maitland described them in 1887 (*Dictionary of National Biography*, XII).

> In managing recalcitrant "prime donne" and other mutinous persons.

Perhaps the greatest show spectacle of them all is the 'circus' (Latin *circus*, "circle," ring, hence a place for games). The 'circus' was originally a building, oblong, oval, or round, for the exhibition of public spectacles, races, games, and the like. By transference it became the word for the company performing in the building and finally for the company and their equipment. A description of the 'circus' appears in Thomas Langeley's translation of *Polidore Vergile* (II, 9), 1546.

> A place walled about named Circus wher was vsed fyghting and coursyng of horses and running with charettes [chariots].

Here is Oliver Wendell Holmes' version of "bread and circuses," *Pages from an Old Volume of Life; a collection of essays* (1883).

They must have something to eat, and the circus shows to look at.

A most important member of the circus family is the 'clown' (Middle English *cloyne, cloine, clowne,* Swedish dialect *klunn,* a low fellow, and *kluns,* a hard knob, a clumsy fellow, probably allied to English *clump,* mass, block). In the seventeenth century, 'clown' had the meaning merely of a rustic or boor, according to Francis Hawkins' translation of *Youth's behaviour: or, decency in conversation amongst 2 men* (VII), 1646.

> Put not thy meat in thy mouth, holding thy knife in thy hands, as do the countrey clowns.

During this same period, the 'clown' also appeared on the stage as a performer, said Samuel Rowlands c. 1630 (Epigrams, from *Works,* XXX).

> When Tarlton clown'd it in a pleasant vaine Vpon the Stage, his merry humours shop,
> Clownes knew the Clowne, by his great Clownish "slop."

A standard feature of the small, traveling 'circus' is the sideshow with its collections of oddities and titillations. The man who cajoles you to come in is called the 'barker' or 'spieler.' 'Barker' (from Middle English *berkere,* from *beorc, beork, borke,* to bark) was likened to a tout by William Hazlitt in 1884 (*Men and Manners,* series II, 11).

> As shopmen and barkers tease you to buy goods.

'Spieler,' a lesser-known synonym for 'barker,' comes from German *Spiel* (a play).

From the happy, mentally undemanding world of the circus and the clown to the mentally stimulating world of the 'drama' is a giant step, requiring a readjustment of attitudes and expectations. 'Drama' is an omnibus word which covers many types of presentations; it is from the Greek *drama* (deed, act) and had an earlier form, *drame,* as evidenced by this passage ofby Alexander Barclay (*Certayne eglogues,* IV).

> Such rascolde drames promoted by Thais,
> Bacchus, Licoris, or yet by Thestalis.

Samuel Johnson set out the basic creed by which all authors must live when he wrote in the *Prologue at the opening of the Theatre in Drury Lane,* 1747,

> The drama's laws the drama's patrons give,
> For we that live to please, must please to live.

In *The new British theatre; a selection of original dramas not yet acted,* 1814– 15, a distinction was made between 'drama' (including tragedy and comedy) and 'melodrama' (from Greek *melos*, song, and French *drame*, action, drama).

> In tragedy and comedy the final event is the effect of the moral operations of the different characters, but in the melodrama the catastrophe is the physical result of mechanical stratagem.

While its literal meaning is "acting with songs," 'melodrama' has taken on today the idea of an extravagant, emotional, and sometimes violent presentation. Helen Maria Williams used 'melodrama' in this sense in 1815 (*A narrative of the events which have taken place in France, from the landing of Napoleon Bonaparte, till the restoration of Louis XVIII. With an account of the present state of society and public opinion*).

> Strangers seem to arrive in France, as they would go to a melodrame, prepared for extraordinary events.

'Tragedy,' which according to Aristotle acted as a catharsis for our emotions, is a word with a strange origin. It is from Middle English and Middle French *tragedie*, Latin *tragoedia*, and Greek *tragodia*, with the literal meaning of "goat singer," and a derived meaning of a tragic poet and singer. It comes from two Greek words, *tragos* (he-goat) and *oidos* (singer). R. C. Trench, in *On the Study of Words* (lecture V), wrote in 1888:

> There is no question that *tragedy* is *the song of the goat;* but *why* the song of the goat, whether because a goat was the prize for the best performance of that song in which the germs of the future tragedy lay, or because the first actors were dressed, like satyrs, in goatskins, is a question which has stirred abundant discussion, and will remain unsettled to the end.

Other theories have been offered as explanation, some even denying the connection with "goat." Lord Byron wrote a letter to John Murray on April 2, 1817, in which he discussed Voltaire's views on tragedy.

> When Voltaire was asked why no woman has ever written a tolerable tragedy, "Ah (said the Patriarch) the composition of a tragedy requires *testicles*"!

In his *Chronicle of Troy* (II), 1414–20, John Lydgate defined tragedy.

> Tragedie, who so list to knowe,
> It begynneth in prosperite,
> And endeth euer in aduersite;
> And it also doth the conquest trete
> Of riche kynges and of lordys grete.

The counterpart of 'tragedy' is 'comedy'; in many theaters one can still see at the keystone point of the proscenium arch the twin masks of 'tragedy' and 'comedy.' 'Comedy' (Middle English *comedye*, *commedy*, Old French *comedie*, Latin *comoedia* Greek *komodia*, ludicrous spectacle, 'comedy,' from two Greek words, *komos*, banquet, jovial festivity, and *oidos*, singer) was originally a festive spectacle with singing and dancing. Chaucer prayed for the ability to write one (*Troilus and Criseyde*):

> Go, little booke, go, my little tragedie,
> Ther God my maker, yet er that I dye,
> So sende me myght to maken som comedye!

In *Don Juan* (stanza 9), 1818–24, Byron drew his own distinction between 'tragedy' and 'comedy'.

> All tragedies are finish'd by a death,
> All comedies are ended by a marriage.

'Comedy' sometimes slides off into 'farce'; the line of separation may be subtle or gross. The word 'farce' (Middle English *farce*) is from Old French *farcir* (to stuff), and Latin *farcire* (to stuff, cram), and is part of our word 'forcemeat.' In defining 'comedy,' both John Dryden and William Butler Yeats used 'farce' to show where 'comedy' stopped. Dryden wrote in 1668 (*An evening's love; or the Mock Astrologer*, preface)

> Comedy presents us with the imperfections of human nature; farce entertains us with what is monstrous and chimerical; the one causes laughter in those who can judge of men and manners, by the lively representation of their folly and corruption; the other produces the same effect in those who can judge of neither; and that only by its extravagancies.

Yeats (1865–1939) was more succinct in *Dramatis Personae*.

> Comedy is the clash of character. Eliminate character from comedy and you get farce.

'Parody' is still another form of "song." It is from Latin and Greek *parodia* (a comparable song, a parody), made up of *para* (beside, in comparison with) and *ode* (song). Dryden talked about 'parodies' in 1693 (*Juvenal*).

> From some fragments of . . . we may find they were Satirique Poems, full of Parodies; that is, of Verses patch'd up from great Poets and turn'd into another Sense than their Author intended them.

At the extreme end of the comic spectrum is the 'burlesque' (French *burlesque,* Italian *burlesco,* ludicrous, from *burla,* trick, fun, banter). In 1712 John Hughes used the word to describe a form of art in the *Spectator #537.*

> Those burlesque Pictures, which the Italians call Caracaturas.

In his *Thoughts on Laughter* Francis Hutcheson (1694 – 1746) comes down harshly on 'burlesque.'

> This contrast between ideas of grandeur, dignity, sanctity, perfection, and ideas of meanness, baseness, profanity, seems to be the very spirit of burlesque.

Henry Fielding made a comparison in 1742 (*Joseph Andrews,* preface).

> No two species of writing can differ more widely than the comic and the burlesque.

One of the features of a 'burlesque' performance is the 'slapstick' comedy. The 'slapstick' is an implement of two pieces of wood that makes a loud noise when hit against something and is used on the stage. *The World Book Dictionary* (see Bibliography) says:

> In slapstick comedy, the actors knock each other around, throw pies, use other stage properties against each other, and often make jokes about the others' lines to make people laugh.

The American 'burlesque' theater incorporated a feature hardly envisioned by these definers of 'burlesque,' the 'striptease.' H. L. Mencken coined a word for these shapely females; he called them 'ecdysiasts,' from the Greek word *ekdyein* (to cast off or shed — applied, e.g., to the dead skin of snakes). Along with the 'striptease,' there were entertaining 'sketches' or 'skits' presented during the show. 'Sketch' is from Dutch *schets* (draught, sketch, model), Italian *schizzo* (first rough draft of anything), Latin *schedium* (extemporaneous poem, anything hastily made), and Greek *schedios* (sudden, offhand, on the spur of the moment). In *London labour* (III) Henry Mayhew wrote in 1861:

> We always did a laughable sketch entitled "Billy Button's Ride to Brentford," and I used to be Jeremiah Stitchem, a servant of Billy Button's, that comes for a "sitiation."

The word 'skit' is of doubtful origin. It may be from Swedish *skjuta* (to shoot, skittish, full of frisks or capers, fickle); it may also be allied to Danish *skotte tie* (to cast a sly look at). William Combe defined it in 1820 (*The Second tour of Doctor Syntax in search of consolation*, VII).

> A Manuscript with learning fraught,
> Or some nice, pretty little skit
> Upon the times, and full of wit.

When 'skits' and 'sketches' were combined with songs, dances, and other acts, the result was the 'variety show,' the 'minstrel show,' 'vaudeville,' and, at a somewhat more sophisticated level, the 'cabaret.' The 'variety' show (from French *variété*, from Latin *varius*, various, varying, versatile) was well-known in England in the nineteenth century. *Referee* of March 25, 1886, commented:

> The biggest variety company ever seen at the East-end of London.

Chamber's Journal of March 14, 1891, also talked about the variety show.

> Music halls, or, to give them the more recent and appropriate term, variety shows, are quite modern institutions.

A peculiarly American version of the variety show was the 'minstrel show.' The word 'minstrel' is from Middle English *minstrel, minstral,* Old French *menestral,* Late Latin *ministralis, ministerialis* (a retainer — applied to the train of retainers who played instruments, acted as buffoons and jesters, and the like), all from Latin *minister* (servant). The word was in use down to the end of the sixteenth century as defining an entertainer who combined singing and story-telling with buffoonery and juggling. Then the role of the 'minstrel' changed. Around 1800, he had become a singer or musician who sang or recited heroic or lyric poetry composed by himself or others, to his own accompaniment on string instruments.

Chaucer wrote of minstrels in *The Romaunt of the rose*.

> Ther mightest thou see these floutours,
> Minstrales, and eek Iogelours.

In 1559 Archbishop Hethe described King David (as quoted by John Strype, *Annals of the reformation and establishment of religion, and . . . other occurrences in the church of England,* 1708 – 09, I app.).

> Kinge Davyd . . . placed himselfe amongest the mynystrells.

The word was still in common use in 1885, when W. S. Gilbert wrote the lyrics to *The Mikado* (I).

> A wandering minstrel I —
> A thing of shreds and patches,
> Of ballads, songs and snatches,
> And dreamy lullaby!

The pioneer company of 'minstrels' in America was organized in 1843 in the form of a quartet, headed by Daniel Decatur Emmett, who wrote the famous song "Dixie" as a "hooray-song" or "walk-around" in 1859. The most important and best-known of the 'minstrel' companies was the Christy Minstrels, organized in Buffalo, New York, in 1845. The group came to New York City in 1846 and reigned supreme for ten years. Many of Stephen Foster's most important songs were written for Christy's Minstrels. Negro minstrelsy was popular in England as well during this period. The 'minstrel' vogue reached its zenith between 1850 and 1870, but very soon afterward the professional companies disappeared from the stage.

There are three Englishmen whose comments on the 'minstrel show' bear repeating. In 1871 M. Schele DeVere wrote *Americanisms; the English of the New World,* in which he said:

> The Negro-minstrel is the artist who blackens his face, adopts the black man's manner and instruments, and recites his field and plantation songs.

John Ruskin made figurative use of the minstrel concept in *Fors Clavigera; letters to the workmen and labourers of Great Britain,* 1871 – 74.

> You have all made Artificial Blacks of yourselves, and unmelodious Christys.

Hallberger's Illustrated Magazine was patronizing in tone, in 1876.

> Christy Minstrelsy . . . a rather unclassical but popular species of concert in America.

Before the onset of television, the place to see the great variety of performers such as singers, dancers, jugglers, magicians, contortionists, and especially comedians was at the 'vaudeville' show. Randle Cotgrave defined 'vaudeville' in *Dictionarie,* 1611.

> Vaudeville, a countrey ballade, or song; a Roundelay or Virelay: so tearmed of Vaudevire, a Norman towne wherein Olivier Bassel, the first inuenter of them, liued; also a vulgar proverb, a countrey or common saying.

As Cotgrave's definition indicates, a 'vaudeville' was originally a light, popular song, sung on the stage. Horace Walpole wrote of one in 1739, in *Letter to R. West* (June 18).

> I will send you one of the vaudevilles or ballads which they sing at the comedy after their *petites pièces.*

Later on it became a play or stage performance interspersed with songs, which is how it was used by Bulwer-Lytton in 1833 (*Godolphin,* IX).

> Fanny . . . was inimitable in vaudeville, in farce, and in the lighter comedy.

'Cabaret' is a word of unknown derivation; it was originally a drinking house, and today it is still a drinking house with music added. Archbishop John Bramhall referred to a 'cabaret' in 1655 (*Against Hobbes*).

> Suppose this servant passing by some cabaret, or tennis court, where his comrades were drinking or playing.

What kind of performers make up the program in these variety show? There are musicians, singers, dancers, ventriloquists, contortionists, acrobats, tumblers, jugglers, magicians, prestidigitators, thaumaturgists, comedians, and straight men.

The 'musician' (from Middle English *musik, musyk,* French *musique,* Latin *musica,* Greek *mousike,* the art belonging to the Muses) might play a variety of instruments. He might at times accompany a 'singer' (from Middle English *singen,* Anglo-Saxon *singan*), who might sing alone or with other singers in a group. One particular group native to America is the 'barbershop quartet.'

There might be 'dancers' (from Middle English *daunce, dawnce,*

Old French *dance, danse*), who would perform a 'soft shoe' or 'tap' dance. Welcoming the spring is an annual rite that goes back in time. In *King Alisaunder,* written around 1300, girls are described as greeting the spring with dance.

> Mery time it is in May . . .
> Maydens so dauncen and thay play.

The art of 'ventriloquism' was known back in 1661 when T. Ady defined it (*Discovery of Witches*).

> "Ventriloquium," a speaking in the belly.

The word is from Latin *venter* (belly) and *loqui* (to speak). One does not see the 'contortionist' very much today, but he used to be popular at the vaudeville show. The word is from the Latin *contortus* (turned, brandished), from *con* (together) and *torquere* (to twist, hurl, turn). Charles Cornwallis, in 1840, cited a notice for performers wanted for a local show (*The New World*, I).

> Cremorna Gardens — Wanted, male and female Equestrians, Tumblers . . . Acrobatic Performers, Contortionists.

The word 'acrobat' might perhaps be used more appropriately to describe a ballet dancer; it is from the Greek *akrobatos* (walking on tip-toe, or on a point). It is made up of two Greek words, *akros* (at the end, outermost) and *bainein* (to walk). The word 'acrobat' seems to have had a narrower meaning, as used by Thomas D. Fosbrooke in 1825 (*The Encyclopaedia of Antiquities,* II).

> "Acrobates" . . . were Rope Dancers of which there were four kinds.

In 1846 *Punch* used the word to make an acid comment (January 24).

> We have no doubt that the performances at St. Stephen's during the coming "session" will be enlivened by feats of agility and strength on the part of the three great Political Acrobats.

Gifted with physical agility like the acrobat is the 'tumbler' (from Middle English *tumblen,* Anglo-Saxon *tumbian*). Sir Walter Raleigh described, in 1624, some performers he had seen in his travels (*The History of the World,* V, 6).

> A tricke of climbing vpon mens heads, somewhat after the manner of our tumblers.

Incidentally, the common drinking glass, the 'tumbler,' got its name because of an unusual custom in certain households, as reported by William F. Collier in 1876 (*Pictures of the periods: a sketch-book of old English life*).

> The guests were supplied with tumblers, or glass vessels, which, being rounded at the base, could not stand upright, and must, therefore, be emptied at a draught.

The 'juggler' (Middle English *iogelour, iuglur, juglar*) was originally a jester, as indicated by the origin of the word; it is from the Latin *joculus,* a diminutive of *jocus* (joke). By the time the word arrived in Old French as *jongleur,* through *jogleor, jugleor,* and *jougler,* it had taken on the meaning of 'juggler.' Ben Jonson described one in *Volpone* (act II, scene 3), in 1605.

> A juggling, tooth-drawing, prating mountebank.

The old adage "The hand is quicker than the eye" clearly applies to the 'juggler' but reaches its finest hour in the feats of the 'magician' (from Middle English *magike, magyke,* Old French *magique,* 'magic,' from Late Latin *magica,* all from Greek *magos,* magician or Magus, a member of the priestly caste of the ancient Medes, reputed to be skilled in enchantment). John Gower (*Confessio,* III) described one who put 'magic' to a use other than to entertain the public.

> Magique he useth forto winne
> His love.

A synonym for 'magician' is a word that is not very common today, 'prestidigitator' from two Latin words, *preste* (quick, sharp) and *digitus* (finger). Robert Southey spoke of one in 1843 (*Commonplace book,* IV).

> Dr. M. G. Ferizer the celebrated enchanter . . . prestidigitateur, and author of several experiments adapted to public amusement.

There is a synonym for 'magic' which is rarely used today, 'thaumaturgy.' The word is from Greek *thaumatourgia,* made up of *thauma* (wonder) and *ergein* (to work). Here is how Thomas Carlyle described a practitioner of the art c. 1850 (*Cagliostro*).

> The foreign Quack of Quacks, with all his thaumaturgic Hemp-silks, Lottery-numbers, Beauty-waters.

No matter what kind of variety show is being presented, there is certain to be in the cast a comedian with his 'straight man' (presumably so-called because he utters the straight lines, which set up the comic situation and provide the comedian with an opening for the punch line, or joke).

Part of the routine of the comedian is his 'patter,' a running commentary which is interspersed with jokes. 'Patter,' as glib and rapid speech, has nothing to do with 'patter' as light tapping sounds (from *pat,* an onomatopoeic word); rather, this kind of speech is short for *paternoster,* Latin for Our Father, the Lord's Prayer, often uttered in a rapid mumble. 'Patter' is used in this sense by Sir Thomas More in 1573 (*A dialogue of comforte against tribulation,* fol. 44).

> But when men are wealthy, & wel at their ease, while our tung pattereth vpon our praiers a pace: good God, how many mad waies our minde wandereth the while!

W. S. Gilbert, whose operattas were highlighted by comic "patter songs," poked fun at them in *Ruddigore* (1887).

> This particularly rapid unintelligible patter,
> Isn't generally heard, and if it is it doesn't matter.

Another stock-in-trade of the comedian is the 'gag' (Middle English *gaggen,* of imitative origin meaning to suffocate). The word has had three meanings other than the current one of a joke. In the midnineteenth century it referred to expressions not occurring in the written piece, but interpolated or substituted by the performer. John Hotten defined it in 1859 (*A dictionary of modern slang, cant, and vulgar words*).

> In certain pieces this [gagging] is allowed by custom, and these are called gag-pieces.

Earlier in the century, it had the sense of a made-up story. John G. Lockhart discussed the gag (*Peter's letters to his kinsfolk,* III) in 1819.

> Whether the Gag come in the shape of a compliment to the Gaggee, or some wonderful story, gravely delivered with every circumstance of apparent seriousness.

Meanwhile in the United States 'gag' took on an altogether different meaning, that of a laughing stock. In 1840 Thomas C.

Haliburton used it in this sense (*The clockmaker; or the sayings and doings of Samuel Slick of Slickville,* III, 2).

> "Sam," says he, "they tell me you broke down the other day in the house of representatives, and made a proper gag of yourself."

There is a performer who does not necessarily need a show to exhibit his talents, the 'jester' or 'buffoon' or, to give him a name that is now obsolete, a 'Merry-Andrew.' According to Skeat (see Bibliography), the name 'Merry' (Middle English *merie, mirie, murie,* Anglo-Saxon *mery, merge,* from *myrge,* making the time short) plus the proper name 'Andrew' originated this way.

> ... where "Andrew" is a personal name, asserted by Hearne to have been given to jesters in remembrance of the once famous "Andrew Boorde," Doctor of Physic in the reign of Henry VIII: several jest-books were ascribed to him, perhaps wrongly. . . .

Both the *Oxford English Dictionary* and the *Century Dictionary* (see Bibliography) disagree with this etymology, claiming that there is no evidence whatever for this assertion. But that 'Merry-Andrew' was a generic term is clear from this citation from John Dryden's *Epilogue to the university of Oxford* (I), 1673.

> Th'Italian Merry-Andrews took their place,
> And quite Debauch'd the Stage with lewd Grimace.

Chaucer wrote about 'jesters' (Middle English *gestour,* teller of tales, from *geste,* exploit, 'gesture,' tale, romance, Latin *gesta,* a plural noun, related to *res gesta,* deed, exploit, all from *gerere,* to carry out, do, perform) in *The House of Fame* (I).

> Gestiours, that tellen tales
> Bothe of wepinge and of game.

John Baret embroidered the role of the 'jester' in *An alvearie or triple (quadruple) dictionarie,* 1573 – 80.

> A Gester, or dizard faining [feigning] and counterfeiting all men's gestures, "pantominius."

(A *dizard* or *dizzard* was another word for 'jester.') Don Marquis (1878 – 1937) felt for the 'jester' (*The Tavern of Despair*).

> The saddest ones are those that wear
> The jester's motley garb.

The last of this trio is the 'buffoon,' a word from French *buffon* ('buffoon,' jester, sycophant) and *bouffer* (to puff). King James VI of Scotland (afterward James I of England) wrote of his times (*The essayes of a prentise, in the divine art of poesie*) in 1585.

> We remaine With Iuglers, buffons, and that foolish seames [seems].

Another kind of musical entertainment is presented by the 'chorus' or 'choir.' 'Chorus' is from the Greek *choros* (a band of dancers or singers). In Grecian times the 'chorus' was a band of performers who provided explanations of the main action through their words, singing, or dancing. In English drama the 'chorus' became a single person who spoke the prologue and explained or commented upon the course of events, but in 1656 Blount (*Glossographia*) was defining 'chorus' as

> a Company of Singers or Dancers, a Quire.

'Choir' (Middle English *quere, quire, queir*) is also from the Greek *choros,* through Latin *chorus,* Old French *cuer,* and Middle French *choeur. Pedler's Prophecie* described a 'choir' in 1595.

> We foure will make an honest quere;
> I will follow, if the Pedler will begin.

A number of theatrical companies across the country have as their name or part of their name the words 'Sock and Buskin.' The *Oxford English Dictionary* explains the origin of this phrase.

> The high thick-soled boot (cothurnus) worn by the actors in ancient Athenian tragedy; frequently contrasted with the "sock" (soccus) or low shoe worn by comedians.

The word 'buskin,' referring to a kind of legging, is from the Old French *bousequin* and may be allied to the Middle Italian *borzachine* (fine boots, 'buskins'), but the origin of the word is disputed. In 1871 John Morley (*Critical Miscellanies,* I) observed actors after a show as they

> Doff the buskin or the sock, wash away the paint from their cheeks, and gravely sit down to meat.

A theatrical company is often called a 'troupe' (Old French *trope*). Richard Brinsley Sheridan spoke of such a group in *The critic, or a tragedy rehearsed* (act I, scene 1) in 1779.

Your first inquiry would be, whether they had brought a theatrical troop with them.

When *The New York Evening Post* of December 6, 1825, printed a review of a performance, it said:

The whole troupe were equally excellent.

One wonders whether the writer used the French spelling 'troupe' to distinguish the word from the word "troop" for a group of soldiers.

All resident companies and some traveling ones have a 'repertory' of productions to offer. The word is also used to describe the range of characters an actor has mastered. For the former use we go to Henry James (*The Tragic Muse*, XXIX), 1890.

A great academic, artistic theatre, . . . rich in its repertory, rich in the high quality and the wide array of its servants.

In 1847 *Illustrated London News* (June 16) offered this critique of a currently performing actor on the London stage.

The part . . . , with the exception of the renowned Robert Macaire, is the best character in his "répertoire."

The word 'repertory' is from Middle French *repertoire* (roll, repertory list), from Latin *repertorium,* consisting of *re* (again) and *parere* (to produce).

What constitutes a 'repertory'? A group of 'plays' (Middle English *pleyen,* Anglo-Saxon *pleya,* game, sport, and *plegian,* to 'play') is needed. The 'play' as propaganda is illustrated in the *Acts of Henry VIII* (C, 1), 1542 – 43.

By . . . balades, plaies, rimes, songes, and other phantasies, subtilly and craftely instructing his highnes people.

The Woman of Fashion (I), 1767, went to a theater and was not impressed.

I went to the Play, as they call it — Play, indeed! Faith, Brother, I think it was past a Joke.

George Bernard Shaw turned his wit on the playgoer in *Fanny's First Play* (epilogue), in 1911.

You don't expect me to know what to say about a play when I don't know who the author is, do you? . . . If it's by a good author, it's a good play, naturally. That stands to reason.

The 'playbill' was the notice posted around town to announce a forthcoming play and give details about the cast and the perform-ance. Frances Burney (Madame D'Arblay) wrote of 'playbills' in 1778 (*Evelina, or the history of a young lady's entrance into the world*, letter 20).

> "Do you come to the play without knowing what it is?"
> "O yes, Sir, very frequently: I have no time read to play-bills; one merely comes to meet one's friends, and show that one's alive."

Who writes a play? Not a "playwrite" but a 'playwright.' The 'wright' part of the word is the English word 'to wright' (to work, fashion), from the Anglo-Saxon *wrycan* (to work), and is now used only in combinations such as 'playwright' or 'wheelwright.' Frederic Reynolds had advice to budding authors in 1789 *(The Dramatist)*.

> Now do take my advice, and write a play — if any incident happens, remember, it is better to have written a damned play, than no play at all — it snatches a man from obscurity.

In 1687 M. Clifford suggests, on the contrary, that playwriting is one occupation that should be avoided at all costs (*Notes upon Mr. Dryden's poems*, IV).

> Wherein you may . . . thrive better, than at this damn'd Trade of a Play-wright.

If, however, you are determined to be a 'playwright' in spite of Mr. Clifford, then Erich Maria Remarque (the author of *All Quiet on the Western Front*) has this advice for you, writing in the *New York Herald-Tribune* of October 24, 1957.

> Every playwright ought to try acting just as every public prosecutor should spend some weeks in jail to find out what he is meting out to others.

T. S. Eliot was quoted in *Time* magazine of March 6, 1950, on the major problem for a 'playwright.'

> My greatest trouble is getting the curtain up and down.

The word 'bard' (Celtic *bard*, poet) originally had the meaning of poet or singer; he was felt by some to have other special attributes. David Powel's translation (along with Humphrey Lhuyd) of Caradoc's *Historie of Cambria*, 1584, spoke of the 'bard.'

> This word Bardh signified such as had knowledge of things to come.

The profession of 'bard' in Scotland in the sixteenth century was precarious, according to the words of Kenneth Stat, as quoted in Sir James Balfour's *Practicks; or a system of the more ancient law of Scotland*, c. 1575.

> All vagabundis, fulis [fools], bardis, scudloris [kitchen scullions], and sicklike idile pepill, sall be brint [burnt] in the cheek.

A constant concern of authors is the possibility of being accused of 'plagiarism' (Middle English *plagiairie*, French *plagiaire*, Latin *plagiarius*, plunderer, kidnapper — "one that steals or takes free people out of one country and sells them in another for slaves, . . . also, a bookstealer, a book-theef," Cotgrave, *Dictionary*). Samuel Johnson and William Hazlitt discussed the plight of one who is accused of 'plagiarism.' Johnson wrote (*Adventurer*, #95)

> Nothing . . . can be more unjust than to charge an author with plagiarism merely because he . . . makes his personages act as others in like circumstances have done.

Hazlitt wrote in 1820 (*Lectures chiefly on the dramatic literature of the age of Elizabeth*)

> If an author is once detected in borrowing, he will be suspected of plagiarism ever after.

Ben Jonson treated the problem with a lighter touch in 1601 (*Poetaster, or the araignment*, IV).

> Why, the ditty's all borrowed; 'tis Horace's; hang him, plagiary!

The expression 'steal my thunder' derives from a case of 'plagiarism' in the eighteenth century. John Dennis, who was an English critic and playwright, invented a new kind of thunder for a play which failed after a few performances. Later, at a showing of *Macbeth*, when Dennis heard his own thunder being made use of, he exclaimed, "See how the rascals use me. They will not let my play run, and yet they steal my thunder!"

A playwright writes a 'script' (Middle English *escript*, a writing, Latin *scriptus*, written composition, from *scribere*, to write), a shortened form of 'manuscript' (from Latin *manus*, hand — thus "written by hand"). In 1897, the *Westmoreland Gazette* used 'script' in connection with the theater (May 13).

> Hearing of the success of the play from a friend, Macready wrote asking to see the "script."

A play, generally, except for some modern, avant-garde concoctions, has a 'plot.' There are various possible origins of this word; it may come from the French *complot* (conspiracy), or from *plotform*, a variety of *platform*, with the meaning of a map or sketch of a place; and some authorities say that the origin is unknown. John Lyly used 'platform' with the sense of "plan" in *Campaspe* (V) in 1584.

> I am devising a platform in my head.

Shakespeare used 'complot' with its French meaning *(Richard II,* act I, scene 3).

> Nor never by advised purpose meet
> To plot, contrive, or complot any ill
> 'Gainst us, our state, our subjects, or our land.

By the seventeenth century, 'plot' had come to its current meaning as the scheme of the play. Richard Lovelace had a suggestion as to the nature and shape of a 'plot' in 1649 (*Lucasta's epodes, odes, sonnets, songs, etc. To which is added Aramanths, a pastorall*).

> Th'other [Comedy] for the Gentlemen oth' Pit,
> Like to themselves all Spirit, Fancy, Wit
> In which plots should be subtile as a Flame.

In 1759 Oliver Goldsmith made fun of a particular poem (*Miscellaneous Works,* III).

> The whole plot of these five cantos is no more than a young lady happening to prick her finger with a needle.

A common current phrase occurred in George Villiers' *The rehersal* (II) in 1672.

> Ay, now the plot thickens very much upon us.

Behind it all and pulling the strings is a female, said Sheridan in 1775 (*The Rivals,* epilogue).

> Thro' all the drama — whether damned or not —
> Love gilds the scene, and women guide the plot.

The use of the word 'dialogue' (Middle English and Old French *dialoge,* Latin *dialogus,* Greek *dialogos,* conversation) in discussion of plays and the drama seems to have originated in the midnineteenth century. Mountstuart Elphinstone was one of the first to use it in this connection in 1841 (*History of India,* I).

> The plots are generally interesting; the dialogue lively.

Some plays have a 'prologue'; others have an 'epilogue'; and some have both. 'Prologue' comes from Latin *pro*, (in front of), and *loqui*, (to speak), while 'epilogue' has one direct root in Greek *epi* (upon, after). In *The old batchelour,* 1693, William Congreve longed for the good old days.

> How this vile World is chang'd! In former Days Prologues were serious Speeches before Plays.

Shakespeare, who tended to have both 'epilogues' and 'prologues' in many of his plays, desired no 'epilogue' for his play within a play in *A Midsummer Night's Dream* (act V, scene 1).

> No epilogue, I pray you; for your play needs no excuse.

Before a play can be put on the stage it must be 'cast' (Middle English *casten, kesten,* to do, throw); the people who will act in it must be chosen. The connection of the word 'cast' to the stage must have been sufficiently uncommon in 1779 so that Sheridan had to qualify his usage of it in *The Rivals* (act I, scene 1).

> I should have thought, now, that it [the piece] might have been cast (as the actors call it) better at Drury-Lane.

Today we call members of the cast 'actors' and 'actresses,' but in 1666, when Pepys wrote about a female on the stage in his diary (December 27), he used 'actor' to apply to her.

> Doll Common doing Abigail most excellently, & Knipp the widow very well, & will be an excellent actor, I think.

A pretentious synonym for 'actor' is 'thespian,' an eponym from *Thespis,* the poet, traditionally the father of Greek tragedy, in the sixth century B.C. The life of an actor has always been difficult, but never more so than when the play in which he appeared offended the reigning authorities. John Doran reported in 1864 (*"Their majesties' servants," annals of the English stage*).

> The angry Lord Chamberlain . . . clapped the unoffending Thespian [Powell] for a couple of days in the Gate House.

Pat O'Brien put acting in a different perspective when, in 1961, he was quoted in the *New York Journal-American* (December 6).

> You know, acting makes you feel like a burglar sometimes — taking all that money for all that fun.

An actor is one who practices the 'histrionic' art (from Latin *histrio,* from Etruscan *hister,* actor). The meaning of the word has been corrupted or narrowed over the years so that it now has a negative meaning, referring to one who overacts, who is "theatrical" or "stagey" in his behavior. William Cowper pinpointed this meaning in 1784 (*The Task,* II).

> Foppish airs And histrionic mumm'ry, that let down The pulpit to the level of the stage.

Prior to this period, however, the word had another sense which may have contributed to the meaning outlined above. In 1658 Edward Phillips defined it in *The new world of English words; or, a general dictionary).*

> "Histrio," a Player of Farces, a Buffoon.

One hundred years before Phillips, John Alday used the word with an altogether different meaning (in his translation of Boaystuau's *Theatrum mundi, the theatre or rule of the world,* S, IV), around 1566.

> Histrians that we have seene in our time flie on a rope in ye ayre.

Some members of the cast have names which describe in general terms their roles in the play; they are called 'ingénue,' 'protagonist,' 'hero,' and 'villain.' The 'ingénue' (French *ingénue,* from Latin *ingenuus,* free-born, frank, candid, from *in* plus *gignere,* to beget) is the young, charming, naive female member of the cast as described in 1889 in *The Academy* (April 6).

> He must be entreated . . . to permit us more of beauty and of charm than is vouchsafed by the scanty utterances of the ingénue of the present play.

We use the term 'protagonist' (from Greek *protos,* first, and *agon,* assembly, contest) to refer to the chief personage in a drama or story. It has become a standard term for such characters, but, strangely enough, its antonym, 'antagonist,' has not achieved the same status in our theatrical vocabulary (from Greek *anti,* opposite, against). John Dryden argued, in 1668, that the occupation or moral character of the 'protagonist' should not be an issue (*An evening's love: or the mock astrologer,* I).

> 'Tis charg'd upon me that I make debauch'd Persons (such as they say my Astrologer and Gamester are) my protagonists, or the chief persons of the drama.

In *The Claverings* (XXVIII) Anthony Trollope discussed in 1867 the dilemma of the author in the handling of his protagonists, or 'hero' and 'heroine' (Middle French *heroe*, a worthy, demigod, Latin *heros*, Greek *heros*, hero, demigod).

> Perhaps no terms have been so injurious to the profession of the novelist as those two words, hero and heroine. In spite of the latitude which is allowed to the writer in putting his own interpretation upon these words, something heroic is still expected; whereas, if he attempt to paint from Nature, how little that is heroic should he describe.

Rather than the term 'antagonist,' we might use the word 'villain' (Middle English *vilein, vileyn*, Old French *vilein*, from Late Latin *villanus*, all meaning a farm laborer). As we see, this word has changed over the years, going from social debasement to moral debasement. In 1602, when Thomas Middleton used it in *Blurt, master Constable, or the Spanish night-walke* (act II, scene 1), there was no connotation of evil.

> Villain? by my blood,
> I am as free-born as your Venice Duke!

By 1822 the word had taken on its modern meaning as seen in Charles Lamb's "On Some of the Old Actors."

> The fact is, you do not believe in such characters as Surface — the villain of artificial comedy — even while you read or see them.

Every actor or actress must perform somewhere for the first time; we call this occasion the 'debut,' a word with an interesting origin. It is from the French *début*, which had meant either the first play in a game of bowls or billiards, or the first cast in a game of dice. These meanings came from the earlier one of displacing an opponent's ball (bowl) and therefore having first play in the next round. The word is made up of two Middle French words, *de* (from Latin *dis*, apart) and *but* (an aim). Byron described poetically the first essay on the stage on some actors in 1806 (*Occasional prologue*).

> Tonight you throng to witness the "debut"
> Of embryo actors, to the Drama new.

It is an extremely rare occasion, one that happens in fiction more often than in reality, for a 'debut' to produce a 'star' (Middle English *sterre*, Anglo-Saxon *steorra*). Most often it takes years of hard work and a little luck to become a 'star.' The word began to take on a theatrical connotation around the end of the eighteenth century. In 1827 the *Edinburgh Weekly Journal* (February 28) carried the following item.

> He had hitherto been speaking of what, in theatrical language, was called "stars."

We have talked about the actor, let us now look at what he does — 'acting.' George Moore, in 1884, didn't think much of the profession (*A Mummer's Wife*).

> Acting is therefore the lowest of the arts, if it is an art at all.

The 'mummers' of George Moore's title were masked players who put on shows of various kinds. The word is of imitative origin; men would put on masks and pretend to frighten children by saying "mum" or "boo." It comes from Middle English *mommerye, mommynge,* Middle French *mommeur,* Middle Dutch *mommen* (to go "moming," in a mask). Alexander Pope described some mummers in 1712 (*The Dunciad,* III, 1).

> Peel'd, patch'd, and piebald, linsey-woolsey brothers,
> Grave Mummers! sleeveless some and shirtless others.

The 'supernumerary' is one who appears on the stage but does not speak any lines. The word is from Latin *super* (beyond) and *numerus* (number). In 1836 in *Brokers' Shops,* one of the *Sketches by Boz,* Charles Dickens gave a subtle twist to this meaning of the word.

> Purchased of some wretched super-numeraries or sixth-rate actors.

What does an actor do when he is on the stage? He assumes a 'role,' tries to 'portray' a 'character' with 'dialogue' and 'gestures.' If he is not very good at this, he may earn the epithet 'ham actor.' 'Role' is from Middle English *rowle, roll,* and French *rôle* (paper roll containing the actor's part). An actor must search his inner being to bring out the 'portrayal' of the character he is playing. It is this process that the origin of the word 'portrayal' defines. It comes from Middle English *purtreye,* Old French *portraire,* Late Latin *portrahere* (to drag or bring forward, expose, reveal). That which the actor is 'portraying' is a 'character' (Latin *character,* mark, sign). John Dryden set the place of the hero in drama (*Parallel of poetry and painting*) c. 1700.

> In a tragedy, or epick poem, the hero . . . must outshine the rest of all the characters.

There is sometimes more eloquence and force in a 'gesture' than in a word. (We have already seen the origins of 'gesture' when we talked about 'jesters.' R. Parker feared the 'gesture' in 1607 *(A scholasticall discourse against symbolizing with Antichrist in ceremonies,* II, 10).

> The player hath no purpose to commit the acte of adulterie: his sinne is in that he gestureth and expresseth the dalliances of it.

John Evelyn spoke of the appeal of the 'gesture' in 1697 *(Numismata; a discourse of medals antient and modern,* IX).

> The Tongue spoke to Men's Ears, but it was the Gesture which spoke to their eyes.

Pity the poor actor who is not very good and who may exaggerate his acting in order to get his portrayal across. We often call him a 'ham actor.' The phrase is from a Black American song, *The Hamfat Man,* described by Edward B. Marks (1865– 1945) in *They All Sang.*

> "Ham," a poor, and generally fatuous performer, was originally "ham fatter," a neophyte in the minstrel ranks, forced to sing "Ham Fat," an old ditty of the George Christy days.

The play is written; the cast is assembled; it is time to 'rehearse' — a word from Middle English *rehercen, rehersen,* Old French *reherser* (from *re,* again, and *hercier,* to rake or harrow the ground), leading to the sense of going over and over the same ground again, or repetition, which is exactly what a 'rehearsal' is. (The same idea is conveyed in the phrase 'to rake up an old story.') The word was used in connection with the theater back in the sixteenth century by Peter Cunningham *(Extracts from the accounts of the revels at court, with an introduction and notes by Peter Cunningham)* 1579– 80.

> Rehersinge of dyvers plaies . . . and their sondry Rehersells.

'Rehearsal' was also used as a synonym for narration, recounting, or telling, as seen in John Lyly's *Euphues,* 1579.

> You have made mine eares glow at the rehearsall of your love.

While learning his 'lines' the actor must also learn his 'cues,' and he may think about his 'makeup.' The word 'line' in this sense is from the French *ligne* and the Latin *linea* (line, stroke, mark). Although the word is old, its usage in the theater is fairly modern. *The Daily Telegraph* of December 7, 1882, carried this item.

> He [an actor] said, "Do let me get in some of my 'lines.' "

The generally accepted version of the origin of 'cue' is that it stands for the Latin *quando* (when), which was abbreviated as *q* or *qu* in the sixteenth century. The sound "cue" denotes the Anglicized pronunciation of the French name of the Latin letter *q*. John Strype used it in his call for greater piety at prayer in 1721 (*Ecclesiastical memorials, relating chiefly to religion and the reformation of it . . . under Henry VIII, Edward VI, and queen Mary the first*, III, app. 11).

> Amen must be answered to the thanksgevying not as to a mans q in a playe.

There are two other versions of the beginnings of 'cue,' but supporting evidence for either one is nonexistent. John Minsheu defined it in 1625 (*The guide into tongues, etc.*).

> "Q," A "qu," a terme vsed among Stage-plaiers, à Latin "Qualis," i. at what manner of word the Actors are to beginne to speake one after another hath done his speech.

'Cue' has also been taken as equal to the French *queue* (tail) on the ground that it is the tail or ending of the preceding speech. Unfortunately for this theory, the French word for 'cue' is not *queue* but *réplique*.

When an actor misses his 'cue,' he is happy to have the services of a 'prompter' (French *prompt*, prompt, Latin *promptus*, brought to light, at hand, ready, from *pro*, forward, and *emere*, to gain, take). The 'prompter,' or at least the box in which he stands, is visible at the opera, but he may be present at plays as well, although not seen by the audience. Thackeray referred to one function of the prompter around 1860 (*The End of the Play*).

> The play is done; the curtain drops,
> Slow falling to the prompter's bell.

George Eliot, in 1858, marveled at how 'makeup' could change one's appearance (as quoted in John W. Cross' *George Eliot's life as related in her letters and journals*, II).

> The Zouaves, with their wondrous make-ups as women.

The essential ingredient of 'makeup' is 'greasepaint,' 'grease' coming from Middle English *grece, grese,* Old French *graisse, gresee,* and Latin *crassus* (thick, fat); and 'paint' coming from Middle English *peinten,* Old French *peint,* and Latin *pingere* (to paint). 'Greasepaint' is tallow or some lard grease melted and colored by stirring into it various pigments. In 1888 the *Pall Mall Gazette* (September 4) discussed an actor in the process of making up his face.

> He only used such materials as [are] in every actor's make-up box — grease-paint, rouge, lining-pencil, and powder.

The final rehearsals have been held, and all is in readiness for the 'performance,' which could be in the evening or might be presented as a 'matinee.' If there are several acts, there would be 'intermissions,' 'interludes,' or 'entr'actes' between them. 'Performance' is from Middle English *parfournen, perfournen,* Old French *parfournir* (to accomplish, achieve, complete, consummate).

Since *matin* is the French word for "morning," why do we use the word 'matinee' for an afternoon performance? In earlier times, the day was considered to start at sunup, not midnight, and the ninth hour, the hour of 'noon' (Latin *nonus,* ninth), came at three o'clock, three hours after midday. In the great society houses the heavy meal was served at 'noon' (i.e., our three o'clock). To amuse the guests who were waiting for dinner, the host hired minstrels and other entertainers who passed among them to take their minds off their hunger — hence 'matinee.'

The 'interlude' (Middle English *enterlude, entyrlude,* Latin *interludium,* from *inter,* between, and *ludus,* a play) was originally a light dramatic or mimic representation between acts of long mystery-plays or moralities. Life was strict in the early seventeenth century, at least according to Michael Dalton (*The countrey justice, conteyning the practise of the justices of the peace out of their sessions,* XXIII), 1618.

> There shall be no . . . Enterludes, Common Plays or other unlawful exercises of pastimes.

A synonym for 'interlude' is 'entr'acte,' from the French *entre* (between) and *acte* (act). Ouida (Louise de la Ramée) observed an odd practice while watching a play (*"Held in bondage"; or Granville de Vigne; a tale of the day*) in 1863.

> That old man there, who droops his head, takes snuff during the entr'actes.

The time between acts is no longer devoted to performances of any kind; it is merely a rest period for performers and audiences alike, and it is now called 'intermission' (from Latin *intermittere,* to inter- rupt, pause, from *inter,* between, and *mittere,* to send).

As the performance ends, there is a reaction from the audience. It may 'applaud' in approval either as individuals or in an organ- ized group called a 'claque'; it may 'boo' or remain silent or 'hiss' in disapproval. John Florio defined 'applaud' (from Latin *ad,* toward, and *plaudere,* to clap, especially the hands) in his *A worlde of wordes,* 1598.

> "Applaudere" . . . to applaude or clap hands for ioy.

In 1820–22 Charles Caleb Colton waxed philosophical about 'applause' (*Lacon: or many things in few words*).

> Applause is the spur of noble minds, the end and aim of weak ones.

A 'claque' (French *claque,* a smack or clap of the hand) is a group organized to support or defeat a play or any kind of show. In 1884 the *Boston* (Massachusetts) *Journal* reported on the employment of a 'claque' in another sphere (June 6).

> Shutting out delegates in order to admit doorkeepers' friends, or the claquers of candidates.

Both 'boo' and 'hiss' are onomatopoeic or imitative words, the former echoing the lowing sound of oxen, the latter the sound of snakes. Audiences today are usually too well-mannered to utter either sound, but in John Alday's time, in 1566, they were less restrained in their reactions (*Theatrum mundi*).

> Subject, as in a playe to be hissed at, and chased awaye with shame.

John Dryden outlined the rights of an audience in 1683 (*Vindication of the Duke of Guise,* in *Works,* V).

> To clap and Hiss are the Privileges of a Free-born Subject in a Play-house.

The play is over, the audience has gone home, leaving behind its reactions to the quality of both the play and the performance. It now remains to see what the 'critics' or 'reviewers' will say about it, and what will be its fate. Will it be a 'flop' or a 'hit'? What is the function of a 'critic' (from Latin *criticus,* Greek *kritikos,* able to discern, from *krinein,* to discern)? Richard Bentley outlined his view in 1697 (*A dissertation upon the epistles of Phalaris,* introduction).

> To pass a censure on all kinds of writings, to shew their excellencies and defects, . . . was the chief Province of the ancient Critics.

Oscar Wilde, in 1890, said that this function was the exclusive property of the 'critic'; the publisher should keep hands off (letter in *St. James Gazette,* June 28).

> No publisher should ever express an opinion of the value of what he publishes. That is a matter entirely for the literary critic to decide . . . A publisher is simply a useful middleman. It is not for him to anticipate the verdict of criticism.

The harshest 'critics' of the 'critics' are, as one would expect, the authors. Here is Benjamin Disraeli on the subject (*Lothair,* XXXV), in 1870.

> "Tomorrow," he said, "the critics will commence. You know who the critics are? The men who have failed in literature
> and art."

George Bernard Shaw resorted to what some have called "the lowest form of humor" in his definition of a critic in 1950 (*The New York Times,* November 5).

> A drama critic is a man who leaves no turn unstoned.

A synonym for 'critic' is 'reviewer' (from Latin *re*, again, and *videre,* to see). The Reverend Sydney Smith had his own technique (as quoted in H. Pearson's *The Smith of Smiths,* 1934).

> I never read a book before reviewing it; it prejudices a man so.

As an appropriate parting touch to this section on 'critics' and 'reviewers' here is a 'critic' in action — Eugene Field reviewing the performance of Creston Clarke as King Lear (attributed to the *Denver Tribune,* c. 1880).

> He played the King as though under momentary apprehension that someone else was about to play the ace.

The word 'hit' (from Middle English *hitten,* Icelandic *hitta,* to strike, hit) for a successful play began to be used at the beginning of the nineteenth century. It appeared in 1815 in William H. Ireland's *Scribbleomania; or the printer's devil's polichronicon, a poem.*

> One of Mr. Lane's most fortunate hits.

In 1866 Mrs. Adeline D. T. Whitney described a happy occasion (*A summer in Leslie Goldthwaite's life*).

The actors crowded round her. "We'd no idea of it!" "Capital!" "A great hit!" they exclaimed.

A slang or informal word to describe a play that does not succeed is 'flop,' an imitative variation of *flap*, related to the Provincial Dutch *flop* (the sound of a blow or fall).

"All the world" may be a "stage," but we have chosen to put on stage in this chapter not "the world" but "a world of words." Through these words we have seen the world of entertainment as presented in its many guises on an assortment of stages, a world that varies from the single performer in the intimacy of a small café or drawing room to the massed crowds on the streets performing in a carnival. We have viewed many facets of the human condition from comedy to tragedy, from cabaret to opera, from vaudeville to circus.

As with all those involved with a production of any sort after the curtain falls on opening night, we await a verdict. We will let Ben Jonson state our case (Epilogue from *Volpone*, act V, scene 12).

> The seasoning of the play is the applause.
> Now, though the fox be punished by the laws,
> He yet doth hope there is no suff'ring due
> For any fact which he hath done 'gainst you.
> If there be, censure him: here he doubtful stands.
> If not, fare jovially, and clap your hands.

THE LAST WORD

The word "last" in "The Last Word" should not be construed as being the end of the matter. We have seen repeatedly throughout this book that there is never a "last word" on words. They keep changing their meaning, pronunciation, and spelling. Words become obsolete; new ones arise to meet the needs of the day.

In the twenties, it was quite common to refer to a night out on the town as "having a gay old time." The word 'gay' today is used almost exclusively to refer to homosexuals. 'Fetch' is a useful word meaning "to go and get and bring back"; it is rarely used today. Pronunciation, too, is changing. About two hundred years ago, the poet Alexander Pope, in his *Essay on Man,* wrote this couplet which includes one of the most famous lines in English literature.

> Good-nature and good-sense must ever join;
> To err is human, to forgive, divine.

It is clear that in Pope's time the word 'join' was pronounced as if it were spelled "jine."

A corollary to one of Parkinson's laws might be "Language expands to meet the needs of the people." Part of this continual expansion are contemporary idioms and the vernacular. Time was, when people parted, they said "God be with you." Only yesterday it was shortened to "Good-bye." Today for many it is "Have a nice day!" What will they say tomorrow? A trendy equivalent of being "interested in" is being "into" something. Is this the last word?

There are many obsolete words in English which are delightfully described by Susan Kelz Sperling in *Poplollies and Bellibones, A Celebration of Lost Words*. They were, at one time, "the last word"; no counterparts exist for them today. Also books like *Mrs. Byrne's Dictionary of Unusual, Obscure, and Preposterous Words* list many that we would not even recognize today. Here are a choice few.

embracery *n.* the attempt to influence a court by bribery or other means.

groak *v.i.* to watch people silently while they're eating, hoping they will ask you to join them.

bedswerver *n.* an unfaithful spouse (obs.) [as though *all* these words were not "obsolete"!]

mulligrubs *n.pl.* 1. abdominal pain; colic. 2. the blues.

snollygoster *n.* a burgeoning politician with no platform, principles, or party preference.

prickmedainty *adj.* goody-goody. *n.* goody-goody person.

And if you wonder about 'poplollies' and 'bellibones' — the former is a little darling, from French *poupelet* (little doll), the latter is a lovely maiden, from French *belle et bonne* (beautiful and good). Ms. Sperling will also tell you that a 'lip-clap' is a kiss and that a 'windsucker' is an envious, covetous character.

When these words were in use, no one believed that they would ultimately disappear. Which of the words in vogue today will still be in use tomorrow?

In the early nineteenth century, there was an unbridled growth of language in America, and new words like 'blizzard,' 'caucus,' 'notions,' 'immigrant,' 'noncommittal,' 'belittle,' 'reckon,' 'whitewash,' 'bunk,' and 'gerrymander' were being added at an unprecedented rate. Concerned with the future of the language, an anonymous writer who signed himself "An American" proposed in a letter to the *Royal American Magazine* in January 1774 the formation of a society, modeled after the Académie Française, to be called Fellows of the American Society of Language. Its function would be to protect, preserve, and perfect the English language in America. John Adams, the future President of the United States, made a similar proposal to the Congress in a letter written from Amsterdam on September 5, 1780.

These proposals, along with the continued growth of the language in America, infuriated the purists in England. In 1808 an article in *The Annual*

> Excoriated "the torrent of barbarous phraseology" pouring from America, which threatened "to destroy the purity of the English language."

In 1834 Noah Webster took up the challenge and threw down one of his own, in *Dissertations on the English Language*.

> As an independent nation our honor requires us to have a system of our own, in language as well as government. Great Britain, whose children we are, should no longer be *our* standard; for the taste of her writers is already corrupted, and her language on the decline. But if it were not so, she is at too great a distance to be our model, and to instruct us in the principles of our own tongue.

Throughout the nineteenth and twentieth centuries, words like 'cafeteria,' 'electrocute,' 'highbrow,' 'egghead,' 'filling station,' and 'O. K.' continued to drift back across the Atlantic to England. The hitherto normal flow of the English language had been reversed; the upstart "colony" was now exporting its words and expressions to the "mother country," and she and the "King's English" would never be the same again.

BIBLIOGRAPHY

Adams, Franklin Pierce. *FPA Book of Quotations*. New York: Funk & Wagnals, 1952.

American Heritage Dictionary of the English Language, The (William Morris, ed.; Norman Hoss, managing ed.). Boston: Houghton Mifflin, 1969, 1980. ["the AHD"]

Americanisms: A Dictionary of Selected Americanisms on Historical Principles (Mitford M. Mathews, ed.). Chicago: University of Chicago Press, 1966.

Barnett, Lincoln. *The Treasure of Our Tongue*. New York: Alfred A. Knopf, 1964.

Bartlett, John. *Familiar Quotations*. 15th ed. Boston: Little Brown, 1980. ["the Bartlett"]

Baugh, Albert C. *A History of the English Language*. New York: Appleton-Century-Crofts, 1957.

Berrey, Lester, and Melvin van den Bark. *The American Thesaurus of Slang*. New York: Thomas Y. Crowell, 1953

Brewer, Ebenezer Cobham. *Brewer's Dictionary of Phrase and Fable*. Centenary Edition (Ivor H. Evans, ed.). New York: Harper & Row, 1970.

Brown, Ivor. *Random Words*. London: Bodley Head, 1971.

Byrne, Josepha Heifetz. *Mrs. Byrne's Dictionary of Unusual, Obscure, and Preposterous Words*. Secaucus, NJ: University Books, 1974.

Cassell's French Dictionary: French-English, English-French (Denis Girard, ed.). New York: Macmillan, 1978.

Cassell's Latin Dictionary: Latin-English, English-Latin (D. P. Simpson, ed.). New York: Macmillan, 1977.

Century Dictionary and Cyclopedia. 12 vol. New York: Century Company, 1911. ["the Century"]

Chambers Biographical Dictionary (J. O. Thorne, T. C. Collocott, eds.). Edinburgh: W. & R. Chambers, 1974.

Chambers Etymological Dictionary (A.M. MacDonald, ed.) New York: Pyramid Books, 1968 (W. & R. Chambers, 1966).

Cohen, J. M., and M. J. Cohen. *The Penguin Dictionary of Quotations.* New York: Atheneum Press, 1962.

Craige, William A., and James Hulbert. *A Dictionary of American English on Historical Principles.* 4 vol. Chicago: University of Chicago Press, 1936, 1966.

Dictionary of American Biography. 21 vol. New York: Scribner (for American Council of Learned Societies), 1943. ["the DAB"]

———. Supplement vol. 1–4. New York: Scribner, 1944–74.

Dictionary of American English on Historical Principles: See Craige, William A., and James Hulbert.

Dictionary of American Slang: See Wentworth, Harold, and Stuart Berg Flexner.

Dictionary of Quotable Definitions. Englewood Cliffs, NJ: Prentice-Hall, 1970.

Dictionary of the Vulgar Tongue: See Grose, Frances.

Duden: Etymology (Günter Drosdowski, Paul Grebe, eds.). Vol. 9 of *Der Grosse Duden.* Mannheim: Bibliographisches Institut, 1963.

Dunkling, Leslie Alan, *First Names First.* New York: Universe Books, 1977.

———. *The Guinness Book of Names.* Enfield, Middlesex: Guinness Superlatives, 1974.

ENCYCLOPAEDIA BRITANNICA: *The New Encyclopaedia Britannica in 30 Volumes (Warren E. Preece,ed.; Donald E. Stewart, managing ed.). 15 ed.* Chicago: Encyclopaedia Britannica, 1974. ["the EB," "the Britannica 3"]

———: *Encyclopaedia Britannica.* 24 vol. Chicago: Encyclopaedia Britannica, 1962. ["the EB"]

———: *Encyclopaedia Britannica; or, a Dictionary of Arts and Sciences, Compiled upon a New Plan In which The different Sciences and Arts are digested into distinct Treatises or Systems; and The various Technical Terms, etc. are explained as they occur in the order of the Alphabet. By a Society of Gentlemen in Scotland.* 3 vol. Edinburgh, 1771.

Eponyms Dictionaries Index (James A. Ruffner, ed.). Detroit: Gale, 1977. ["the EDI"]

Espy, Willard R. *The Game of Words.* New York: Bramhall House, 1971, 1972.

Evans, Bergen. *Comfortable Words.* New York: Random House, 1959, 1961.

———. *Dictionary of Quotations.* New York: Delacorte Press, 1968.

Flexner, Stuart Berg. *I Hear America Talking: An Illustrated Treasury of American Words and Phrases.* New York: Van Nostrand Reinhold, 1976.

Folger Book of Shakespeare Quotations, The (Burton Stevenson, ed.). New York: Funk & Wagnalls (for Folger Books), 1979.

Follett, Wilson. *Modern American Usage.* New York: Grosset & Dunlap, 1966.

Fowler, H. W. *Modern English Usage.* New York and Oxford: Oxford University Press, 1973.

Funk, Charles Earle. *A Hog on Ice and other Curious Expressions.* New York: Harper and Brothers, 1948.

Funk & Wagnalls New Standard Dictionary of the English Language, Complete in One Volume (Isaac K. Funk, ed. in chief; Frank H. Vizetelly, managing ed.). New York: Funk & Wagnalls, 1963.

Geisinger, Marion. *Plays, Players, & Playwrights.* New York: Hart, 1971.

Granville, Wilfred. *The Theater Dictionary.* Westport, CT: Greenwood Press, 1952.

Grose, Frances. *A Classical Dictionary of the Vulgar Tongue* ([1796 ed.] Eric Partridge, ed.). Freeport, NY: Book for Libraries Press, 1971.

——. *1811 Dictionary of the Vulgar Tongue: A Dictionary of Buckish Slang, University Wit, and Pickpocket Eloquence* (Bob Cromie, ed.). Northfield, IL: Digest Books, 1971.

Hazon, Mario. *Dizionario Inglese-Italiano, Italiano-Inglese.* Milan: Garzanti, 1963. ["the Garzanti"]

Hendrickson, Robert. *Human Words.* Philadelphia: Chilton Book Company, 1972.

Holt, Alfred A. *Phrase and Word Origins.* New York: Dove Publications, 1961.

Hunsberger, I. Moyer. *The Quintessential Dictionary.* New York: Hart Publishing Company, 1978.,

Johnson, Samuel. *A Dictionary of the English Language in which The Words are deduced from their Originals, and Illustrated in their Different Significations by Examples from the best Writers, to which are prefixed, A History of the Language, and An English Grammar. By Samuel Johnson, A.M. In Two Volumes.* London: W. Strahan, 1755.

Klein, Ernest. *A Comprehensive Etymological Dictionary of the English Language.* Amsterdam, London, New York: Elsevier, 1971.

Larousse: See *Petit Larousse Illustré.*

Levinson, Leonard Louis. *Bartlett's Unfamiliar Quotations.* Chicago: Cowles Book Company, 1971.

Lexis: Dictionnarie de la Langue Française (Jean Dubois, ed.). Paris: Librairie Larousse, 1975.

Longman Dictionary of English Idioms (Thomas Hill Long, editorial director; Della Summers, managing ed.). London: Longman, 1979.

Lounsbury, Warren C. *Theater Backstage from A to Z.* Seattle and London: University of Washington Press, 1967.

Marckwardt, Albert H. *American English.* New York: Oxford University Press, 1958.

Matthews, C.M. *English Surnames.* New York: Scribner, 1967.

Mencken, H. L. *A New Dictionary of Quotations on Historical Principles.* New York: Alfred A. Knopf, 1977.

Moore, John. *You English Words.* Philadelphia and New York: Lippincott, 1961.

Morris, William, and Mary Morris. *Morris Dictionary of Word and Phrase Origins.* New York: Harper & Row, 1977.

New Century Cyclopedia of Names, The (Clarence L. Barnhart, ed.). 3 vol. Englewood Cliffs: Prentice-Hall, 1954. ["the CCN"]

New Century Handbook of English Literature, The (Clarence L. Barnhart, ed.). New York: Appleton-Century-Crofts, 1956, 1967.

O'Brian, M.A. *New Engligh-Russian and Russian-English Dictionary.* New York: Dover Publications, 1944.

Oxford Classical Dictionary, The (N. G. L. Hammond, H. H. Schullard, eds.). 2nd ed. Oxford: Oxford University Press, 1970, 1978.

Oxford Companion to the Theater, The (Phyllis Hartnall, ed.). London: Oxford University Press, 1967.

Oxford Dictionary of English Etymology, The (C. T. Onions, ed.). New York and Oxford: Oxford University Press, 1966, 1974.

Oxford Dictionary of Quotations, The. 3rd ed. London and New York: Oxford University Press, 1980

OXFORD ENGLISH DICTIONARY: *The Compact Edition of the Oxford English Dictionary* (R. W. Burchfield, ed. in chief). 2 vol. Oxford: Oxford University Press, 1971. ["the OED," "the Compact OED"]

———: *A Supplement to the Oxford English Dictionary* (R. W. Burchfield, ed.). Oxford: Oxford University Press, vol. I (A-G) 1972, vol. II (H-N) 1976.

———: *The Shorter Oxford English Dictionary on Historical Principles* (C. T. Onions, ed.). 2 vol. Oxford: University Press, 1933, 1973. [" the Shorter Oxford," "the Shorter OED"]

Palmer, A. Smythe. *Folk-Etymology: A Dictionary of Verbal Corruptions or Words Perverted in Form or Meaning, by False Derivation or Mistaken Analogy.* New York: Henry Holt, 1890.

Partridge, Eric. *A Charm of Words.* New York: Macmillan, 1960.

———. *A Dictionary of Slang and Unconventional English.* New York: Macmillan, 1970.

———. *Origins: A Short Etymological Dictionary of Modern English.* 4th ed. New York: Macmillan, 1958, 1977.

———. *Slang, To-day and Yesterday.* New York: Bonanza Books, 1950.

Pei, Mario. *Words in Sheep's Clothing.* New York: Hawthorn Books, 1969.

Penguin Dictionary of Quotations: See Cohen, J. M., and M. J. Cohen.

Petit Larousse Illustré (Paul Augé, ed.). Paris: Librairie Larousse, 1979.

Pyles, Thomas. *The Origins and Development of the English Language.* New York: Harcourt Brace and World, 1964.

Random House Dictionary of the English Language, The (Jess Stein, ed. in chief; Laurance Urdang, managing ed.). Unabridged ed. New York: Random House, 1966, 1981. ["the RHD"]

Roget's International Thesaurus. 4th ed. New York: Thomas Y. Crowell, 1977.

Scribner-Bantam English Dictionary, The (Edwin B. Williams, general ed.; Walter D. Glanze, managing ed.). New York: Bantam Books, 1977, 1979.

Simpson, James B. *Contemporary Quotations.* New York: Thomas Y. Crowell, 1964.

Skeat, Walter W. *A Concise Etymological Dictionary of the English Language.* Oxford: Oxford University Press, 1976.

———. *An Etymological Dicationary of the English Language.* Oxford: Oxford University Press, [1879,] 1963, 1974.

Smith, Elsdon C. *American Surnames.* New York: Chilton Book Company, 1969.

Sperling, Susan Kelz. *Poplollies and Bellibones: A Celebration of Lost Words.* New York: Clarkson N. Potter, 1977.

Stevenson, Burton. *The Home Book of Quotations.* New York: Dodd, Mead, 1967.

Stewart, George R. *American Place Names: A Concise and Selective Dictionary for the Continental United States of America.* New York: Oxford University Press, 1970.

———. *Names on the Globe.* New York: Oxford University Press, 1975.

———. *Names on the Land.* Boston: Houghton Mifflin, 1958.

Stratman, Francis Henry. *A Middle English Dictionary.* London: Oxford University Press, 1967.

Traupman, John C. *The Bantam New College German & English Dictionary.* New York: Bantam Books, 1981.

——. *The New College Latin & English Dictionry*. New York: Bantam Books, 1966.

Tripp, Rhoda Thomas. *The International Thesaurus of Quotations*. New York: Thomas Y. Crowell, 1970.

Viking Book of Poetry, The (Richard Aldington, ed.). New York: Viking Press, 1941.

Wahrig, Gerhard. *Deutsches Wörterbuch*. Gütersloh: Bertelsmann Lexikon-Verlag, 1966. ["the Wahrig"]

Webster's New World Dictionary of the American Language (David B. Guralnik, ed. in chief). 2nd ed. Cleveland: William Collins + World Publishing Co., 1953, 1976. ["the New World," "the NW"]

Webster's Third New International Dictionary of the English Language, Unabridged (Philip Babcock Gove, ed. in chief). Springfield, MA: G. & C. Merriam, 1971, 1981. ["Webster's Third," "the W3," "the Third International"]

Webster's New International Dictionary of the English Language. Second Edition. Unabridged (William Allan Neilson, ed. in chief; Paul W. Carhart, managing ed.). Springfield, MA: G. & C. Merriam, 1934, 1948. ["Webster's Second," "the W2"]

Webster's Biographical Dictionary (William Allan Neilson, ed. in chief; Lucius Holt, managing ed.). Springfield, MA: G. & C. Merriam, 1943, 1976.

Weekley, Ernest. *An Etymological Dictionary of Modern English*. 2 vol. New York: Dover Publicatons, 1967.

Wentworth, Harold, and Stuart Berg Flexner. *Dictionary of American Slang*. New York: Thomas Y. Crowell, 1960, 1975.

Whiting, Bartlett Jere. *Early American Proverbs and Proverbial Phrases*. Cambridge, MA: Belknap Press of Harvard University Press, 1977.

——. *Proverbs, Sentences, and Proverbial Phrases from English Writings Mainly Before 1500*. Cambridge, MA: Belknap Press of Harvard University Press, 1968.

World Book Dictionary, The (Clarence L. Barnhart, Robert K. Barnhart, eds.). New York: Doubleday, 1977.

INDEX

271